STILL WATERS DEEP WATERS

STILL WATERS DEEP WATERS

Edited by Rowland Croucher

AN ALBATROSS BOOK

Published in Australia and New Zealand by
Albatross Books Pty Ltd
PO Box 320, Sutherland
NSW 2232, Australia
and in the United Kingdom by
Lion Publishing plc
Peter's Way, Sandy Lane West
Oxford OX4 5HG, England

First vinyl edition 1987
Reprinted 1988, 1991, 1992, 1993
This paperback edition 1998

National Library of Australia
Cataloguing-in-Publication data

Still waters, deep waters.

Bibliography.
ISBN 0 7324 1070 3

1. Meditations. I. Croucher, Rowland.

242

Printed by Kyodo Printing Co. Pte Ltd, Singapore

Contents

Preface

THERE ARE FEW RESOURCES AROUND to help more thoughtful Christians in their devotions. For many, their daily Bible reading is either associated with a specific task such as preparation for preaching or it is a hit-and-miss affair conducted on a semi-regular basis.

This book aims to satisfy the needs of those many people seeking something more in their devotional life. The idea is to spend one day a week, perhaps your day off, in a more leisurely and protracted quiet time — 'wasting time with God' as Sheila Cassidy beautifully expresses it in *Prayer for Pilgrims*.

These meditations are offered by a range of people (clergy and lay people, scholars and self-educated) from a variety of Christian denominations. A list of contributors may be found at the back, but we haven't revealed who wrote what: let us hear God speaking to us, whatever the personal style or stance of the author/compiler.

Special thanks are due to World Vision of Australia which, through its commitment to leadership enhancement, has made it possible for me to give time to editing and compiling this book. My secretary and research assistant, Grace Thomlinson, has given tireless attention to the many administrative and creative details involved. And my loving gratitude is always owing to Jan, Amanda and Lindy, for allowing their husband and father the freedom to keep his head in a book.

Rowland Croucher
John Mark Ministries
7 Bangor Court
Heathmont, Victoria 3135
Australia

A life all turbulence and noise may seem
To him that leads it wise and to be praised,
But wisdom is a pearl with most success
Sought in still waters.

William Cowper
The Task, Book III

Theme: Quietness

'Beside quiet waters' (Psalm 23:2)

The Lord is my shepherd;
  I shall lack nothing.
He makes me lie down in green pastures,
  he leads me beside quiet waters,
  he restores my soul.
He guides me in paths of righteousness
  for his name's sake.

Psalm 23:1-3, NIV

WEEK

Stillness and quietness bring strength

Be still and know that I am God. Tremble with fear and stop sinning; think deeply about this when you lie in silence on your beds.

How precious to me are your thoughts, O God! How vast is the sum of them! When I awake, I am still with you.

Jesus stood up and commanded the wind, 'Be quiet!' and he said to the waves, 'Be still!' The wind died down, and there was a great calm.

You rule over the surging sea; when its waves mount up, you still them. You calm the roar of the seas and the noise of the waves; you calm the uproar of the peoples. The Lord is my shepherd; I shall want nothing. He makes me lie down in green pastures, and leads me beside the waters of peace.

He stilled the storm to a whisper; the waves of the sea were hushed. This is what the Sovereign Lord, the Holy One of Israel, says: 'In repentance and rest is your salvation; in stillness and in staying quiet, there lies your strength.'

(Ps.46:10, RSV; Ps.4:4, GNB; Mark 4:39, GNB; Ps.139:17,18b, NIV; Ps.89:9, NIV; Ps.65:7, GNB; Ps.23:1-2, NEB; Ps.107:29, NIV; Is.30:15, NIV, NEB)

We spend most of our lives, said Evelyn Underhill, conjugating three verbs: to want, to have and to do. But none of these verbs has any ultimate significance until it is transcended by and included in the fundamental verb, to be.

The culmination of our being, according to the New Testament, is 'union with Christ'. Not justification by faith, sanctification in the Spirit, or even reconciliation with the Father. These are spiritual means to the great end of my 'living, yet not I, but Christ living in me' (Galatians 2:20). 'He who is united to the Lord,' says Paul, 'becomes one spirit with him' (1 Corinthians 6:17).

So what is to be my desire? In practical terms, as *The Cloud of Unknowing* suggests, it is neither what you are nor what you have been that God sees with his all-merciful eyes, but what you desire to be. The life of the Christian is a love affair, a life of love given freely in response to the Father's love. Thus the main aim of prayer is to know God through love: 'affective knowledge'.

How does that happen? Paul,describing his 'beatific vision', tells his Corinthian friends how it came — fourteen years ago, he says — and passed (2 Corinthians 12:1-10). He had, then, an experience of God which was very precious, and heard divine secrets he was not at liberty to reveal. However, the 'normal Christian life' is rather the daily affair of a soldier's hardships, an athlete's training, a farmer's toils (2 Timothy 2:1-6).

So knowing God through love involves obedient sacrifice, or, to change the metaphor, the spiritual baptism of all we are, and do, and think.

The analogy of water is a marvellous one for our meditation in this regard. Water is the stuff of life: if you're buried alive during an earthquake, its presence or absence is crucial. Saints were made — in biblical times and since — in waterless wildernesses. But even in water-full seas — where water is everywhere but not a drop to drink — angels may minister to us. Water can be a blessing or a curse, a life-giving or destructive force; it may quench our thirst or ruin our landscape. It is essential for our survival and yet may sometimes terrorise us. God 'who is present in all his works though still unseen' (Justin Martyr) is with us when waves and billows threaten us or when we enjoy the tranquillity and peace of 'the still waters'.

But our friendship with God is not an end in itself. We are called to service as well as to piety. We are shaped in our communion with the Father so that the world may experience his glory in these frail human vessels. Although 'there is only one sorrow, not to be a saint', a saint, like cathedral windows, is someone the light shines through. A saint is useful, as well as decorative. Saints love not just humanity but persons. They are God's saving agents in the world: wounded healers, incarnating the love of God among those who are being threatened in the storms of their lives.

Silence is the simple stillness of the individual under the Word of God... We are silent at the beginning of the day because God should have the first word, and we are silent before going to sleep because the last word also belongs to God... 'Seek God, not happiness' is the fundamental rule of all meditation. If you seek God alone, you will gain happiness: that is its promise... Prayer [ought] to be guided by the word of the Scriptures... in this way we shall not become the victims of our own emptiness.

Dietrich Bonhoeffer, *Life Together*

Be still and know that I am God. 'Let be,' reads a marginal notation, but in a colloquialism we have it even more clearly: 'Relax'. Psychology has something to say about the relationship of relaxation to sanity, and the familiar exhortation is rendered in the Vulgate, *Vacate, et videte*. Indeed, the treatment of minds broken by the cataclysms of earth, and the inhumanity, fancied or real, of one's fellows, demands relaxation as the first step in therapy. 'Give place and see!'

Edwin McNeill Poteat, *The Interpreter's Bible*

You must turn to him, the Lord, with all your heart... if your soul is to find rest. Christ is ready to come to you, with what kindness in his glance! But you must make room, deep in your heart, to entertain him as he deserves. Where he finds someone whose thoughts go deep, he is a frequent visitor; such pleasant converse, such welcome words of comfort, such deep repose, such intimate friendship, are well-nigh past belief.

Up with you, then, faithful soul, get your heart ready for the coming of this true Lover... You must make room for Christ and shut the door upon all intruders.

Thomas à Kempis, *The Imitation of Christ*

Silence [is]... a gift, one which is 'promising' in the true sense of the word. The promise of this silence is that new life can be born. It is this silence which is the silence of peace and prayer, because you are brought back to the other who is leading you. In this silence you lose the feeling of being compulsive and you find yourself a person who can be himself along with other things and other people.

Then you realise that you can do many things, but it isn't necessary. It is the silence of the 'poor in spirit', where you learn to see your life in its proper perspective. In this silence, the false pretences fade away and you can see the world again with a certain distance, and, in the midst of all your cares, you can pray with the psalmist:

> If Yahweh does not build the house,
> in vain the masons toil;
> if Yahweh does not guard the city,
> in vain the sentries watch. (Psalm 127)

Henri Nouwen, *With Open Hands*

For the first time, Alain tells me the words he has repeated to himself over and over again for many years: 'Jesus my joy, my hope, my life.'

Brother Roger of Taizé, *The Wonder of a Love*

Even if a man is deeply versed in the understanding and knowledge of all spiritual things ever created, he can never by such understanding come to know an uncreated spiritual thing... which is none else than God!... That is why St Dionysius said, 'the most godlike knowledge of God is that which is known by unknowing'.

The Cloud of Unknowing

'Attend' and 'obey': these two principles underlie all Christian sanctity... *absorbing* attention and *utter* obedience. The saints attend to God. There is no instance of one great in sanctity who was not great in prayer... Holiness can never be an aim in itself... The saints do not set out for ethical perfection. They set out for God. They gaze on God in love and longing. Sanctity is given by God to those who want nothing but himself, and who know no higher bliss than just to be with him.

Not only do the saints attend to God. They obey him — utterly, instantly, gladly. They will *one* will with him. 'Do not consult me' they say in effect: 'Command me.'

Well, those are the two basic principles of sanctity: attention and obedience. To those who were looking for something hidden and mysterious, they will seem simple to the point of absurdity. To those who say 'We knew it all the time', it will be enough to ask, 'How are you getting on in the practice of them?'

W.E. Sangster, *The Pure in Heart: A Study in Christian Sanctity*

Recollection opens our soul to heaven, *but also to others*. The contemplative life or the active life — this problem is somewhat artificial, says St Serapion. The real problem is that of the heart's dimension. Acquire inner peace and a multitude will find their salvation near you... This is an interesting statement. The saint does not say 'through' you but 'near' you.

Catherine de Hueck Doherty, *Poustinia*

(2)

Hear my prayer, O Lord; let not my soul faint under thy discipline, nor let me faint in confessing unto thee thy mercies, whereby thou hast saved me from all my most wicked ways till thou shouldst become sweet to me beyond all the allurements that I used to follow. Let me come to love thee wholly, and grasp thy hand with my whole heart that thou mayest deliver me from every temptation, even unto the last.

Augustine, *Confessions*

Thanks, thanks to thee, O Eternal Father, for thou hast not despised me, the work of thy hands, nor turned thy face from me, nor despised my desires. Having known the truth through thy clemency, I have found thy charity, and the love of my neighbour. What has constrained me? Not my virtues, but only thy charity... Who can attain to thy greatness, and give thee thanks for such immeasurable gifts and benefits thou has given me...Thou hast been willing to condescend to my need and to that of thy creatures — the need of introspection. Having first given the grace to ask the question, thou repliedst to it, and satisfiest thy servant, penetrating me with a ray of grace, so that in that light I may give thee thanks. Clothe me, clothe me with thee, O Eternal Truth, that I may run my mortal course with true obedience and the light of holy faith, with which light I feel that my soul is about to become inebriated afresh.

Catherine of Siena, *The Dialogue of the Seraphic Virgin*

Be exalted, Lord, above the heavens,
  let your glory cover the earth.
Keep our nation under your care,
  and guide us in justice and truth.
Let your way be known on earth,
  your saving power among the nations.
Send out your light and your truth
  that we may tell of your saving works.
Hear our prayers, O Lord,
  for we put our trust in you.

An Australian Prayer Book

God of our fathers, of Abraham, Isaac and Jacob
God of our Lord and Saviour Jesus Christ
God of ocean storms and rippling creeks
God of our ecstasies and of our mundane commonplaces,
who, mysteriously, yearns for me,
wants me,
even 'needs' me . . .
Lord, it is not so much I who am seeking you, but you are seeking me.
You are the 'water of life',
the source of serenity amidst turbulence,
the great Creator of all the grandeurs of our world,
Rescuer, Companion, Father, Provider.
Help me to love you above all else,
to desire only you, and enjoy your gifts as an unexpected 'bonus',
to be pure in heart, so that I may 'see' you,
to be ready for all your perfect will
to be brother/sister to all I meet in this 'bent world',
particularly those who cannot enjoy your good gifts,
through poverty, hunger, sickness, oppression, ignorance or sin.

A Benediction

May God be in my whole being, before he is in my ministry.
May God be in my heart as well as my head.
May God be in my loving and my knowing and my willing and my speaking and my acting.

May I readily see Christ in others,
And may my life be itself a benediction
For your glory, Lord. Amen.

God the Father enrich you with his grace,
God the Son make you holy in his love,
God the Holy Spirit strengthen you with his joy.
The Lord bless you and keep you in eternal life. Amen.

WEEK

The desert in the marketplace

One of those days Jesus went out into the hills to pray, and spent the night praying to God. When morning came he called his disciples to him and chose twelve of them, whom he also designated apostles: Simon (whom he named Peter), his brother Andrew, James, John, Philip, Bartholomew, Matthew, Thomas, James son of Alphaeus, Simon who was called the Zealot, Judas son of James, and Judas Iscariot, who became a traitor.

He went down with them and stood on a level place. A large crowd of his disciples was there, and a great number of people from all over Judea, from Jerusalem, and from the sea-coast of Tyre and Sidon, who had come to hear him and to be healed of their diseases. Those troubled by evil spirits were cured, and the people all tried to touch him, because power was coming from him and healing them all.

(Luke 6:12-19, NIV)

Australian Christians often follow a lifestyle symbolised by the pattern of white settlement in their country. In the centre are the arid, desert regions where it is difficult to see signs of life. On the perimeter are the fertile plains. Most live busily on the fertile plains, occasionally longing to find desert time and space to be alone with God, but secretly afraid that this desert would not provide nourishment.

We are invited to find our own desert space within the marketplace of daily living. The rhythm of life demonstrated by Jesus helps us to understand the importance of this lifestyle.

The passage from Luke 6 has much to say to us: Jesus' activity and his prayers were complementary to one another. Neither was allotted to whatever time was left over. He knew that the source of his power and wisdom came from communion with his Father.

Our complex lifestyles can be transformed if we understand the basic simplicity of Christian living, which is to *be* and to *do*. God calls us to our true vocation, which is to be his children, and to express that vocation by doing his will.

We are invited to live both in the desert (being) and the marketplace (doing). Our response to that invitation will involve some conscious decisions about our use of time. Often we self-consciously leave prayer for 'left-over time', fearing we shall appear over-pious if we withdraw during what are traditionally 'active' daytime hours.

Our desert is found in moments when we give undivided attention to God. Then we receive spiritual nourishment, forgiveness, healing and grace, growth in wisdom and a call to serve.

Circumstances and moods change: sometimes the daily desert is a consolation and at others it is a painful and lonely place. Yet as we persist in spending time there, so we sense changes in our lives and eventually we become more deeply dependent upon the grace of God. The desert begins to provide our daily bread, and the marketplace becomes our opportunity to express the life of Christ which now abides within us.

Early in December 1984 twelve people met in France to begin an on-going search for a spirituality for our times. This was initiated by the World Council of Churches. Amongst the issues the group discussed was the relationship between 'moments of withdrawal and moments of engagement'. Participants concluded that the church was called to a costly spirituality that was Christ-centred and which enabled people to live more effectively in the world.

This demanded constant conversion and on-going formation and discipleship. It was rooted in a life of prayer and in solidarity with the poor and oppressed. It would lead to suffering. In it Christians who were encouraged and challenged by a community nourished by word and sacrament would discover that 'this life is one of joy and hope in the risen Lord'.

Our century thirsts for the authenticity of simplicity, the spirit of prayer and the life of obedience.

Richard Foster, *The Freedom of Simplicity*

The time of business does not differ from the time of prayer; and in the noise and chatter of my kitchen while several persons are at the same time calling for different things, I possess God in as great a tranquillity as if I were upon my knees at the blessed sacrament.

Brother Lawrence, *The Practice of the Presence of God*

[Poustinia is]. . . a place where we can raise the arms of prayer and penance towards God in expiation, intercession and reparation for our own sins and the sins of our brothers. The desert is the place where we gather courage, where we pronounce words of truth remembering that God is truth. The desert is the place where we purify ourselves and prepare ourselves to act as if touched by the burning coal that was placed by the angel on the lips of the prophet.

Catherine de Hueck Doherty, *Poustinia*

Make yourself a little 'poustinia' in your house, in your garden, in your attic. Do not dissociate the concept of desert from the places where men and women lead their lives. Try both in your thoughts and in your lives to put this glorious phrase into practice: 'the desert in the heart of the city'.

Carlo Carretto, *The Desert in the City*

When you are able to create a lonely place in the middle of your actions and concerns, your successes and failures slowly can lose some of their power over you. For then your love for this world can merge with a compassionate understanding of its illusions. Then your serious engagement can merge with an unmasking smile. Then your concern for others can be motivated more by their needs than your own. In short: then you can care. Let us therefore live our lives to the fullest, but let us not forget once in a while to get up long before dawn to leave the house and go to a lonely place.

Henri Nouwen, *Out of Solitude*

It is as much our duty to live in the beauty of the presence of God on some mount of transfiguration until we become white with Christ, as it is for us to go down to men where they grope and grovel and groan, and lift them to new life.

Frank Laubach, *Open Windows, Swinging Doors*

'Action' is no longer a matter of resigning ourselves to works that seem alien to our life in God: for the Lord himself places us exactly where he wants us to be and he himself works in us. 'Contemplation' is no longer merely the brief and satisfying interlude of reward in which our works are relieved by recollection and peace. Action and contemplation now grow together into one life and one unity. They become two aspects of the same thing. Action is charity looking outward to other men, and contemplation is charity drawn inward to its divine source. Action is the stream and contemplation is the spring. The spring remains more important than the stream, for the only thing that really matters is for love to spring inexhaustibly from the infinite abyss of Christ and of God.

Thomas Merton, *No Man is an Island*

God himself is present,
let us now adore him
as with awe we come before him.
God is in our midst, now
in our hearts keep silence,
worshipping in deepest reverence.
Him we know,
him we name,
come and let us make him
our renewed surrender.

O majestic Being,
I would praise you duly
and my service render to you
in the selfsame spirit
as the holy angels,
ever standing in your presence.
Grant me now
so to strive
evermore to please you
dearest God, in all things.

Australian Hymn Book, No.47
Words, Gerhard Tersteegen

Lord, in the stillness of these sacred moments before you, help me to remember that you are present to me in love. Grant me the inner serenity which allows me to lose myself in contemplation of you. I am a person created to reflect your glory: with all my frailties and failures you still love me, and desire to keep company with me. Most wonderful Lord, my heart leaps with joy when I recall this truth! (Pause)

Forgive me, for those occasions when I have kept busy to satisfy myself or to escape from loneliness. Forgive me, for being tempted to think that you only require me to be in the marketplace, and for allowing the desert to be pushed aside.

Lord, I long to discover my desert and my marketplace. Help me to order my days with a divine rhythm.

Before you I recall the marketplace of my life. You have placed me there to offer Christ to others. Humbly I wait before you now, looking for your wisdom, your gifts. You are the well-spring in my desert. I seek you. I worship you. (Pause)

Teach me, Lord, to be your person and to do your will, that both desert and marketplace may be sacred ground. Amen.

A Benediction

Go now, in the peace and strength of God, ready to impart to others what you have first received from him: and may the presence and power of God, Father, Son and Holy Spirit, go with you. Amen.

WEEK

3

We know in part

Be still, and know that I am God.

Now this is eternal life: that they may know you, the only true God, and Jesus Christ, whom you have sent.

I want to know Christ.

And I pray that you, being rooted and established in love, may have power, together with all the saints, to grasp how wide and long and high and deep is the love of Christ, and to know this love that surpasses knowledge.

Oh, the depth of the riches of the wisdom and knowledge of God! How unsearchable his judgments, and his paths beyond tracing out! Who has known the mind of the Lord? Or who has been his counsellor?... For from him and through him and to him are all things. To him be the glory for ever! Amen.

(Psalm 46:10; John 17:3; Philippians 3:10; Ephesians 3:17-19; Romans 11:33-36 — all NIV)

Do you realise that many of the world's greatest inspirational books have come from extremely busy people? Thousands have benefited from the masterly studies on the inner life written by A.W. Tozer, who had a crowded schedule as a Chicago pastor and editor. Augustine, J.I. Packer and others have demonstrated the possibility of being both busy and deeply conscious of God's presence at the same time. The Quaker poet, J.G. Whittier, held out the following promise:

Not to ease and aimless quiet
Doth that inward answer tend,
But to works of love and duty
As our being's end

Not to idle dreams and trances,
Length of face, and solemn tone,
But to faith, in daily striving
And performance shown.

O'er life's humblest duties throwing
Light the earthling never knew,
Freshening all its dark waste places,
As with Hermon's dew.

Not a vain and cold ideal,
Not a poet's dream alone,
But a presence warm and real,
Seen and felt and known.

J.G. Whittier

My intention is to instruct those who live in towns, in households . . . and who, by reason of their circumstances, are obliged to lead an ordinary life in outward show: who very often, under colour of an alleged impossibility, are not willing even to think of undertaking the devout life . . . while living in the midst of the pressure of worldly occupations. And I show them that . . . a vigorous and constant soul can live in the world without receiving any worldly taint, can find springs of sweet piety in the midst of the briny waters of the world . . .

St Francis de Sales, *The Devout Life*

How *well*, and with what *practical* results, do we know God?

Divine knowledge is not as the light of the moon to sleep by, but as the light of the sun to work by.

William Secker, *The Nonesuch Professor*

Some don't know *better* as they grow older; they merely know *more*.

H.H. Munro

How can we turn our knowledge *about* God into knowledge *of* God? The rule for doing this is demanding, but simple. It is that we turn each truth that we learn *about* God into matter for meditation *before* God, leading to prayer and praise *to* God.

J.I. Packer, *Knowing God*

'Be still and know'. How can God give us visions when life is hurrying at a precipitate rate? I have stood in the National Gallery and seen people gallop round the chamber and glance at twelve of Turner's pictures in the space of five minutes. Surely we might say to such trippers, 'Be still, and know Turner!'

J.H. Jowett, *Thirsting for the Springs*

When Christ comes in, the wonder is not that one has emotion, but the wonder is that one can be so restrained.

E. Stanley Jones

Has *the wonder* of God broken in upon us in a vital way?

Wonder is the opposite of cynicism and boredom; it indicates that a person has heightened aliveness, is interested, expectant, responsive. It is essentially an 'opening' attitude . . . an awareness that there is more to life than one has fathomed, an experience of new vistas of life to be explored as well as new profundities to be plumbed.

Rollo May

In the divine Scriptures, there are shallows and there are deeps; shallows where the lamb may wade, and deeps where the elephant may swim.

John Owen, *Works*

When we cannot, by searching, find the bottom, we must sit down at the brink and adore the depths.

Matthew Henry, *Commentary*

The larger the island of knowledge, the longer the shoreline of wonder.

Ralph Sockman

I seem to have been only a boy playing on the seashore, and diverting myself in now and then finding a smoother pebble or a prettier shell than ordinary, whilst the great ocean of truth lay all undiscovered before me.

Isaac Newton

(We) need no longer pause in fear to enter the Holy of Holies. God wills that we should push on into his presence and live our whole life there. This is to be known to us in conscious experience. It is more than a doctrine to be held, it is a life to be enjoyed every moment of every day.

The world is perishing for lack of the knowledge of God and the church is famishing for want of his presence. The instant cure of most of our religious ills would be to enter the presence in spiritual experience, to become suddenly aware that we are in God and that God is in us.

What a broad world to roam in, what a sea to swim in is this God and Father of our Lord Jesus Christ.

A.W. Tozer, *The Pursuit of God*

Knowledge is proud that he learned so much;
Wisdom is humble that he knows no more.

W. Cowper, *Poems*

Great saints and spiritual leaders have often displayed glaring differences from each other. Are we able to identify a common factor in their lives? I venture to suggest that the one vital quality which they had in common was *spiritual receptivity*. Something in them was open to heaven, something which urged them Godward... They had spiritual awareness and they went on to cultivate it until it became the biggest thing in their lives. They differed from the average person in that when they felt the inward longing, *they did something about it*. They acquired the lifelong habit of spiritual response. They were not disobedient to the heavenly vision.

A.W. Tozer, *The Pursuit of God*

O God, You are my God, earnestly I seek you; My soul thirsts for you, my body longs for you, in a dry and weary land where there is no water.

Psalm 63:1, NIV

Give to every believer a sweet sense of pardoned sins, a blessed consciousness of divine love, a holy peace of mind, a blessed restfulness in Christ. Give also perfect consecration, strong resolve to serve the Lord while here below to the utmost of our capacity. Give more receptiveness that we may be ready to hold. Lord, enlarge us; give much faith to believe great things and to lay hold of great things. Amen .

C.H. Spurgeon, *Behold the Throne of Grace*

O Lord, one thing I desire and seek, that I shall dwell in your presence and gaze, not glance, upon your beauty all the days of my life, in whatever circumstances of bustle and pressure I may find myself. I have tasted your goodness, and it has both satisfied me and made me thirsty for more. Draw me on to enter more deeply into a conscious sense of your presence, to know you in a more ravishing way that I may be a worshipper before I am a worker, that your work may be done in your way and that rivals for your affection may be diverted from my soul. Amen .

A Benediction
May his love be poured out into your heart by his Holy Spirit, may the knowledge of him be deeply impressed upon your mind, and may his strength enable you to keep on keeping on. Amen.

WEEK

Jogging in triangles

Guard your steps when you go to the house of God; to draw near to listen is better than to offer the sacrifice of fools.

It is vain that you rise up early and go late to rest, eating the bread of anxious toil.

Be still before the Lord, and wait patiently for him.

Fear not, stand firm, and see the salvation of the Lord . . .

The Lord will fight for you, and you have only to be still.

Fear not, for I am with you; be not dismayed, for I am your God.

For God has not given us a spirit of fear, but a spirit of power and love and a sound mind.

Peace I leave with you; my peace I give you . . . Do not let your hearts be troubled and do not be afraid.

So do not worry, saying, 'What shall we eat?' or 'What shall we drink?' or 'What shall we wear?' For the pagans run after all these things.

Don't worry about anything, but in all your prayers ask God for what you need, always asking him with a thankful heart.

Rejoice always, pray constantly, give thanks in all circumstances; for this is the will of God in Christ Jesus for you.

(Ecclesiastes 5:1, RSV; Psalm 37:7, RSV; Exodus 14:13,14, RSV; Isaiah 41:10, RSV; 2 Timothy 1:7, Phillips; John 14:27, NIV; Matthew 6:31-32, NIV; Philippians 4:6, TEV; 1 Thessalonians 5:16-18, RSV)

We in Western society are very much into doing and achieving, and as Christians we sometimes embrace in practice a kind of salvation by works despite what we claim in our theoretical theology.

We seem to despise remaining, resting and abiding as being almost non-Christian. The protestant work ethic has still got us firmly by the throat.

In the words of Psalm 127 we still eat 'the bread of anxious toil' of our own efforts.

Jesus invites us to consider the lilies, not just in order to examine their beauty, but to note how they grow. They grow spontaneously without conscious effort or concern, cared for by their Master and Creator.

How far removed is this tranquil scene from the life of many of us, trying so hard to grow and be 'productive', spurring ourselves on to more and more frantic efforts 'for the Lord'.

Many Christians are great workers for God's cause, volunteering for difficult jobs, out many nights in the week, attending church committees. However, when it comes to sitting still for a moment and relaxing in God's presence to receive his directions, empowering and resources, they are unable to do so. They become what has been described as 'rocking chair Christians', plenty of motion but little real progress, doing what they think God would have them do but not taking time to ask him for guidance and taking time to listen to him.

The 'hyperactive' prophet Elijah had to go through the valley of depression, anger, bitterness and physical exhaustion before he was prepared to listen to the still, small voice of God for his direction.

'Be still and know . . .' (Psalm 46:10). The Hebrew term used here is *rapah*, which means relax! 'Relax and know that I am God.'

'But, but,' the Christian 'workaholics' protest, 'What about running the race, fighting the fight, subduing the body . . . aren't you just copping out?'

No, I don't think so. I am just trying to re-discover that fine balance between action and contemplation, the inward journey and the outward journey. In my reading of the Old and New Testaments for every challenge to action there is at least one other command to rest, remain, wait or abide.

Also in our 'busyness' we have lost a sense of praise and thanksgiving. We are so busy doing things for God that we do not have time to stop and comprehend what he has done and is willing to do for us, and so we have little that consciously we can praise him for.

How long is it since you (or I) have stopped for a prolonged period of time to praise and thank God for his blessings? Life indeed has become very serious.

Slow me down Lord,
Ease the pounding of my heart by the quietening of my mind,
Steady my hurried pace with the vision of the eternal reach of time.
Give me, amid the confusion of the day, the calmness of the everlasting hills.
Break the tension of my nerves and muscles with the soothing music of the singing streams that live in my memory . . .
Slow me down Lord, and inspire me to send
my roots deep into the soil of life's enduring values,
that I may grow towards my greater destiny.
Remind me each day that the race is not always to the swift; that there is more to life than increasing its speed.

Orin L. Crain in Tim Hansel, *When I Relax I Feel Guilty*

Freedom from anxiety is characterised by three inner attitudes. If what we have we receive as a gift, and if what we have is to be cared for by God, and if what we have is available to others, then we will possess freedom from anxiety.

Richard Foster, *Celebration of Discipline*

If I had my life to live over again,
I'd try to make more mistakes next time:
I would relax, I would limber up, I would
be sillier than I have been this trip.
I know of very few things I would take seriously.
I would take more trips, I would be crazier . . .
I would eat more ice cream and less beans
I would have more actual troubles and fewer imaginary ones.
You see I'm one of those people who lives life

prophylactically and sensibly hour after hour,
day after day.
Oh, I've had my moments, and if I had
to do it over again, I'd have more of them...

Anonymous monk, in Tim Hansel,
When I Relax I Feel Guilty

Far and away, the most important benefit of celebration is that is saves us from taking ourselves too seriously... Our spirit can become weary with straining after God, as our body can become weary with overwork.

Richard Foster, *Celebration of Discipline*

Do something unusual. Be an experimenter. Meet new people, try new experiences. Let people think you're loony. Wear a funny hat or put your shirt on backwards for a day... Hug a tree, fly a kite, wear a button, jog in triangles. Go for a long walk in your bare feet. Poke some holes in your rigidity. This is not a time to be timid. Take a chance, it's worth it.

Tim Hansel, *When I Relax I Feel Guilty*

Oh Lord, I laugh aloud as I think of jogging in triangles; it's a long time since we laughed like that. Lord, I take myself too seriously.

I think I'm mostly responsible for making things happen, not you. Please forgive me for such arrogance and pride.

Lord, let me learn to rest, await, abide; to relax in you, enjoy you and the life you've given me.

As I relax and slow down may I see what I have missed in my frenzied activities — you — and as I see you more may I praise you more.

A Benediction

God grant me the serenity to accept the things I cannot change, the courage to change the things I can, and the wisdom to know the difference. Amen.

WEEK

5

The waiting game

Wait for the Lord; be strong and let your heart take courage; yes, wait for the Lord.

For God alone my soul waits in silence, for my hope is from him.

It will be said on that day 'Lo this is our God; we have waited for him, that he might save us.'

From of old no one has heard or perceived by the ear, no eye has seen a God besides thee, who works for those who wait for him .

Be ready for action with belts fastened and lamps alight. Be like men who wait for their master's return . . . ready to let him in the moment he knocks.

When he was abused he did not retort with abuse. When he suffered he uttered no threats, but committed his cause to the one who judges justly.

We ourselves, who have the first fruits of the Spirit, groan inwardly as we wait for adoption as sons.

For to us, our hope of attaining the righteousness which we eagerly await, is the work of the Spirit through faith.

Be patient my brothers until the Lord comes. The farmer looking for the precious crop his land may yield can only wait in patience, until the autumn and spring rains have fallen.

(Psalm 27:14, RSV; Psalm 62:5, RSV; Isaiah 25:9, RSV; Isaiah 64:4, RSV; Luke 12:35-36, NEB; 1 Peter 2:23, NEB; Romans 8:23, RSV; Galatians 5:5, NEB; James 5:7-8, NEB)

Between our work and the fruit of it there is always a distance, the time of waiting. We all know this and we all have found it hard to bear. Yet waiting is built into the structures of living.

Expectation of good is a joy that we could not have without waiting. Crises of courtship, birth, promotion, all make demands upon our patience. Would it have been better if these changes had fallen upon us, like Newton's apple? Would we have been better people? Something persuades us otherwise. We appreciate the good that has come to us the more when it comes, not by plain sailing, but through heavy seas; over the edge of the falls.

All the same, we do not like being kept waiting; not for appointments, not for service at stores, restaurants or government offices. This understanding of the importance of not having to wait is reinforced by what we experience in hospitals and nursing homes. Patients (by definition sufferers, those who must wait) have to wait for everything — for food, drink, nursing; wait even to be moved. Unemployed people are 'waiters'. People who work are 'doers'. The unemployed lack this apparent worth.

We notice in the scriptures that there is a premium set upon waiting for God. Waiting is a form of faithfulness, of endurance. It is the other side of seeking him. Waiting is so important that its demands are placed upon Jesus, who carries it up to the Father. He works steadily, patiently, in the day God has given him. He has time for people, time for God. When he is handed over to the Jews and to Pilate he accepts for himself exactly those marks of waiting which we see in the hospital and nursing-home patient. He waits for others, others serve him as they will; move him, push him, give him food or drink or not, as they decide. Waiting thus is hallowed by God who voluntarily sets aside his rule *over* us and in Christ comes under its rule. So he encourages and blesses our waiting, our patience, our endurance.

When our experience of waiting... comes home to us we speak of our frustration and, in doing so disclose our assumption that the waiting role, the condition of dependence, the status of patient, is improper to us, a diminution of our true function or status in the world, an affront to our human dignity.

W.H. Vanstone, *The Stature of Waiting*

Faith means just that blessed unrest, deep and strong, which so urges the believer onward that he cannot settle at ease in the world, and anyone who was quite at ease would cease to be a believer.

Soren Kierkegaard, *Gospel of Sufferings*

Perhaps, indeed, the better the gift we pray for, the more time is necessary for its arrival. To give us the spiritual gift we desire, God may have to begin far back in our spirit... He may be approaching our consciousness from behind, coming forward through regions of our darkness into our light, long before we begin to be aware that he is answering our request — has answered it and is visiting his child.

George MacDonald, *Unspoken Sermons* Second series

'Passion' does not mean exclusively or even primarily 'pain': it means dependence, exposure, waiting, being no longer in control of one's own situation, being the object of what is done... If the truth of God is disclosed and the glory of God is manifest in Jesus, then the truth of God must be this, and the glory of God must appear in this — that God so initiates and acts that he destines himself to enter into passion, to wait and to receive.

W.H. Vanstone, *The Stature of Waiting*

God himself cuts himself off from himself, he gives himself away to his people, he suffers with their sufferings, he goes with them into the misery of the foreign land, he wanders with their wanderings.

Fritz Rosenweig, quoted by Jurgen Moltmann in *Experiences of God*

Christ is our hope because Christ is our future. That means that we are waiting and hoping for his second coming, praying 'Come, Lord Jesus, come to the world, come to us'. Without the expectation of Christ's second coming there is no hope.

Jurgen Moltmann, *Experiences of God*

(With the example of Christ) before my mind, I will begin to desire with all the power of my will to practise this same patience according to my capacity in my own trials. Knowing at the same time the weakness and imperfection of my own soul fettered by attachments, I will above all pray earnestly and humbly for the grace without which I can never hope to conquer my impatience, irritability, aggressiveness and self-righteous impulses to judge and punish other men.

Thomas Merton, *Spiritual Direction and Meditation*

When we love we hand ourselves over to receive from another our own triumph or our own tragedy.

W.H. Vanstone, *The Stature of Waiting*

Father, thank you for the hope you give me in Jesus, which makes me restless to go on and upwards in his calling of me, and impatient for change among the people with whom I work. May more of them come to love and serve you. I confess, Lord, that there are times when my impatience with them makes me judgmental. I forget how patient you have been with me, watching and waiting for me through times of dullness and rebellion and loss, waiting for me to grow up in all things into Christ.

Because you love us you hand yourself over to us, giving us power over you. Help me to be modest, humble, and patient with them all.

A Benediction

I go on today, Lord, singing and making melody to you in my heart, ready to do and to suffer all that you ask of me, in Jesus Christ. I seek you in all things, I wait for you so. Amen.

WEEK

On sabbatical

By the seventh day God had finished the work he had been doing; so on the seventh day he rested from all his work. And God blessed the seventh day and made it holy, because on it he rested from all the work of creating that he had done.

Six days you shall do your work, but on the seventh day you shall rest; that your ox and your ass may have rest, and the son of your bondmaid, and the alien, may be refreshed . . . in ploughing time and in harvest you shall rest.

Take heed for the sake of your lives, and do not bear a burden on the sabbath day.

If you turn your foot from the sabbath, from doing your business on my holy day, and call the sabbath a delight and the holy day of Yahweh honourable; if you honour it, not going your own ways, or pursuing your own callings, or talking idly; then you shall take delight in Yahweh, and I will make you ride upon the heights of the earth.

'The Sabbath was made for man, not man for the Sabbath. So the Son of Man is Lord even of the Sabbath.'

Come to me, all you who are weary and burdened, and I will give you rest. Take my yoke upon you and learn from me, for I am gentle and humble in heart, and you will find rest for your souls. For my yoke is easy and my burden is light.

One man considers one day more sacred than another; another man considers every day alike. Each one should be fully convinced in his own mind.

Therefore do not let anyone judge you . . . with regard to a religious festival, a New Moon celebration or a Sabbath day. These are a shadow of the things that were to come; the reality, however, is found in Christ.

There remains, then, a Sabbath-rest for the people of God; for anyone who enters God's rest also rests from his own work, just as God did from his. Let us, therefore, make every effort to enter that rest, so that no-one will fall...

Then I heard a voice from heaven say, 'Write: Blessed are the dead who die in the Lord from now on.' 'Yes,' says the Spirit, 'they will rest from their labour, for their deeds will follow them.'

(Genesis 2:2-3, NIV; Exodus 23:12, RSV; Exodus 34:21, RSV; Jeremiah 17:21ff, RSV; Isaiah 58:13-14, RSV; Mark 2:27-28, NIV; Matthew 11:28-30, NIV; Romans 14:5-6, NIV; Colossians 2:16-17, NIV; Hebrews 4:9-11, NIV; Revelation 14:13, NIV)

The Sabbath is, in a sense, a peep-hole into eternity, a glimpse of the good times God has in store for us.

It's a day to let our hair down in honour of God — a day of sheer surprise. As Andreasen says, 'it's like a bouquet of flowers when there is no anniversary, birthday or Mother's Day.'

It's a day of daring non-doing, when we put a distance between ourselves and our deeds, a day to let the washing wait and leave the phone off the hook. A day of gracious living, a day when we remind ourselves that we rest not on our own laurels but on Christ's, because Jesus is our Sabbath: our relationship with him is our rest.

Some Christians may give practical expression to this one day a week: usually Sunday. Others think it's Saturday. Pastors usually have Monday. Some have parts of every day. Whatever we do, Paul says in Romans 14:5-10 and Colossians 2:16-17 that we're free to do so as long as we remind ourselves of our relationship with Christ.

The Old Testament stresses the role of remembering God's deeds so that like a rower we move forward towards the future by facing backwards and getting our bearings. Times to remember function like a traffic island in the rush of time.

A sabbatical style of life is also a standing protest against the tyranny of things. It can come so far but no further. Five or six days we turn time into things. On the seventh there is a reservation for relationships. Then the rich don't get richer and the poor, poorer. Everyone is theoretically equal in time. The professor and the student, the boss and the worker can share the same beach or park bench. The Sabbath keeps us in step with the slow coaches, the old, the handicapped, the children. We can all meet on the level of the lowest common denominator. This is very much in line with the Sabbath's concern for the sojourner, and even the animals and the earth.

The Sabbath — our rest in Christ — is both an historical hangover from paradise and a preview of heaven. It is an oasis in the desert of our days, an oasis for time with God, others and ourselves.

The work which has been laid upon man is not his goal. His goal is the eternal rest which has been suggested in the rest of the seventh day.

Claus Westermann, *Creation*

It is remarkable that the Sabbath, in the Old Testament, is not understood as the day on which some special service of worship is held. We hear nothing of any special religious practices from which the special importance of the Sabbath day might be derived. No, the Sabbath day is the day of rest; for rest it has been appointed and for nothing else . . . Modern man may well find strange the idea that God can be honoured simply by doing no work. But the men of old time regarded work not as something holy in itself, but rather as something that can set up a wall of separation between even God and man. We sometimes feel that the duty to work has unchallenged sovereignty over men; but this rest that is imposed upon man from without denies the exclusive claim that work would sometimes make . . . But the Sabbath could also be described as the normal day . . . 'Upon the whole course of the world's history rests like a benediction God's repose of the seventh day of creation, which knows no evening,' says one modern writer. But if man no longer pays attention to this rest, his life falls victim to all manner of slavery.

Gerhard von Rad, *Moses*

Man's first working day will begin only after God's day of rest, with its contemplation of the fullness of creation. Early Christianity showed theological wisdom in decreeing that the first day of the week was to be the day of rest instead of the seventh. For liberated man who is the receiver of God's gifts, the week does not end with the day of rest; it begins with it. The working days can then take on rather more of the character of play — even the character of protest against the principle of judging performance by results and against the demand for those results. What can man do more in his work than to see to it that whatever the Creator has prepared for him is rightly harvested and rightly used — is not spoiled, but is protected from being ruined by man's misuse? Without the focus on the work that God has already completed, man cannot find a right relationship either to his own work or to rest.

Was it not precisely this that early Christianity grasped when it associated the day of rest with the resurrection of Jesus Christ? No power, not even the power of death, can conquer the liberator of man any longer. Because of Jesus' work of redemption, no pressure to produce results is now to torment man, no transgressions are to rise up to accuse him, not even the imperfections and incompletions of a past week.

Hans Walter Wolff, *Anthropology of the Old Testament*

Listen to Spurgeon: 'Repose is as needful to the mind as sleep to the body . . . If we do not rest, we shall break down. Even the earth must lie fallow and have her Sabbaths, and so must we.' Jesus said: 'Come apart and rest awhile.' (If you don't rest awhile, you'll soon come apart!)

Arch Hart, *Grid* Magazine

The meaning of the Sabbath is to celebrate time rather than space . . . It is a day on which we are called upon to share in what is eternal in time, to turn from the results of creation to the mystery of creation.

The Sabbath is an example of the world to come.

Abraham Heschel, *The Sabbath*

I heard the voice of Jesus say:
  Come unto Me and rest;
Lay down, thou weary one, lay down
  Thy head upon My breast!

I came to Jesus as I was,
  Weary, and worn, and sad;
I found in Him a resting-place,
  And He has made me glad.

Horatius Bonar, *The Voice of Jesus*

O Sabbath rest by Galilee!
O calm of hills above,
where Jesus knelt to share with thee
the silence of eternity,
interpreted by love.

John Greenleaf Whittier, in
the *Australian Hymn Book*

My spirit longeth for thee
  Within my troubled breast;
Although I be unworthy
  Of so divine a Guest.
Of so divine a Guest,
  Unworthy though I be;
Yet has my heart no rest,
  Unless it come from thee.
Unless it come from thee,
  In vain I look around;
In all that I can see,
  No rest is to be found.
No rest is to be found,
  But in thy blessed love;
O, let my wish be crowned,
  And send it from above.

John Byrom, *My Spirit Longeth for Thee*

The Lord is my pace-setter, I shall not rush;
he makes me stop and rest for quiet intervals,
he provides me with images of stillness,
which restore my serenity.
He leads me in the way of efficiency,
through calmness of mind;
and his guidance is peace.
Even though I have a great many things to accomplish each
  day
I will not fret, for his presence is here.

His timelessness, his all-importance will keep me in balance.
He prepares refreshment and renewal
in the midst of activity,
by anointing my mind with his oils of tranquillity;
my cup of joyous energy overflows.
Surely harmony and effectiveness shall be
the fruits of my hours
and I shall walk in the pace of my Lord,
and dwell in his house for ever.

Toki Miyashina, *Psalm 23 For Busy People*

In this era of conflicts
  and mountainous problems,
we know what it is to labour
  and be heavy laden.
You have called us to go out
  into all the world
and immerse all nations
  in the gospel of divine love.
We have tried, Lord,
  and have become tattered and tired,
  despondent, even a bit cynical.
We, the heavy-laden,
  come to you, Lord,
needing your rest.
As the native hen nests
  in the clumps of tussocks
  at the edge of quiet waters;
so give us a nesting place
  in the quiet places of your kingdom,
that our hope may be renewed
  as your mothering Spirit broods over us,
protecting us through
  every dark night of the soul,
until morning comes again
  and we are renewed —
  as if born again —
to learn from you the holy way
  that leads to life
for all humanity.

Bruce Prewer, *Australian Prayers*

Take my tired body, my confused mind, and my restless soul into your arms and give me rest, simple quiet rest. Do I ask too much too soon? I should not worry about that. You will let me know. Come, Lord Jesus, come. Amen.

Henri Nouwen, in *Lion Book of Famous Prayers*

Carpenter and easy yoke-maker, we confess that we are restless, chafing under yokes of our making... we admit that like Pharisees we add burdens to the backs of others, sometimes deliberately, sometimes unwittingly... sometimes we carry chips on our shoulders that rub against your yoke and rub other people up the wrong way... Lord forgive us, help us to be and become more like you, release us from feeling we always have to do, and grant us the grace to rest in our relationship with you.
Unhurried God, help us to take time to remember you as we remember the Sabbath day, help us to remember what Eden was like, and grant us a preview of what Paradise will be. On our days off, on our days of rest, in all our days, grant us a glimmer of your glorious new world. Amen.

A Benediction
Now, may the Father who works and rests (and invites us to join him in his work and in his rest), the Son who cried, 'It is finished' and the Spirit who completes his work in us maintain a right rhythm of work and rest in us this day and evermore. Amen.

WEEK

Talking it through

'Come now, let us talk this over,' says Yahweh.

'Yahweh,' he said, 'I have had enough. Take my life; I am no better than my ancestors.' Then he lay down and went to sleep... But the angel of Yahweh came back a second time and touched him and said, 'Get up and eat, or the journey will be too long for you.' So he got up and ate and drank, and strengthened by that food he walked for forty days and forty nights until he reached Horeb, the mountain of God... And after the fire there came the sound of a gentle breeze. And when Elijah heard this, he covered his face with his cloak and went out and stood at the entrance of the cave. Then a voice came to him, which said, 'What are you doing here, Elijah?'

I thank you, Yahweh, with all my heart, because you have heard what I said... The day I called for help, you heard me and you increased my strength.

But when you pray, go to your private room and, when you have shut your door, pray to your Father who is in that secret place.

In the morning, long before dawn, he got up and left the house, and went off to a lonely place and prayed there.

But he said in answer, 'My mother and my brothers are those who hear the word of God and put it into practice.'

Then he took them with him and withdrew to a town called Bethsaida where they could be by themselves.

So I say to you: Ask, and it will be given to you; search, and you will find; knock, and the door will be opened to you. For the one who asks always receives; the one who searches always finds; the one who knocks will always have the door opened to him.

Jesus turned round, saw them following and said, 'What

do you want?' They answered, 'Rabbi,' — which means Teacher — 'where do you live?' 'Come and see,' he replied; so they went and saw where he lived, and stayed with him the rest of that day.

(Isaiah 1:18; 1 Kings 19:4, 7-8 and 12-13; Psalm 138:1 and 3; Matthew 6:6; Mark 1:35; Luke 8:21, 9:10, 11:9-10; John 1:38-39 — all JB)

One of the greatest problems facing Christians today — and perhaps particularly Christian clergy — is that we are so busy doing God's work that we forget about him.

He's left us a lot of work: preaching his word and visiting the needy and comforting the oppressed, changing evil structures and fighting injustice, stressing that good is alive in our world and evil needn't be the victor.

The trouble is that work can turn into busyness, and God's work can very subtly become mine.

We need to be reminded forcefully day by day that it is his work, that he has asked us to be his partners in his ongoing work of redemption.

There's an old Latin tag — *nemo dat quod non habet* — you can't give what you haven't got. What we are called to give — who we are called to give — is God himself: his compassion, love, mercy, listening. If I don't know him I can't give him.

I can know him through his creation, through study, through reading scripture, through interaction with others. These are good, but there is one way that is essential. We have traditionally called it prayer.

It seems self-evident. But if we are ruthlessly honest with ourselves we know that busyness can force prayer out. The prayer with the congregation may remain, but the prayer which is my Lord and I alone together can be forced further and further to the limits of my life, and one day just quietly disappear. When it does, there's an emptiness.

We need that time with him each day. We need to talk over our life with him. We need to tell him of our desires and disappointments, our doubts and our strivings. We need to be quiet, to listen, to wait. We need to be with him in our sinfulness and forgiveness. We need to let him know who we are and how we are, to let him be our strength in our weakness.

We need to let him be God to us in the way we need it, a different way each different day. We need to let him be the God he wants to be through us.

Call it talking it through, conversation with God, just being with him as I am. Call it waiting, listening. Call it, as Karl Rahner does, an encounter with silence, the silence of the God who waits on me. Call it prayer, daily. Call it life.

Jesus does.

We need no wings to go in search of him, but have only to find a place where we can be alone and look upon him present within us.

St Teresa of Avila

It is not for his gifts that I continue in my prayers, but because he is true life.

Gregory of Narek,
source unknown

The question of how or when to pray is not the most important one. The crucial question is whether you should pray always and whether your prayer is necessary. Here the stakes are all or nothing! If someone says that it's good to turn to God in prayer for a spare moment, or if he grants that a person with a problem does well to take refuge in prayer, he has as much as admitted that praying is on the margin of his life and that it doesn't really matter. Whenever you feel that a little praying can't do any harm, you will find that it can't do much good either. Prayer has meaning only if it is necessary and indispensable. Prayer is prayer only when we say that without it a man could not live.

Henri Nouwen, *With Open Hands*

Prayer is nothing more than a conversation with God, who loves me.

St Teresa of Avila

Prayer is the sum of our relationship with God. We are what we pray. The degree of our faith is the degree of our prayer. Our ability to love is our ability to pray.

Carlo Carretto, *Letters from the Desert*

I know, my God, that my prayer need not be enthusiastic and ecstatic to succeed in placing me so much in your power and at your disposal that nothing is held back from you. Prayer can be real prayer, even when it is not filled with bliss and jubilation or the shining brilliance of a carefree surrender of self. Prayer can be like a slow interior bleeding, in which grief and sorrow make the heart's-blood of the inner man trickle away silently into his own unfathomed depths.

Karl Rahner, *Encounters with Silence*

The implication would seem to be that silence is a kind of death to communication because it disrupts social intercourse. (But) when the Son of God became man he gave to silence and solitude a new meaning and a perennial value. Christ's loneliness in Nazareth and on the mountainside is meaningful as an aspect of his communion with his Father and with all men through him. Since Christ's action is our instruction, no matter how demanding on our time and energy the needs of our neighbour may be, if we are to follow him we must discover a time for silence. There are many ways in which Christ can express his love in and through men; but there must be a listening to him if that life is to be Christlike. Christian listening is an aspect of Christian knowing; it is not the titillation of curious ears; it is a waiting on the Lord and a laying open of the heart to his commands.

Nicholas Madden,
source unknown

Well, let's now at any rate come clean. Prayer *is* irksome. An excuse to omit it is never unwelcome. When it is over, this casts a feeling of relief and holiday over the rest of the day. We are reluctant to begin. We are delighted to finish. While we are at prayer, but not while we are reading a novel or solving a crossword puzzle, any trifle is enough to distract us. And we know that we are not alone in this. The fact that prayers are constantly set as penances tells its own tale. The odd thing is that this reluctance to pray is not confined to periods of dryness. When yesterday's prayers were full of comfort and exaltation, today's will still be felt as, in some degree, a burden. Now the disquieting thing is not simply that we skimp and begrudge the duty of prayer. The really disquieting thing is it should have to be numbered among duties at all. For we believe that we were created 'to glorify God and enjoy him forever.'

C.S. Lewis, *Prayer: Letters to Malcolm*

In the lonely place Jesus finds the courage to follow God's will and not his own; to speak God's words and not his own; to do God's work and not his own. He reminds us constantly: 'I can do nothing by myself . . . my aim is to do not my own will, but the will of him who sent me' (John 5:30), and again, 'The words I say to you I do not speak as from myself: it is the Father, living in me, who is doing this work' (John 14:10). It is in the lonely place where Jesus enters into intimacy with the Father that his ministry is born. Somewhere we know that without a lonely place our lives are in danger. Somewhere we know that without silence words lose their meaning, that without listening speaking no longer heals, that without distance closeness cannot cure. Somewhere actions quickly become empty gestures. The careful balance between silence and words, withdrawal and involvement, distance and closeness, solitude and community forms the basis of the Christian life.

Henri Nouwen, *Out of Solitude*

I'm very busy, Lord. There is so much to do for you, so many meetings, so many sermons to get ready, so many people to see. There's a service to prepare for next Sunday, it's important and. . .

Just a minute — no, not you Lord, me. The service for next Sunday, the sermon: the preachers are concerned with you, they're to make your word present in the hearts and lives of others. So, I guess, are the meetings and the visiting. And what am I doing? I'm planning them — I'm organising them — I'm wondering about their effect.

I'm doing all this, Lord. I've just realised that that dreaded personal pronoun keeps cropping up. Isn't it your work, Lord? Shouldn't the 'I' merge into 'We'?

Am I giving it enough chance to, Lord? When did you and I last meet, just you and I? When did I last make time just to be with you, to sit quietly with you, even to tell you about my day and how I felt and what fears I had? When did I last make an appointment with you?

I don't think I want to remember, Lord — I feel guilty about it. Make me remember.

Give me the gift of making time each day for you. Remind me that it is you who are the soul of my activity. Jolt me into a continual realisation that you must be with me if what I do is to be truly your work, not mine.

Give me the courage to set me and my interests aside each day, and just be before you, with you, open to you.

Let me be silent with you, my waiting God.

A Benediction

Go, and know the Lord goes with you. Let him lead you each day into the quiet place of your heart, where he will speak to you. Know that he blesses and watches over you — that he listens to you in gentle understanding — that he is with you always, wherever you are and however you may feel. Amen.

WEEK

Still waters... deep waters

He lets me rest in fields of green grass and leads me to quiet pools of fresh water.

A person's thoughts are like water in a deep well, but someone with insight can draw them out.

Tremble with fear and stop sinning; think deeply about this, when you lie in silence on your beds. Offer the right sacrifices to the Lord, and put your trust in him.

Very early the next morning, long before daylight, Jesus got up and left the house. He went out of the town to a lonely place, where he prayed.

(Jesus said) 'How is it that you three were not able to keep watch with me even for one hour? Keep watch and pray that you will not fall into temptation. The spirit is willing but the flesh is weak.'

But when you pray, go to your room, close the door, and pray to your Father, who is unseen. And your Father, who sees what you do in private, will reward you.

Come to me, all of you who are tired from carrying heavy loads, and I will give you rest.

(Psalm 23:2; Proverbs 20:5; Psalm 4:4-5; Mark 1:35; Matthew 26:40-41; Matthew 6:6; Matthew 11:28 — all GNB)

Any action of Jesus was preceded by prayer: first he had to be both rested and sure of God's will. Any prayer of Jesus was followed by effective action: preaching, teaching, healing, demonstrating to those with eyes to see the in-breaking of the kingdom of God.

The inner quiet that Jesus needed he offers to us. This inner quiet calls up the image of a deep rock pool high in the Blue Mountains, the placid clarity of fresh water, not the fetid stagnation of an old billabong. Inner quiet is no complacent acceptance of fate, no resignation in the face of hardship, no escape from the realities of life; it is a 'still point of the turning world' (T.S. Eliot), a creative and energising 'contemplation in a world of action' (Thomas Merton). In whatever ways we are called to our Lord's service, release from outer stress and 'inner strife' were never more needed than today. To find and nurture that inner resource of the Spirit is absolutely essential for effective ministry, for basic Christian discipleship.

Hesychasm, from the Greek word for quiet, stillness, tranquillity, refers to the way of prayer taught and practised in the Christian East from the fourth century on. More specifically it refers to prayer that is as far as possible free from concepts and the verbiage of discursive reason. It points us to contemplative prayer, seeking the kingdom within (compare with Luke 17:21), that state of being where Christ truly dwells in us (2 Corinthians 13:5).

In a narrower sense still, *hesychasm* refers to the use of the Jesus Prayer, 'Lord Jesus Christ, Son of God, have mercy on me,' and to the linking of the act of praying with the control of the act of breathing: that with every breath we may praise our Lord. Anthony de Mello's *Sadhana: A Way to God,* among other recent books, has given us access again to this ancient way of praying. The contemplatives of the Christian era have found in the Jesus Prayer a way of becoming quiet so that they can find a relationship with God at depth, and may be reshaped by it. It can become a tool for carving out an inner stillness so that the Spirit can be heard, and the conscious and unconscious dimensions of the mind harmonised. That deep stillness, with a place and time uncluttered by physical noise, emotional stress or cerebral musings, is where the Holy Spirit can create, renew, refresh and inspire.

Muddy water,
Let stand,
Becomes clear.

Lao Tse (Chinese philosopher, 5th Century BC),
source unknown

Settle yourself in solitude and you will come upon him in yourself.

Teresa of Avila

I said to my soul, be still, and wait without hope
For hope would be hope for the wrong thing;
  wait without love
For love would be love of the wrong thing;
  there is yet faith
But the faith and the love and the hope are all
  in the waiting.
Wait without thought, for you are not ready for thought:
So the darkness shall be the light, and the stillness
  the dancing.

T.S. Eliot, 'East Coker', III, *Four Quartets*

Words, after speech, reach
Into the silence. Only by the form, the pattern,
Can words or music reach
The stillness.

T.S. Eliot, 'Burnt Norton', V, *Four Quartets*

Elected Silence, sing to me
And beat upon my whorled ear,
Pipe me to pastures still and be
The music that I came to hear.

Gerard Manley Hopkins, 'The habit of perfection',
in *A Selection of Poems and Prose*

All is still and gentle
as if all creation shares
with tender empathy
the last whisper
of this dying day.
The lights are low now,
and everything is suspended
as if waiting
for some final word.

Bruce Prewer, 'Vespers by the Murray River',
in *Australian Prayers*

Drop thy still dews of quietness,
till all our strivings cease;
take from our souls the strain and stress,
and let our ordered lives confess
the beauty of thy peace.

John Greenleaf Whittier, in the
Australian Hymn Book, No.519

Jesus calls us from loneliness to solitude... Loneliness is inner emptiness. Solitude is inner fulfilment. Solitude is not first a place but a state of mind and heart... There is an old proverb to the effect that 'the man who opens his mouth, closes his eyes!' The purpose of silence and solitude is to be able to see and hear.

Richard Foster, *Celebration of discipline*

To be calm and quiet all by yourself is hardly the same as sleeping. In fact, it means being fully awake and following with close attention every move going on inside you. It involves a self-discipline where the urge to get up and go is recognised as a temptation to look elsewhere for what is really close at hand... To pray means to open your hands before God. It means slowly relaxing the tension which squeezes your hands together and accepting your existence with an increasing readiness, not as a possession to defend, but as a gift to receive. Above all, therefore, prayer is a way of life which allows you to find a stillness in the midst of the world where you open your hands to God's promises, and find hope for yourself, your fellowman and the whole community in which you live.

Henri Nouwen, *With Open Hands*

Stillness and quiet, freedom from the demands of others, becoming inner-directed, these are not goals in themselves. They are steps on the way to learning the meaning of God's love for us. As one finds the reality of that love, it becomes possible to offer oneself to God in a mature way and to give some of the same love and understanding to others, self-giving love without strings attached... Whatever else it involves, one finds in this process of detachment and reattachment the meaning of being born again, of giving up an old life and being given a new one.

Morton T. Kelsey, *The Other Side of Silence*

Choose a suitable time for recollection and frequently consider the loving-kindness of God. Do not read to satisfy curiosity or to pass the time, but study such things as move your heart to devotion. If you avoid unnecessary talk and aimless visits, listening to news and gossip, you will find plenty of suitable time to spend in meditation on holy things.

Thomas ã Kempis, *The Imitation of Christ*

John Climacus of Mt Sinai in the sixth century said: 'When you pray do not try to express yourself in fancy words, for often it is the simple, repetitious phrases of a little child that our Father in heaven finds most irresistible. Do not strive for verbosity lest your mind be distracted from devotion by a search for words . . .' This is a very helpful suggestion for us, people who depend so much on verbal ability. The quiet repetition of a single word can help us descend with the mind into the heart. This repetition has nothing to do with magic . . . On the contrary, a word or sentence can help us to concentrate, to move to the centre, to create an inner stillness and thus to listen to the voice of God. When we simply try to sit silently and wait for God to speak to us, we find ourselves bombarded with endless conflicting thoughts and ideas. But when we use a very simple sentence such as 'O God, come to my assistance,' or 'Jesus, Master, have mercy on me,' or a word such as 'Lord' or 'Jesus', it is easier to let the many distractions pass by . . . [and] slowly empty out our crowded interior life and create the quiet space where we can dwell with God.

Henri Nouwen, *The Way of the Heart*

Lord, I have many excuses ready for not finding the opportunity to be still, for not making the time to be quiet. I have high expectations of myself. I hear, sometimes too seriously, the expectations of others. I even blame you sometimes, thinking you want me to do more, for 'more's sake' alone. It's easier to read, or plan, or act, even easier to doodle or admire the view, than to stop and listen. I'm more accustomed to praying in thanks and in intercession than in adoration and submission. I bring you my baggage of activity: these are the things that make the waters muddy: may your Spirit move upon the waters and still them . . .

Muddy water, let stand, becomes clear.

Lord, I would be immersed in the tranquillity of your presence. I give you these minutes of solitary, concentrated prayer-in-your-presence. Shut out the distractions of noise and anxious thought. Relieve and relax the pressures of posture and the demands of the body. My very breathing I put under your command:

* *that its intake may infuse me with your Spirit*
* *that its expulsion may signify my cleansing*
* *that its rhythm may match your vibrant rekindling of my deepest being.*

Lord Jesus Christ, Son of God, have mercy on me (to be repeated, in whole or in part, for the time allotted for silent prayer).

A Benediction

Go into the demands of the day released from inner strife and outer stress. After the quiet joy of encounter in the stillness, may the Holy Spirit remain an inner resource in the dullest routine and the greatest challenge.

The Lord bless you and keep you. Receive his peace. Amen.

Theme: Maturity

'Planted by streams of water' (Psalm 1:3)

Happy are those who reject
  the advice of evil men,
  who do not follow the example of sinners
  or join those who have no use for God.
Instead, they find joy in obeying
  the Law of the Lord,
  and they study it day and night.
They are like trees that grow beside a stream,
  that bear fruit at the right time,
  and whose leaves do not dry up.
They succeed in everything they do.

Psalm 1:1-3, GNB

WEEK

Growing up is growing down!

Blessed is the one who trusts in the Lord, whose confidence is in him. He will be like a tree planted by the water that sends out its roots by the stream. It does not fear when heat comes; its leaves are always green. It has no worries in a year of drought and never fails to bear fruit.

So then, just as you received Christ Jesus as Lord, continue to live in him, rooted and built up in him, strengthened in the faith as you were taught, and overflowing with thankfulness.

Grow in the grace and knowledge of our Lord and Saviour Jesus Christ. Therefore let us leave the elementary teachings about Christ and go on to maturity.

One thing I do: forgetting what is behind and striving toward what is ahead, I press on towards the goal to win the prize for which God has called me heavenwards in Christ Jesus. All of us who are mature should take such a view of things.

To each one of us grace has been given as Christ apportioned it... to prepare God's people for works of service, so that the body of Christ may be built up until we all reach unity in the faith and in the knowledge of the Son of God and become mature, attaining to the whole measure of the fullness of Christ. Then we will no longer be infants... instead, speaking the truth in love, we will in all things grow up into him who is the Head, that is, Christ.

(Jeremiah 17:7-8; Colossians 2:6-7; 2 Peter 3:18; Hebrews 6:1; Philippians 3:13b-15a; Ephesians 4:7,12-13 — all NIV)

Many of us have a yearning to know something of our historical roots. We all, no doubt, know some individuals who have painstakingly researched their family history. Many of those adopted — and their natural parents — are eagerly taking advantage of recent legislation allowing greater access to adoption records. And in many parts of the world there is a burgeoning pride in racial heritage, exemplified by such slogans as 'black is beautiful'. One's roots are important to one's identity.

But more important than our biological and social roots are our spiritual roots. As Christians, we are exhorted to be like trees planted by streams of water, with roots that dig deeply enough to make us strong and stable, and that draw enough regular nourishment to sustain our life and fruitfulness whatever threats our environment brings. However, because we are human beings, not trees, we have a choice as to where we want to be planted, how deeply we will allow our roots to grow, and how liberally we will drink from the water source. If we so choose, we can be planted in an arid area, or near foul water; we can be content with a shallow root system; and we can try to make do with a spasmodic sip of water. Hardly a recipe for a maturing spiritual life!

Further, spiritual roots are nurtured by both historical and contemporary elements, by 'theory' and 'experience'. It is stimulating for us to develop the ability to ponder the nature of God, and his working in history from creation to consummation: but that has minimal value unless we also let our roots go down deeply into the spiritual life that only comes from him. We are enriched by widening our understanding of the atonement as an historical and theological event: but that cannot nourish our souls unless it motivates us to drink freely of the water of life offered to us by Christ in his atonement. There is a place for discussion about the coming of the Holy Spirit and the significance of his work: but that can never be a substitute for allowing him to grow his fruit in our lives, and equip us with the gifts he wishes us to use in the building up of the Body into maturity.

So we face a paradox: growing up is growing down! Whether we identify more readily with the 'riverside tree' or the 'downtown tree' of Ken Medema's 'Tree Song' — the one with its visibly lush surroundings, the other with its hidden water source — we can experientially affirm:

I've got roots growing down to the water,
I've got leaves growing up to the sunshine,
And the fruit that I bear is a sign of the life in me.
I am shade from the hot summer sundown,
I am nest for the birds of the heaven.
I'm becoming what the Lord of trees has meant me to be,
a strong young tree.

Many Christians never grow up. They remain beginners in the faith. The time and effort required to secure the treasures of the spiritual life call for too much effort; the moral and social demands of loyalty to Christ are more than they are prepared to pay; so they remain children in the faith.

E. Ernest Thomas

To some people maturity seems to mean questioning everything and being agnostic on all things. Surely, however, the mark of maturity is to arrive at firm convictions instead of remaining forever in an attitude of adolescent questioning and scepticism. There is a distinction to be drawn between open-mindedness (the willingness to *examine* basic convictions) and empty-mindedness (the principle of throwing everything overboard and then trying to make a fresh start). The [Christian] need not be afraid to submit his deepest convictions to scrutiny, for the truth can stand scrutiny. Nor will he let himself be swept off his feet by superior argument, so that he continually vacillates like a broken weather-vane. Rather he will hold fast to the Word of God, and from this position he will have a proper stance to exercise his critical and self-critical faculties.

I. Howard Marshall, from an article 'Towards Maturity'

If prayer were just an intelligent exercise of our mind, we would soon become stranded in fruitless and trivial inner debates with God. If, on the other hand, prayer would involve only our heart, we might soon think that good prayers consist in good feelings. But the prayer of the heart in the most profound sense unites mind and heart in the intimacy of the divine love... It is indeed like a murmuring stream that continues underneath the many waves of every day and opens the possibility of living in the world without being of it and of reaching out to our God from the centre of our solitude.

Henri Nouwen, *Reaching Out*

Maturity begins to grow when you can sense your concern for others outweighing your concern for yourself.

John MacNaughton,
source unknown

The growth and final maturity of the individual Christian contributes to the growth and final maturity of the church, the society of which he is a member. Conversely, this growth and maturity can only be fully attained in the unity of faith and knowledge which typifies the corporate experience of the church. The Christian individual and the Christian society are, therefore, through their mutual organisation about Christ, interdependent.

W.E. Andersen, *The Christian Concept of Maturity*

Ethical development, as well as intellectual and emotional development, is a necessary condition of maturity... Since ethics always asserts that one kind of conduct is better than another, an ultimate basis for comparison is implied. Therefore, ethical choices are basically theological, since they imply loyalty to God or to some principle that stands in the place of God as an ultimate referent... The intellectual and emotional components of maturity can be developed by effort, such as self-discipline, devotion to learning, and the cultivation of habit. But theological questions demand commitment.

Orville S. Walters, in an article 'Maturity: When?'

Temptation is a factor in the psychological and spiritual growth process everyone must go through if we are to become mature individuals, capable of living a full and meaningful life. The function of temptation is always to trigger a choice and provoke a definite stand or action.

Bob Mumford, *The Purpose of Temptation*

The one who is mature is not he who has achieved all his goals, but who has his goals clearly in mind, and who is, in addition, pursuing them with vigour.

W.E. Andersen, *The Christian Concept of Maturity*

Real maturity comes when we say to ourselves and to others: 'We know in part and prophesy in part... our seeing now is as through a glass darkly.' This means while I don't now know everything, I do know something, and on the basis of what I do know I can act constructively in the present toward the future... If we will respond in this way, that will be the best proof I know that we have 'put away childish things' and are functioning as mature human beings.

John Claypool, in a sermon 'Absurdity, Causality and Mystery'

Where did the idea ever come from that we should reach total maturity quickly or without lots of falling down and getting up? If we abandon the expectation that our growth should be another way, then we can live into where we are and use it as an occasion 'to press on to the mark' as St Paul said, rather than giving up in discouragement... Being a slow learner does not disqualify one. It may be death to pride, but not to hope. Listen, the issue is not how long it takes us to be fully graced, but trust in him who, having begun a good work, will see it through to completion.

John Claypool, from a sermon 'Slow Learners and Hope'

The Lord is often in less of a hurry than we are... It was fourteen years from the time of Paul's conversion to the time of his departure with Barnabas from Antioch. Those largely 'hidden' years were not wasted. God was preparing his instrument: tempering and hardening him, hammering him into shape, teaching him. Paul was learning about discipleship.

Michael Griffiths, *Give Up Your Small Ambitions*

Superficiality is the curse of our age. The doctrine of instant satisfaction is a primary spiritual problem. The desperate need today is not for a greater number of intelligent people, or gifted people, but for deep people. The classical Disciplines of the spiritual life call us to move beyond surface living into the depths. They invite us to explore the inner caverns of the spiritual realm. They urge us to be the answer to a hollow world... Our world is hungry for genuinely changed people. Leo Tolstoy observed, 'Everybody thinks of changing humanity and nobody thinks of changing himself.' Let us be among those who believe that the inner transformation of our lives is a goal worthy of our best effort.

Richard Foster, *Celebration of Discipline*

Our Father, we confess that too often we've put down our roots in the wrong places; we've been more concerned with our human heritage and resources than we have been to experience the riches of our inheritance in Christ; we've not really grown up, because we've not really grown down.

Father forgive us.

Lord Jesus, we want to have more than an intellectual understanding of our faith: we want to know you; *we want to grow up to be mature in you, to be nourished by the water of life you offer us; we want to be made willing to accept the commitment and discipline of being your disciples.*

Lord, inspire us by your example of growth in obedience, so that our goal will be to grow up into you, our Head.

Holy Spirit, we don't want to remain infants, grieving you by our immaturity; we don't want to have such shallow roots that we are unable to produce the fruit you wish to see in our lives; we don't want to ignore the challenges of receiving and using the gifts you allocate to us so we can fulfil our proper functions as part of the Body of Christ.

Spirit, thank you for your power which enables us to grow down, in order that we may grow up.

Our God, Father, Son and Holy Spirit, we accept your forgiveness, your inspiration and your empowering with grateful hearts. Amen.

A Benediction

I pray that out of his glorious riches he may strengthen you with power through his Spirit in your inner being, so that

Christ may dwell in your hearts through faith. And I pray that you, being rooted and established in love, may have power, together with all the saints, to grasp how wide and long and high and deep is the love of Christ, and to know this love that surpasses knowledge: that you may be filled to the measure of all the fullness of God (Ephesians 3:16-19, NIV).

WEEK

'Just add water and shake' — but can the bubbles last?

We proclaim him... so that we may present everyone perfect in Christ.

Be perfect, therefore, as your heavenly Father is perfect.

Not that I have already obtained all this, or have already been made perfect but I press on to take hold of that for which Christ Jesus took hold of me.

That you may be filled to the measure of all the fullness of God... attaining to the whole measure of the fullness of Christ... be filled with the Spirit.

Others... produce a crop... even a hundred times what was sown.

(Colossians 1:28; Matthew 5:48; Philippians 3:12; Ephesians 3:19, 4:13 and 5:18; Mark 4:20 — all NIV)

We live in 'a day of the issue' — smoking, feminism, uranium mining. Good issues: but we can easily be side-tracked from the one quoted in these scriptures. George Bernard Shaw once said, 'A fanatic is one who having forgotten his objectives redoubles his efforts.'

Is Christian maturity forgotten as we are full of overwork rather than overflow? Our Christian booksellers have all the answers but our Christian counsellors report tragedies in our family and church life, many of which stem from shallow Christian experience. Perhaps we need the 'issue' Paul talked about when he said, 'This one thing I do ' (Philippians 3:13).

Every age has its unique conditions which militate against the Christian's reaching his or her full potential. Today, we have an instant society, a paper war, endless demands for seminars and workshops, but rarely do we hear the compulsive call of the Master, 'Be therefore perfect!' So many of us become spiritual dilettantes, avoiding the absoluteness of Christ's demands.

Where then do we start? 'There is nothing unnatural in an increase of temptations, conflicts and pressures as the Christian goes on with God' (J.I. Packer).

E.M. Bounds says, 'We need an insatiable yearning for the fullness of God.'

A.W. Tozer says, 'The great god entertainment has taken hold of the minds of the retarded saints of our day and life is intolerable without some form of entertainment.'

Os Guinness believes that 'we have a "copy cat" syndrome so that we do not have to think or evaluate seriously. It is all done for us.'

Let us 'gird up the loins of our minds' (1 Peter 1:13, KJV) or in today's idiom 'grasp the nettle'. It is a false dichotomy to separate our devotional life from Christian maturity, but the former must develop into the latter, rather than the former being our daily 'dosage' to meet the current day's 'aches and pains'.

'I wish you wouldn't squeeze so,' said the Doormouse, who was sitting next to her. 'I can hardly breathe.'

'I can't help it,' said Alice very meekly: 'I'm growing.'

'You've no right to grow *here*,' said the Doormouse.

'Don't talk nonsense,' said Alice more boldly: 'you know you're growing too.'

'Yes, but *I* grow at a reasonable pace,' said the Doormouse: 'not in that ridiculous fashion.'

Lewis Carroll, *Alice in Wonderland*

A rosebud is perfect in its season, with its delicate folds overlapping each other, but when you observe it a little later, another perfection has appeared; a full bloom with a captivating fragrance has replaced the bud.

There is no such thing as a once-for-all fullness; it is a continuous appropriation of a continuous supply from Jesus Christ himself. . . as I trust him he fills me, so long as I trust him he fills me. The moment I begin to believe that moment I begin to receive.

Chas. Inwood,
source unknown

The world belongs to the disciplined.

Paul Rees

Although evangelical Christians pay lip service to the principle of the 'quiet time' it seems to be less important in practice in the lives of many than it has been in past years.

Rev. Francis Foulkes, 'In touch with God: The Devotional Life of the Messenger'. An occasional paper.

Nothing less than a whole Bible can make a whole Christian.

A.W. Tozer, *Of God and Men*

Prayer is vital — our prayers are the measure of our Christianity. To fail in prayer is to fail in everything else.

Professor E.M. Blaiklock, '*Our Lord's Teaching on Prayer*'

Above all, George Fox excelled in prayer . . . the most awful, living reverent frame I ever felt and beheld I must say, was his when in prayer.

William Penn,
source unknown

Nothing great was ever achieved without enthusiasm.

Ralph Waldo Emerson

Mary had a little lamb
It should have become a sheep
It joined a local Bible church
And died of lack of sleep.

Gary Inrig, *Life in His Body*

If thou could'st empty all thyself of self,
Like to a shell dishabited
Then would he find thee on the ocean shelf
And say 'This is not dead'
And fill thee with himself instead.

But thou art so replete with vanity
And hast such rude activity
That when he comes, he says

'This is enough unto itself
Better to let it be
It is too small, and full;
There is no room for me.'

Author unknown

Batter my heart, three person'd God; for, you
As yet but knocke, breathe, shine, and seeke to mend;
That I may rise, and stand, o'erthrow mee, and bend
Your force, to breake, blowe, burn and make me new . . .
Take mee to you, imprison mee, for I
Except you enthrall mee, never shall be free,
Nor ever chast, except you ravish mee.

John Donne

Indwelt:

Not merely in the words you say,
Not only in your deeds confessed,
But in the most unconscious way
Is Christ expressed.

And from your eyes he beckons me
And from your heart his love is shed
Till I lose sight of you and see
The Christ instead!

Beatrice Cleland,
source unknown

Father, I thank you for the joy of every new beginning; 'In the beginning God' and so you gave me a life which was absolutely new when I came into the world, and then a new life in Christ when I was born from above.

Father, do help me to grow in grace as I have grown in my human life. Let me see the hindrances clearly. Keep me from rationalising what may grieve you. Give me grace to allow prejudices, narrowness, bigotry, the spirit of the Pharisee, to drop out of my life and enable me to reach out for all the fullness of God. As one of your saints prayed, 'Make me as holy as it is possible for a saved sinner to be.'

A Benediction

May the God of peace who through the blood of the eternal covenant brought back from the dead our Lord Jesus, that great Shepherd of the sheep, equip you with everything good, for doing his will, and may he work in us what is pleasing to him, through Jesus Christ, to whom be glory for ever and ever. Amen (Hebrews 13, NIV).

To him who is able to keep you from falling and to present you before his glorious presence without fault and with great joy, to the only God our Saviour be glory, majesty, power and authority through Jesus Christ our Lord, before all ages now and forever more. Amen (Jude 24, NIV).

WEEK

So much dying to be done!

Have this mind among yourselves, which you have in Christ Jesus, who... emptied himself, taking the form of a servant.

Be careful, however, that the exercise of your freedom does not become a stumbling-block to the weak... When you sin against your brothers in this way and wound their weak conscience, you sin against Christ.

If others have this right of support from you, shouldn't we have it all the more? But we did not use this right. On the contrary, we put up with anything rather than hinder the gospel of Christ.

'Everything is permissible' — but not everything is beneficial. 'Everything is permissible' — but not everything is constructive. Nobody should seek his own good, but the good of others.

If any man would come after me, let him deny himself and take up his cross and follow me.

But in your society... if anyone wishes to be great he must be your servant; if anyone wishes to hold the first place, he must be everyone's slave.

I, your Lord and Teacher, have just washed your feet. You, then, should wash one another's feet.

(Philippians 2:5-7, RSV; 1 Corinthians 8:9,12, NIV; 1 Corinthians 9:12, NIV; 1 Corinthians 10:23-24, NIV; Mark 8:34, RSV; Matthew 20:26-27, Barclay; John 13:14, GNB)

We live in a world that is drunk with rights. Women's rights, children's rights, land rights, human rights, animal rights, civil rights, the rights of the unborn: the varieties crowd around us like bottles on the shelves of a liquor shop. And having imbibed, we reel down the street, unable to distinguish tree from lamppost, unable to walk a straight line. Like alcohol, 'rights' have become for some a panacea for all our social ills.

Into this intoxicating environment, the words of the Bible crash with all the gentleness of an axe wielded by a temperance crusader in a bar.

Jesus and Paul are not wowsers on a rampage, however: the concept of 'rights' has some value for expressing spiritual truth and focussing efforts for social change. But their calls to servanthood move us beyond the chimera of self-assertion to the reality of a love so concrete it is prepared to sacrifice for the sake of others even things to which we have a right.

Here is one of the touchstones of true servanthood. Are we prepared to give up legitimate and treasured pastimes, possessions, prerogatives if love for someone, Christian or non-Christian, asks it?

The idea is appallingly practical, appalling because it is practical. We know that in so many ways we are capable of it. But time and again we refuse it, choosing instead the road of self- indulgence and pride and delusion.

Giving up our 'rights' is a kind of death: a death to self. And dying is hard. But in the end, despite our unwillingness to believe so, it is the way to life. The only way.

I need to be so utterly God's, that he can use me or hide me, as he chooses, as an arrow in his hand or in his quiver. I will ask no questions: I relinquish all rights to him who desires my supreme good.

Helen Roseveare, *Living Sacrifice*

We are neither big nor small but what we are in the eyes of God, and as long as we surrender ourselves totally then God can use us without consulting us. We like to be consulted but letting him use us without consultation is very good for us. We must accept emptiness, accept being broken in pieces, accept success or failure.

Mother Teresa of Calcutta

Following Christ has nothing to do with success as the world sees success. It has to do with love.

Madeleine L'Engle, *Walking on Water*

The Learner: How often am I to surrender myself, Lord, and in what matters am I to leave my own preferences behind?
The Beloved: Always; at every moment, in small things as much as in great.

Thomas ā Kempis, *The Imitation of Christ*

...our whole personality can be established, strengthened, settled, given a sure confidence, only when there is a basis of abundant love.

Leon Morris, *1 and 2 Thessalonians*

Mechanical, the
Amber cricket makes her way
Across the concrete:

Eggs must be laid and there is
So much dying to be done!

Andrew Lansdown, *Counterpoise*

We must see the difference between choosing to serve and choosing to be a servant. When we choose to serve we are still in charge. We decide whom we will serve and when we will serve... But when we choose to be a servant we give up the right to be in charge.

Richard Foster, *Celebration of Discipline*

...condescend to all the weaknesses and infirmities of your fellow-creatures, cover their frailties, love their excellencies, encourage their virtues, relieve their wants, rejoice in their prosperities, compassionate their distress, receive their friendship, overlook their unkindness, forgive their malice, be a servant of servants, and condescend to do the lowest offices to the lowest of mankind.

William Law, *A Serious Call to a Devout and Holy Life*

Oh, beware of the mistake so many make, who would fain be humble, but are afraid to be too humble. They have so many qualifications and limitations, so many reasonings and questionings, as to what true humility is to be and to do, that they never unreservedly yield themselves to it. Beware of this. Humble yourself unto death. It is in the death of self that humility is perfected.

Andrew Murray, *Humility*

But the Christian knows from the outset that the salvation of a single soul is more important than the production or preservation of all the epics and tragedies in the world: and as for superiority, he knows that the vulgar since they include most of the poor probably include most of his superiors.

C.S. Lewis, article on 'Christianity and Literature'

The Church . . . will have to take a strong line with the blasphemies of *hubris*, power-worship, envy and humbug, for these are the roots of evil. She will have to speak of moderation, purity, confidence, loyalty, steadfastness, patience, discipline, humility, content and modesty.

Dietrich Bonhoeffer, *Letters and Papers from Prison*

No man has any right to claim a right, to indulge in a pleasure, to demand a liberty which may be the ruination of someone else . . . A pleasure or an indulgence which may be the ruin of someone else is not a pleasure but a sin.

William Barclay, *The Letters to the Corinthians*

This attitude — the willingness to give oneself away, to give up *good* things for the sake of the better . . . is loss only in a limited sense. On the one hand it is real loss because what we lay aside in redeeming the world is in fact laid aside — time to enjoy an artistic talent, to read a book or to make a garden. This is not insignificant. At times it causes great longing and heart-searching and is a source of temptation just as the devil used life itself to tempt Jesus when Peter said, 'This [suffering] shall never happen to you' (Matthew 16:22). We must not underestimate this loss. Yet in another sense we lose nothing. We do not experience *only* loss now, for God honours the imitation of his love.

Ranald Macaulay and Jerram Barrs, *Being Human*

Lord, your gentle words are strong enough to break me. They ruthlessly expose my duplicity. Deep down, I want to love and serve you; and equally deeply, I resist you.

This double-mindedness has wounded me. Lord: heal me. And it has wounded others, little ones for whom Jesus died: heal them where I have harmed.

I confess that many times I have heard your call to servanthood but have pretended to be deaf to your voice. I confess that often, when I have *committed myself to serve you, as soon as you have faced me in one of your children I have withdrawn my service. I am like the man who put his hand to the plough but looked back; I am not fit for the kingdom of God. Your mercy is my only hope.*

There are things in my life, Lord, that are legitimate and good, but that I have clung to and even now would be reluctant to give up for the sake of love. I name them before you... Lord, these things stand like sea-walls between me and the ocean of your love; I renounce them, and pray for the strength to live out that renunciation.

Jesus, you are king of the universe, yet you wrapped a towel around your waist and washed the smelly feet of your disciples. This is not only an example for me to follow; it is an offer for me to accept. Yet like Peter, I have often refused your service, being strangely reluctant to let the one who drips love like water from his hands touch my feet. Give me a vision of your desire to serve me, so that — like Peter — I will come to accept this astonishing love and be transformed.

A Benediction

Go under God's mercy, knowing that when you are faithless he is faithful, and that when you fail he can redeem your failure. All things are possible for him, and 'he will keep you strong to the end, so that you will be blameless on the day of our Lord Jesus Christ' (1 Corinthians 1:8, NIV).

WEEK

12

Carry me on your shoulders

(Timothy Dudley-Smith)

But by thy saving power, O God, lift me high above my pain and my distress, then will I praise God's name in song and glorify him with thanksgiving.

My flesh and my heart may fail, but God is the strength of my heart and my portion forever...

I was given a painful physical ailment... Three times I prayed to the Lord about this and asked him to take it away. But his answer was: 'My grace is all you need, for my power is strongest when you are weak.' I am most happy, then, to be proud of my weaknesses, in order to feel the protection of God's power over me.

My brothers, think what sort of people you are, whom God has called. Few of you are men of wisdom, by any human standard; few are powerful or highly born. Yet, to shame the wise, God has chosen what the world counts folly, and to shame what is strong, God has chosen what the world counts weakness.

Through faith [they] conquered kingdoms, enforced justice, received promises, stopped the mouths of lions, quenched raging fire, escaped the edge of the sword, won strength out of weakness...

Then one of the elders said to me, 'Don't cry. Look! The Lion from Judah's tribe, the great descendant of David, has won the victory, and he can break the seven seals and open the scroll.' Then I saw a Lamb standing in the centre of the throne, surrounded by the four living creatures and the elders. The Lamb appeared to have been killed.

(Psalm 69:29-30, NEB; Psalm 73:26, RSV; 2 Corinthians 12:7b,8-9, TEV; 1 Corinthians 1:26-27, NEB; Hebrews 11:33-34b, RSV; Revelation 5:5-6a, TEV)

Scripture is the record of God in his great grace reaching out to us who in our weakness are powerless to save ourselves and restore lost communion with God. When redeemed we are most at risk when we seek to live and serve in our own strength. Weakness, whether it be physical, emotional, or a deliberate acceptance of risk as God's people, is more likely to enable the power of God to work in our lives. The implications of such a theology of weakness are most profound.

For us, like Jesus, suffering and helplessness are risks involved in pursuing a vision of God's love and justice. As we are prepared to 'lay down our lives for our friends' we discover that such deliberate weakness becomes a source of creativity.

We do not have to rely upon our own strength; rather we should make 'I can do all things through Christ' a rule of our lives. To cultivate a dependence upon God will mean far greater resources are available to us than our own.

Church life should be firmly based upon God's strength, not ours. How easy it is for us to organise God out of his church! Our expertise — or our schemes — can mean that God is not really needed.

The life of prayer and meditation will help us to depend upon God's strength. Otherwise we are likely to lose our awareness of the divine and find ourselves simply relying upon our own planning and busyness.

When suffering comes to us in any dimension we are able to acknowledge it as a positive experience. We can know God's presence and be covered by his power.

We must all descend into weakness sooner or later. A theology of weakness will help us see that even the ultimate weakness, dying, is opportunity for God to work in our lives. The process of growing old need not hold so many fears for us if we accept the presence of his strong shoulders.

In God's topsy-turvy approach to power, he takes weak, scarred, scared, struggling, failing and ineffective people and accomplishes his mighty work with such miserably inadequate tools.

Robert Girard, *My Weakness: His Strength*

This is the answer — that always it is upon human weakness, not human strength and confidence, that God chooses to build his kingdom; and that he can use us, not merely in spite of our ordinariness and helplessness and disqualifying infirmities, but precisely because of them. . .

J.S. Stewart, *Thine is the Kingdom*

When we were poor, lost and separated from God, we were able to appropriate his grace to cover our sin. It is therefore no surprise to find that this strength is available for his people in any kind of weakness. Our confidence in the ever-present strength of God is based upon that initial work of God in Christ when the Strong One took our weakness, our sin, upon himself.

John Helm, *Weak But Strong*

Behold the tiny Babe in cradle small,
He lies so helpless at our lady's side,
New born to filth and stench of cattle stall,
His heaven reflecting eyes are open wide.
This scene's revived each Christmastide.

See Christ with crown of thorns on gibbet raised,
Too weak to need to suffer broken bones,
In dereliction hung with sad eyes glazed,
Unheard by him the weeping women's moans,
This sacrifice for sin atones.

Regard yourself, O Man, weighed down with sin,
Such that the sacred heart was made to bleed,
Receive Christ's strength and rich new life begin
And all the wisdom of the scriptures heed.
God's grace suffices for your need.

Charles Povey, *The Paradox of Weakness*

Again we heard across the silent night the roaring beasts.

One of the men held his cup toward the ceiling.

'To the great lion,' he said, 'the lion of Judah, the lion of St Mark.' We all brought our cups together in the thin clanking that tin makes on tin. We drank.

'This is the blood of the New Testament!' said Publius.

We smiled at the distant roaring.

Calvin Miller, *The Philippian Fragment*

When we compare the strength and vigour of the Spirit-filled early church with the confused and sometimes feeble performance of the church today, we might perhaps conclude that when man's rigidity attempts to canalise the free and flexible flow of the Spirit he is left to his own devices.

J.B. Phillips, *Young Church in Action*

There are many people who, through long training, have reached a high level of competence in terms of the understanding of human behaviour, but few who are willing to lay down their own lives for others and make their weakness a source of creativity. For many individuals, professional training means power. But the minister, who takes off his clothes to wash the feet of his friends, is powerless and his training and formation are meant to enable him to face his own weakness without fear and make it available to others. It is exactly this creative weakness that gives the ministry its momentum . . .

Henri Nouwen, *Creative Ministry*

The great mystery of ministry is that while we ourselves are overwhelmed by our own weaknesses and limitations, we can still be so transparent that the Spirit of God, the divine counsellor, can shine through us and bring light to others.

Henri Nouwen, *The Living Reminder*

Old age, with all its acknowledged handicaps and limitations can, however, open up new horizons of joyous possibility to us. The very realisation of our own finiteness that comes with the gradual waning of our powers affords us the opportunity of proving in our own experience the validity of Paul's paradoxical claim: 'When I am weak, then I am strong'. We, too, can know the thrill of discovering that our inadequacy is complemented by God's sufficiency . . .

J.O. Sanders, *Your Best Years*

Christian faith, I said to her, does not involve repressing one's anxiety in order to appear strong. On the contrary, it means recognising one's weakness, accepting the inward truth about oneself, confessing one's anxiety, as my sister has so movingly done, and still to believe; that is to say that the Christian puts his trust, not in his own strength, but in the grace of God.

P. Tournier, *Learning to Grow Old*

When I am weak, then I am strong,
Lord, help me sing this triumph song.
Your grace is promised for each day,
Your power upon me, this I pray.

Lord, I do not easily risk myself for the sake of others. Stepping out of the boat as Peter did is scary and I usually opt for greater safety. Yet Jesus spoke about losing oneself for the sake of the gospel and he set the example of suffering servanthood. So help me to be willing to count the cost, to take up my cross, to be less concerned with my own security and more concerned with the Kingdom.

Lord, forgive me that in my ministry I have often relied upon my bright ideas and my carefully laid plans rather than on your guidance and your empowering. Your heart must ache as you see so much 'politicking' and petty ambition in church government. I pray for Christians in countries where the church is under suspicion and your followers must stay close to the Spirit, to survive. But I also pray for your work in countries like mine where there is little external pressure. Many of our problems come from unregenerate desires which are often carefully covered up under the guise of bringing about your will.

Lord, suffering is something which I don't handle well. There are so many negative aspects about it that I find it hard to discern any value in such experiences. As soon as I find myself in a hurting situation I quickly ask you to rescue me. Help me to realise that healing is not always your will and let me be prepared to accept suffering and find in it opportunity to know your perfect strength. All the time I have before me my ultimate weakness — death. May my living day reflect a willingness to depend upon you in all things.

A Benediction

Go forth in the strength which God is able to supply. May God's grace which is brought to completion in your weakness go with you throughout this day. Amen.

WEEK

Free only in God

(Sherwood Eddy)

Not so with you. Instead, whoever wants to become great among you must be your servant, and whoever wants to be first must be slave of all. For even the Son of Man did not come to be served, but to serve, and to give his life as a ransom for many.

So Jesus addressed the Jews who had believed him, saying: 'If you abide by what I say, you are really disciples of mine: you will understand the truth, and the truth will set you free.

Everything is permissible for me — but not everything is beneficial. Everything is permissible for me — but I will not be mastered by anything... Though I am free and belong to no man, I make myself a slave to everyone, to win as many as possible. To the Jews I became like a Jew, to win the Jews. To those under the law I became like one under the law (though I myself am not under the law), so as to win those under the law. To those not having the law I became like one not having the law (though I am not free from God's Law but am under Christ's law), so as to win those not having the law. To the weak I became weak, to win the weak. I have become all things to all men so that by all possible means I might save some. I do all this for the sake of the gospel, that I may share in its blessings.

Freedom is what we have — Christ has set us free! Stand, then, as free people and do not allow yourselves to become slaves again.

For you were called to freedom, brethren; only do not use your freedom as an opportunity for the flesh, but through love be servants of one another. For the whole law is fulfilled in one word, 'You shall love your neighbour as yourself.' But if you bite and devour one another take heed that you are not consumed by one another.

(Mark 10:43-45, NIV; John 8:31-32, Moffatt; 1 Corinthians 6:12 and 9: 19-23,NIV; Galatians 5:1, GNB; Galatians 5:13-15,RSV)

Christian freedom has limits. The Christian only remains free while a servant. When we refuse to obey we lose our freedom. As William Barclay points out, 'Christian freedom is not licence for the simple but tremendous reason that the Christian is not the person who has become free to sin, but the person who by the grace of God has become free not to sin.'

Christians are called to be responsible people. There are two sides to the coin of Christian living: first, Christians have been set free from slavery to sin; second, they are called to serve Jesus Christ. Freedom is one of the most frequently used words in our world. What do we mean by it? Millions are crying out for freedom, with many different ideas of what freedom is. People want to do what they like. Albert Camus once said that basically all rebellion is, at its root, rebellion against God. This truly is the spirit of our age — rebellion, revolt against authority. Ordinary people say, 'I'll do as I like.' In taking such an attitude they become slaves to sin and incapable of real freedom. Believers on the other hand are free to serve Christ (John 8:32 and 34-36; 1 Peter 2:16).

Man is really free only in God, the source of his freedom.

Sherwood Eddy

For the love of God is broader
  Than the measure of man's mind;
And the heart of the Eternal
  Is most wonderfully kind.

But we make his love too narrow,
  By false limits of our own
And we magnify his strictness,
  With a zeal he will not own.

Frederick W. Faber

True freedom comes only through Jesus. The New Testament presents Jesus as the totally free person who can liberate us. Other people and ideas may understand some aspect of freedom, but Jesus incarnated the total freedom offered by God. Jesus inaugurated freedom in his earthly ministry, but the full actualisation of freedom will come at the consummation of history... We are often impatient with the gap between the freedom we experience in Christ now and the final realisation of freedom. Our culture teaches us to demand satisfaction now. Christian freedom is both present and future. Our demand for instant freedom may cause us to ignore the freedom we already have in Christ. Jesus is our guide to freedom.

Warren McWilliams, *Free in Christ*

If we want this freedom, we must pay the price. And the price is unreserved surrender to him, in decisions big and small. It sounds hard, but it is not unreasonable, if you come to think of it. After all, he made us; he gave us the qualities, the aptitudes we possess. He knows how they would be best employed. Is it not wise, therefore, to entrust the choice of your career to him, rather than blunder along with your own guess? Is it not wise to entrust the decision about your marriage to him? That is a sphere where we get so easily carried away, and where we greatly need his guidance. Not that Christ wants to interfere; but he wants the very best for both our personal happiness and for our joint usefulness. Both could be wrecked by a foolish choice of a life-partner. 'Remember any girl can sleep, choose one who is some good when she is awake,' said Martin Luther. Christ will enable you to do just that — if you share the decision with him.

Michael Green, *Choose Freedom*

Karl Barth, the great Swiss theologian, used to preach to prisoners in Basel, Switzerland. These sermons were published under the title, *Deliverance to the Captives*. As he went in and out of that prison he noticed how heavy the doors were and how thick the walls. One Sunday afternoon he said to those prisoners, 'Frankly, we are all together great sinners. I stand ready to confess being the greatest sinner among you all; yet, you may not exclude yourself from the group... And we are prisoners. Believe me there is much worse captivity than the captivity of this house. There are walls much thicker and doors much heavier than those closed upon you.'

Quoted by Chevis F. Horne in his sermon 'Liberation'

Freedom means much more than the opportunity to do what we like or go where we want. A lot of people do what they like but seldom like what they do. Some have all the goods of life, it seems, but no life. They have everything to live with but nothing to live for. Handling freedom is like handling nitroglycerin. It may be a good feeling to have so much power in your hands, but you'd best be careful, or it will destroy you. Too many feed the hunger in their hearts — that appetite for living — with junk food, ways of living that destroy. The result is an unhealthy lifestyle which is anything but free.

Frank Pollard, *Keeping Free*

We talk about our freedom... But we are not free from God... We see this truth when we think of the 'laws of nature'. There is no freedom in this universe except perfect obedience to the laws of the universe. Science seeks to know how the universe behaves, because only by knowing her ways can we know how we must obey. Perfect obedience gives us more 'freedom', not from laws, but through obeying laws. Those who say 'knowledge is power' are half wrong. The truth is that knowledge plus obedience to Nature's laws is power.

Frank C. Laubach, *Christ Liveth in Me*

Lord of all, give me a greater understanding of the fact that my only real freedom is found in Christ; for only when he is in me and I am in him can I really have the power to be free. Only through Christ can I be free from the shackles of serving evil; only when I seek to obey the will of my heavenly Father can I really know what freedom is.

Father, help me to hand over my life more fully to your keeping so that my ways may become your ways, my thoughts your thoughts, my acts your acts. May your image be implanted upon my mind so that I will start living the kind of life you would have me live. Forgive my foolish ways and my past insistence on doing my own thing.

My ways, gracious Lord, are not your ways. My ways lead in the wrong direction and I find myself caught up in failing to do your will. Quickly I become once again a servant to sin. Help me, I pray, to seek your will, obey your will and follow in the ways of Jesus Christ your Son, my Saviour.

A Benediction
O loving Lord, grant that I may much more closely follow in your footsteps and refuse to follow a different way. May your powerful Spirit keep my feet walking in the path you have chosen for me and may I never be found in strange places where I would be ashamed. Amen.

WEEK

14

Better than jewels

Wisdom is supreme; therefore get wisdom. Though it cost all you have, get understanding.

The fear of the Lord is the beginning of wisdom, and the knowledge of the Holy One is insight.

If any of you falls short in wisdom, he should ask God for it and it will be given him, for God is a generous giver who neither refuses nor reproaches anyone.

The wisdom from above is pure first of all; it is also peaceful, gentle, and friendly; it is full of compassion and produces a harvest of good deeds; it is free from prejudice and hypocrisy.

The child (Jesus) grew and became strong, filled with wisdom; and the favour of God was upon him... As Jesus grew up he advanced in wisdom and in favour with God and man.

That they may have the full riches of complete understanding, in order that they may know the mystery of God, namely, Christ, in whom are hidden all the treasures of wisdom and knowledge.

We ask God to fill you with the knowledge of his will, with all the wisdom and understanding that his Spirit gives. Then you will be able to live as the Lord wants and will always do what pleases him. Your lives will produce all kinds of good deeds, and you will grow in your knowledge of God.

Christ's message in all its richness must live in your hearts. Teach and instruct each other with all wisdom. Sing psalms, hymns, and sacred songs; sing to God with thanksgiving in your hearts.

(Proverbs 4:7, NIV; Proverbs 9:10, RSV; James 1:5, NEB; James 3:17, GNB; Luke 2:40, RSV and 52, NEB; Colossians 2:2-3, NIV; Colossians 1:9-10, 3:16, GNB)

It is probably easier to recognise wisdom than it is to define it. It is more than intelligence or know-how and it cannot be produced by education or the collection of data. A peasant might have it and a professor might lack it or vice versa.

Wisdom is obviously moral as well as intellectual. It is a kind of spiritual shrewdness, the ability to see deep into the heart of life and to know what to do. It is 'the practical side of moral goodness' (J.I. Packer).

God is the source of wisdom. But because his wise rule comes to us through the distorted screen of a fallen world his wisdom is often strange and paradoxical. He uses the devious and diabolical plans of humanity to save the world! When sly Herod, weak Pilate, hostile Jews and callous Romans conspired to exterminate his son they opened up a fountain for the washing away of sins (Acts 4:27-28).

Reverence for God is the key that opens the door to wisdom. A humble teachable spirit, a healthy distrust of our own cleverness, will put us where God can share his wise will with us. His word will also show us the way: in a world where the intellectual and moral atmosphere is polluted by anti-God thinking we constantly need to 'oxygenate' our minds with God-thoughts. And, of course, if we are short of wisdom we can always *ask* for it! God gives it very liberally to those who sincerely and earnestly request it.

This is the way of wisdom. Clearly, it is just one facet of the life of faith. For what underlies and sustains it? Why, the conviction that the inscrutable God of providence is the wise and gracious God of creation and redemption. We can be sure that the God who made this marvellously complex world-order, and who compassed the great redemption from Egypt, and who later compassed the even greater redemption from sin and Satan, knows what he is doing, and 'doeth all things well', even if for the moment he hides his hand. We can trust him and rejoice in him even when we cannot discern his path.

J.I. Packer, *Knowing God*

Deep in unfathomable mines
of never-failing skill
he treasures up his bright designs,
and works his sovereign will.

Judge not the Lord by feeble sense,
but trust him for his grace;
behind a frowning providence
he hides a smiling face.

Blind unbelief is sure to err,
and scan his work in vain;
God is his own interpreter,
and he will make it plain.

William Cowper, in the hymn 'God moves in a mysterious way his wonders to perform...'

This universal Voice of God was by the ancient Hebrews often called Wisdom, and was said to be everywhere sounding and searching throughout the earth, seeking some response from the sons of men. The eighth chapter of the Book of Proverbs begins, 'Doth not wisdom cry? and understanding put forth her voice?'... This universal Voice has ever sounded, and it has often troubled men even when they did not understand the source of their fears. Could it be that this Voice distilling like a living mist upon the hearts of men has been the undiscovered cause of the troubled conscience and the longing for immortality confessed by millions since the dawn of recorded history?

A.W. Tozer, *The Pursuit of God*

Do you so love the truth and the right that you welcome, or at least submit willingly to, the idea of an exposure of what in you is yet unknown to yourself — an exposure that may redound to the glory of the truth by making you ashamed and humble?... Are you willing to be made glad that you were wrong when you thought others were wrong?

George Macdonald, *The Final Unmasking*

If thou shouldst say, 'It is enough, I have reached perfection,' all is lost. For it is the function of perfection to make one know one's imperfection.

St Augustine

These Sages had the character of freelances but none could doubt their unswerving loyalty to the heritage that had made Israel the people of God. And the Sages believed that heritage was for all men. Their parish was the world and their message was for Everyman . . . They represented the finest education of their period in combination with the pious spirit of their religion. They shared fully in the international exchange of ideas and their viewpoint was ecumenical. They counted nothing human alien to them. In a day when foreign fashions were threatening to overwhelm the moral and spiritual life of their people they stood forth to 'reprove, correct, and equip men for salvation'.

John Paterson, *The Wisdom of Israel*

If Folly speaks to a young man's passion, Wisdom speaks to his idealism. A generous-hearted youth with his life before him may gladly offer all his powers of mind and body to the highest cause he knows. If that is the cause of God and His wisdom, how happy the man will be! We sometimes speak in metaphor of a man being 'in love with' his work, or a student 'wedded' to his books. So the wise use the language of love and marriage to show how one should give himself to wisdom:

Say to wisdom, 'you are my sister',
and call insight your intimate friend.
Prize her highly and she will exalt you;
she will honour you if you embrace her. (Proverbs 7:4; 4:8)

John Goodwin, *Divine Wisdom*

That low man seeks a little thing to do,
Sees it and does it:
This high man, with a great thing to pursue,
Dies ere he knows it.
That low man goes on adding one to one,
His hundred's soon hit:
This high man, aiming at a million,
Misses a unit.
That, has the world here — should he need the next,
Let the world mind him!
This, throws himself on God, and unperplexed,
Seeking shall find him!

Robert Browning

You have to be good to be wise — though Proverbs is particularly concerned to point out the converse: that you have to be wise to be really good; for goodness and wisdom are not two separable qualities, but two aspects of a single whole. To take it further back, you have to be *godly* to be wise; and this is not because godliness pays, but because the only wisdom by which you can handle everyday things in conformity with their nature is the wisdom by which they were divinely made and ordered.

Derek Kidner, *Proverbs*

A retrospect of my whole life, from the earliest period of my recollection down to the present hour, leaves me with this impression, that I have been, and am being, guided by a gracious and mighty Hand, which has made, and is making, that possible to me which otherwise to me had been impossible. Oh that I had at all times unhesitatingly trusted and yielded myself to its guidance!

Richard Rothe, *Still Hours*

So when Paul prays that his friends may have *wisdom and understanding*, he is praying that they may understand the great truths of Christianity, and that they may be able to apply these truths to the tasks and decisions which meet them in everyday living. A man can quite easily be a master of theology and a failure in living. He may be able to write and talk about the great eternal truths, and yet be quite helpless to apply these truths to the things which meet him every day. The Christian must know what Christianity means, not, as it were, in a vacuum, but in the business of living from day to day.

William Barclay, commentary on Colossians 1:9

Give me my scallop-shell of quiet,
My staff of faith to walk upon,
My scrip of joy, immortal diet,
My bottle of salvation,
My gown of glory, hope's true gage,
And thus I'll take my pilgrimage.

Sir Walter Raleigh, His Pilgrimage

Lord, in this world of getting and spending there are a whole lot of good things going unasked for. You say that wisdom is better than anything, worth any price, and yet there for the asking. O generous Father, give this great gift to your needy child, and keep on giving it. The choking atmosphere of this self-centred, God-denying society shuts off the air that my mind and spirit needs. I can't think straight. I can't act right. I leave you out of decisions. I bungle my relationships with others. Lord, give me wisdom lest I go on making a hash of things!

Help me to see life as you do, to make my calculations from the top down not from the bottom up. Help me to see deep into the heart of life — my own life and the lives of others — and help me to use that as a compass point to steer in the right direction. Make me humble, happy and holy; make me teachable, correctable, reversible; make me wise, make me wise, make me wise.

Lord Jesus, you were filled with wisdom. Fill me with your wisdom and help me day by day to learn to face life as you faced it. Lead me on step by step to unlearn my unwise ways, and to be re-educated into your sensitive and loving insights, into your strong and gentle ways.

A Benediction

The immortal, invisible, only wise God go with you, going before you, behind you, around you and within you; the God who made all things, who sustains all things, rules all things, sees all things, give you insight and understanding from this time forward and forevermore. Amen.

WEEK

You are accepted

(Paul Tillich)

The Lord your God chose you out of all nations on earth to be his special possession. It was not because you were more numerous than any other nation that the Lord cared for you and chose you... it was because the Lord loved you.

Now the word of the Lord came to me saying, 'Before I formed you in the womb I knew you, and before you were born I consecrated you.'

The Lord says, 'When Israel was a child, I loved him and called him out of Egypt as my son... How can I give you up Israel? How can I abandon you?... My heart will not let me do it! My love for you is too strong.

Him who comes to me I will not cast out. Neither do I condemn you; go, and do not sin again.

God puts people right through their faith in Jesus Christ. God does this to all who believe in Christ, because there is no difference at all: everyone has sinned and is far away from God's saving presence. But by the free gift of God's grace all are put right with him through Christ Jesus, who sets them free.

Accept one another, then, for the glory of God, as Christ has accepted you.

(Deuteronomy 7:6-7, NEB; Jeremiah 1:4-5, RSV; Hosea 11:1,8, GNB; John 6:37, RSV; John 8:11, RSV; Romans 3:22-24, GNB; Romans 15:7, GNB)

One of our most basic needs is to be accepted. When others recognise and value us we feel alive and fulfilled. We need acceptance just as birds need air and fish need water.

Who cannot recall the nervous tension of the first day at a new school or a new job? When we move to a strange location how greatly we long to be accepted by our new neighbours. Advertisers can play on this need, telling us that if only we wear this, smoke that or drink this we will be part of the 'in' group.

The church is God's answer for our need to belong. Our gospel speaks of a God who accepts us as we are. Then we are capable of accepting others, even as Christ has accepted us. Barriers are down. We belong. Of course the world has not yet seen it as it ought to be. We are all slow learners in the church, the 'school for sinners': most of us are in the remedial class. But the first and absolute necessity is that we can accept that we are accepted. To grow in that awareness is to grow into the potential of truly accepting others. 'Love your neighbour as you love yourself,' says God.

Whenever one finds an individual who has become a fount of bitterness, taunting and criticising people, saying cruel things that wound the hearts of friends, one may be sure that he is dealing with someone who hates himself, who loathes and despises himself, and that the bitterness manifested by such a person is but the projection of his own contempt for himself.

J.S. Bonnell, *Pastoral Psychiatry*

As for others and the world around him he never ceased in his heroic and earnest endeavour to love them, to be just to them, to do them no harm, for the love of his neighbour was as strongly forced upon him as the hatred of himself, and so his whole life was an example that the love of one's neighbour is not possible without love of oneself, and that self-hate is really the same thing as sheer egoism, and in the long run breeds the same cruel isolation and despair.

Description of Harry Haller, character in *Steppenwolf* by Herman Hesse

The act of self-acceptance is the root of all things. I must agree to be the person who I am. Agree to have the qualifications which I have. Agree to live within the limitations set for me. . . The clarity and the courageousness of this acceptance is the foundation of all existence.

Romano Guardini, from his essay 'The Acceptance of Oneself'

Jesus says to us, in effect: Accept yourself as God accepts you; be yourself, love yourself properly. Take off your dark-coloured glasses and see yourself not as superior or inferior to anyone else, but as you, a person who matters. You were not meant to go through life on your hands and knees, you were meant to walk tall. You are more significant, stronger, wiser and more creative than you think. I am with you to help you, and to give you life to the full.

W. Scott McPheat, *Coping with Life*

The courage to be is the courage to accept oneself as accepted in spite of being unacceptable... this is the genuine meaning of the Paulinian-Lutheran doctrine of 'justification by faith'.

Paul Tillich, *The Courage To Be*

Sometimes at that moment [of despair] a wave of light breaks into our darkness, and it is as though a voice were saying: 'You are accepted. You are accepted, *accepted by that which is greater than you...'*

Paul Tillich, *The Shaking of the Foundations*

There are many religions which know no divine welcome to the sinner until he has ceased to be one. They would first make him righteous, and then bid him welcome to God. But God in Christ first welcomes him, and so makes him penitent and redeems him. The one demands newness of life; the other imparts it. The one demands human righteousness as the price of divine atonement; the other makes atonement in order to evoke righteousness.

J.S. Whale, *Christian Doctrine*

God loves you as though you are the only person in the world, and he loves everyone the way he loves you.

St Augustine

The whole doctrine of justification by faith hinges, for me, upon my painfully reluctant realisation that my Father is not going to be more pleased with me when I am good than when I am bad. He accepts me and delights in me as I am. It is ridiculous of him, but that is how it is between us.

John V. Taylor, *The Go-Between God*

Jesus loves me! This I know
For the Bible tells me so.

Anna Warner

Christ accepts us as we are... But when he accepts us, we cannot remain as we are. Acceptance is nothing but the first step of love. Then it exposes us to a process of growth. Being accepted by the love of Christ means being transformed.

Walter Trobisch, *Love Yourself*

Four stages of growth in Christian maturity:
1. love of self for self's sake
2. love of God for self's sake
3. love of God for God's sake
4. love of self for God's sake

Bernard of Clairvaux

This fourth step was what shocked me at first, but as I reflected on it I realised the medieval saint was exactly right. The hardest thing about God to love is the fact that he made *me*, and to come to accept this and love this is the greatest challenge facing most of us.

John Claypool, *The Light Within You*

Lord, the wonder of your grace always amazes me. There is a part of me which still finds it hard to believe. Somehow it seems to reverse all religious protocol. You love me as I am, grubby and outrageous, and without me first having to wash my hands and comb my hair. You have accepted me, completely. No reserve. Just as I am without one plea.

But! There always has to be a 'But'. This is a 'But' of grace. It does not follow logic but is the dictate of love. 'But that thy blood was shed for me'. So I am accepted, as I am, because of Jesus and not because I am good enough. Even as a child I sang, and believed, 'There was no other good enough to pay the price of sin'.

Why do I still find it so hard to accept acceptance? Is it the pride that is the root of all my sin?

Lord, here today I want to sing of your amazing grace that accepts me. I am so often defeated by the memory of my own rebellion, by disgust at my indifference, by shame at my weakness. How can you love me? I don't even like myself when I see myself as I really am.

But then you really do tell me in Jesus' words that you love the real me. May your word of acceptance lift me to that love of self which is so different from egoism and which is only ever possible because you first loved me.

Help me to accept others just as they are. Not to be indifferent to their need to change but to begin with them just as you have begun with me. Show me how really to open up to others and not to fear my vulnerability.

So may my relationship with you shape my relationships with others — accepting, loving, encouraging.

A Benediction

May the amazing grace of the Lord Jesus Christ be with you, assuring you that in love the Heavenly Father fully accepts you and that the Holy Spirit is changing you into the person who can accept all others as God's children.

WEEK

The Lord is meant for the body

'All things are lawful for me' but not all things are helpful. 'All things are lawful for me,' but I will not be enslaved by anything. 'Food is meant for the stomach and the stomach for food' — and God will destroy both one and the other. The body is not meant for immorality, but for the Lord, and the Lord for the body. And God raised the Lord and will also raise us up by his power. Do you not know that your bodies are members of Christ? Shall I therefore take the members of Christ and make them members of a prostitute? Never! Do you not know that he who joins himself to a prostitute becomes one body with her? For, as it is written, 'the two shall become one.' But he who is united to the Lord becomes one spirit with him. Shun immorality. Every other sin which a man commits is outside the body; but the immoral man sins against his own body. Do you not know that your body is a temple of the Holy Spirit within you...? You are not your own; you were bought with a price. So glorify God in your body.

(1 Corinthians 6:12-20, RSV)

One of the great themes of Christian faith is that God himself made his home in a human body. It is tragic and ironic then, that many of us battle so hard to be at home in our bodies. I am body as well as spirit and I dare not think of myself as split apart. And when I live as though I were, I bring into disrepute the very robe that God himself chose to put on. I wonder what went through your mind as you read this well-known passage from Paul? Unfortunately, Christians in the past have often failed to give the body its rightful place. Taken the wrong way, this passage can lead to a terrible distortion of our faith and our humanity. It has often been interpreted to mean that the pleasures of the body — food, wine, sex, dancing, even sport — must be denied, because, after all, the body is meant for the Lord.

But Paul's emphasis is twofold: 'The body is meant for the Lord' — yes, but 'the Lord is meant for the body'. His riches extend to our bodies as well as our spirits. One reason why Paul condemns prostitution is because it is an act that calls for the fragmenting of the self. It is based on the distortion that I must split myself off from my body in order to gain pleasure. But because it involves this splitting up of the person prostitution is a foretaste of hell, not of heaven. For in heaven all things will be united in Christ, including all our parts: body, mind, spirits, emotions, wills. But, because new life has been born in us, we can already have little tastes of this glorious vision of unity.

How much at home are you in your body? It is an important Christian question to ask yourself. It is one that many non-church people are taking very seriously. In part, the rise of such fads as jogging, aerobics and health foods represents a concern shared by many of our contemporaries to reclaim the body — to give it its rightful place as integral to who I am as a person. The less at home I am in my body, the less possible it is for me to be whole and joyful and the less saved I feel.

I am not talking here about the silly tendency in our society to idolise the so-called 'body beautiful'; that tendency is just as much a distortion as the one that despises the body. Both distortions spring from the same source, the fear of death.

Because our bodies are subject to decay and to wounding of all kinds, they give us probably our most immediate sense of the end to which we are all heading. If we fear death, it is unlikely that we can be at home in this fragile flesh. And so we make the mistake of trying to build it up so that it appears invulnerable or we try to ignore it.

Think for a moment of the last time you had a strong sense of being at one or at home in your body. It may have been an experience in the shower or bath. Perhaps you were playing sport, dancing, bushwalking or holding someone.

Have you ever been by yourself at the beach or in a pool and had that experience of slowly easing yourself into the water? You begin to feel that you are at one with the water, perhaps even with the scene itself. It is exhilarating. And one reason why this is so is because it is a foretaste of heaven. For God intends that we, along with 'the whole of creation', will become one in a new kingdom where our present experiences of fragmentation, separation and suffering come to an end; where our bodies will be new bodies, resurrected bodies.

Then we will have harmony between our new bodies and our new selves, between men and women, between nature and humanity, between humanity and God.

Our bodies provide us right now with a marvellous anticipation of the pleasure and fulfilment that will one day be fully ours. 'The Lord is meant for the body,' says Paul. So, 'glorify God in your bodies.'

It was as hard to explain how this sunlit land was different from the old Narnia as it would be to tell you how the fruits of that country taste. Perhaps you will get some idea of it if you think like this. You may have been in a room in which there was a window that looked out on a lovely bay of the sea or a green valley that wound away among mountains. And in the wall of that room opposite to the window there may have been a looking-glass. And as you turned away from the window you suddenly caught sight of that sea or that valley, all over again, in the looking-glass. And the sea in the mirror, or the valley in the mirror, were in one sense just the same as the real one: yet at the same time they were somehow different — deeper, more wonderful, more like places in a story: in a story you have never heard but very much want to know. The difference between the old Narnia and the new Narnia was like that. The new one was a deeper country: every rock and flower and blade of grass looked as if it meant more. I can't describe it any better than that: if you ever get there you will know what I mean.

C.S. Lewis, from his children's story, *The Last Battle*

The Rainbow

Even the rainbow has a body
made of the drizzling rain
and is an architecture of glistening atoms
built up, built up
yet you can't lay your hand on it,
nay, nor even your mind.

D.H. Lawrence

How fair and pleasant you are,
O loved one, delectable maiden!
You are stately as a palm tree,
and your breasts are like its clusters.
I say I will climb the palm tree
and lay hold of its branches.
Oh, may your breasts be like clusters of the vine
and the scent of your breath like apples,
and your kisses like the best wine
that goes down smoothly,
gliding over lips and teeth.
I am my beloved's,
and his desire is for me.
Come, my beloved,
let us go forth into the fields,
and lodge in the villages;
let us go out early to the vineyards,
and see whether the vines have budded,
whether the grape blossoms have opened
and the pomegranates are in bloom.
There I will give you my love.
The mandrakes give forth fragrance,
and over our doors are all choice fruits,
new as well as old,
which I have laid up for you, O my beloved.

Song of Solomon

A colleague has recently described to me an occasion when a West Indian woman in a London flat was told of her husband's death in a street accident. The shock of grief stunned her like a blow; she sank into a corner of the sofa and sat there rigid and unhearing. For a long time her terrible tranced look continued to embarrass the family, friends and officials who came and went. Then the schoolteacher of one of her children, an Englishwoman, called and, seeing how things were, went and sat beside her. Without a word she threw an arm around the tight shoulders, clasping them with her full strength. The white cheek was thrust hard against the brown. Then, as the unrelenting pain seeped through to her, the newcomer's tears began to flow, falling on their two hands linked in the woman's lap. For a long time that is all that was happening.

And then at last the West Indian woman started to sob. Still not a word was spoken and after a little while the visitor got up and went, leaving her contribution to help the family meet its immediate needs.

That is the embrace of God, his kiss of life. That is the embrace of his mission, and of our intercession. And the Holy Spirit is the force in the straining muscles of an arm, the film of sweat between pressed cheeks, the mingled wetness on the backs of clasped hands. He is as close and unobtrusive as that, and as irresistibly strong.

John Taylor, *The Go-Between God*

O God, you created all things good. Thank you for this flesh — for its beauty, its strangeness, its fragility. Thank you for the warmth of another's arms, for the power of touching, the wonder of holding and being held.

Help me to experience my body in all its splendour; to care for it as I would care for your dwelling-place; to enjoy it, as I would enjoy your nearness; to keep it fit for the tasks to which you call me.

And when it fails me, when it reminds me of the transience of this present life, when it trips me up and warns me of my mortality, may I then have the grace and wisdom to give you thanks — thanks for your unseen purposes, for your great drama of redemption that will one day lift all faltering things into newness of life and riches beyond imagining.

A Benediction

O God, who was pleased to dwell in mortal flesh, raise me with your son to new abundant life in my body. May his body, broken for all, preserve me through the change and decay of this present life. May your indwelling spirit bring me the fullness of joy that is mine in this life and in the life to come. Amen.

Week

17

So moves the Claviger beetle

God [Father, Son, and Holy Spirit] said, make mankind in our image, after our likeness; and let them have complete authority over the fish of the sea, the birds of the air, the [tame] beasts, and over all the earth, and over every thing that creeps upon the earth. So God created man in his own image, in the image and likeness of God he created him; male and female he created them. And God blessed them, and said to them, Be fruitful, multiply, and fill the earth and subdue it [with all its vast resources]; and have dominion over the fish of the sea, the birds of the air, and over every living creature that moves upon the earth. . . And God saw everything that he had made, and behold, it was very good — suitable, pleasant — and he approved it completely. And there was evening and there was morning, a sixth day.

But no helpmate suitable for man was found for him. So Yahweh God made the man fall into a deep sleep. And while he slept, he took one of his ribs and enclosed it in flesh. Yahweh God built the rib he had taken from the man into a woman, and brought her to the man. The man exclaimed: 'This at last is bone of my bones, and flesh from my flesh! This is to be called woman, for this was taken from man.' This is why a man leaves his father and mother and joins himself to his wife, and they become one body. Has not the Lord made them one? In flesh and spirit they are his. And why one? Because he was seeking godly offspring. So guard yourself in your spirit, and do not break faith with the wife of your youth.

God made them male and female. For this reason a man shall leave his father and mother, and be made one with his wife; and the two shall become one flesh. It follows that they are no longer two individuals: they are one flesh. What God has joined together, man must not separate.

(Genesis 1:26-28 and 31 and 1:20b-24, JB; Malachi 2:15, NIV; Mark 10:6-9, NEB)

God did not stop at creating a man; he also created a woman to produce what might be called a divine duet. In creating man and woman, God brought into existence things which had no previous existence. The divine duet formed the crown of creation. Man was made in God's image, with two sexes. The exalted nature of this relationship is shown by the fact that the two sexes were intended to reflect the relationship between Christ and his church as we discover in Ephesians 5:25-33. Within the bounds of a family God's love can be reflected in a beautiful way. God created man and woman for each other in the divinely instituted arrangement called marriage. God made the family the foundation of the social order, and family ties are sacred and should not be tampered with.

The small Claviger beetle moves inside the ant hill, unalarmed by the fact that ants are one of its most ferocious enemies. The ant hill offers easy access to life's necessities: it's warm inside and the ants stock a variety of tasty foods. The beetle soon stops in its tracks — it spots a fast-approaching ant, one of the hungry predators that call this hill home. The ant, in turn, stops when it reaches the motionless beetle. But, instead of striking out, it strokes the beetle. A secretion then appears on the beetle's body; and the ant eagerly consumes this and goes on its way, leaving the visitor unmolested. These two species, the Claviger beetle and the meadow ant, have a pleasant arrangement; biologists call it 'symbiosis'. Though they should be enemies they live together in a mutually beneficial way. The beetle gets a warm home with a lot to eat, and the ant has its portable refreshment stand. We might expect the church and family to display some of this, to work together in a sort of social symbiosis. Yet, these two institutions haven't always gotten along so well, nor contributed to one another's welfare as they should. In fact, I know of many church members who have sacrificed their family life to build the life of the church. And it is quite obvious that many churches fail to offer much to enrich their families.

Charles M. Sell, *Family Ministry*

The problem is not with the institution of marriage. The problem lies with the individuals within that structure and their attitudes toward it. Richard Lessor wrote, 'In the twentieth century it is not a matter of marriages having been tried and found wanting. Marriage is deeply wanted but largely untried.' Today in place of exerting consistent effort and determination to make one's marriage work, the solution is to 'bail out'.

H. Norman Wright, *Premarital Counseling*

It does not hurt any of us to discover our idols have clay feet. Children can tolerate easily and can genuinely grow from a recognition that their parents occasionally make mistakes, become confused and discouraged, and need the support of others. This may even increase the impact of that which is truly solid about us, that which is genuinely our strength. On the other hand there is no need to suggest that we are 'hollow men'. If this is in fact true, it may be hard to hide anyway, but to reveal weakness of such proportions is not to contribute to the stature of those entrusted to our care.

Armin Grams, *Changes in Family Life*

But, there is a romance appropriate for every age and stage, and it is vital that we keep romance in marriage if it is to succeed and if we are to achieve happiness for ourselves and our children. We must take real care, lest 'moonlight and roses' become 'daylight and dishes'! A movie star has been quoted as saying that 'marriage kills romance'. That ought not be and is not true if romance is understood rightly. Someone has defined romance as 'a long story of love'. The dictionary defines it as 'a dreamy imaginative habit of mind tending to dwell on the picturesquely unusual'. Both of these definitions are realistically true! Romance in marriage is to be found in the long story of love that began before marriage and found fulfilment after marriage. It is to be found in the wonder of relationships that are colourful, thrilling and practical. The romance of marriage includes all the joys of marriage as well as the hazards. It is a way of life for a couple within the bounds of responsible marriage.

T. Cecil Myers, *Happiness Is Still Home Made*

Every person needs a sense of personal identity or worth. But we live in a time of great confusion and contention over the question of one's worth. Striking workers insist they are worth more pay. Protesting demonstrators insist they are worth a fairer stake in the economic and social scheme of things. Teenagers insist they are worth more respect and consideration in home and school. Parents feel that they are entitled to more respect. The overall emphasis in much of this is upon one's rights. A person has a certain number of rights which he can claim because he's worth something. God begins at a different point. He begins not with our rights, but with our duties.

Larry Christenson, *The Christian Family*

Gracious Father, as I share with my family day by day, grant me a much deeper insight into what family life is all about. Help me to set aside my selfish desires and my foolish ways so that I may place my family first and not insist on pushing forward my ingrown plans, thus robbing other members of the family of their due rights as part of the family.

Help me, loving Lord, to see Christ in the other members of my family. Give me spiritual eyes to see their needs, spiritual ears to hear them calling for help when they need it. Prevent me from being so busy with myself that I fail to be aware of the needs other members of my family have.

Strengthen me, dear Saviour, so that I may have the courage to live constantly for you in the family. Make me a stepping stone for my family so that I might encourage them in the things of God. Use me to help my family grow in grace and in the knowledge of Jesus Christ as Lord.

A Benediction

Continue to transform this family, O heavenly Father. Mould them more and more into your will. Build them up this day so they may reflect the life and love of your Son our Saviour. Pour out your Spirit on this family so they may uplift your honour and glory. Amen.

Theme: Hope

'Out of deep waters' (Psalm 18:16)

He reached down from on high
  and took hold of me;
  he drew me out of deep waters.
Therefore let everyone who is godly
  pray to you while you may be found;
  surely when the mighty waters rise,
  they will not reach him.
You are my hiding place;
  you will protect me from trouble
  and surround me with songs of deliverance.

Psalm 18:16; 32:6-7, NIV

WEEK

God is a sea

(Ruysbroeck)

God is our shelter and strength, always ready to help in times of trouble. So we will not be afraid, even if the earth is shaken and mountains fall into the ocean depths; even if the seas roar and rage, and the hills are shaken by the violence. I am the Lord: why don't you fear me? Why don't you tremble before me? I placed the sand as the boundary of the sea, a permanent boundary that it cannot cross. The sea may toss, but it cannot go beyond it; the waves may roar, but they cannot break through.

Come and see what God has done, his wonderful acts among men. He changed the sea into dry land; our ancestors crossed the river on foot. There we rejoiced because of what he did. Who is a God like you, who pardons sin... You will tread our sins underfoot and hurl all our iniquities into the depths of the sea.

There will be strange things happening to the sun, the moon, and the stars. On earth whole countries will be in despair, afraid of the roar of the sea and the raging tides... Then the Son of Man will appear... When these things begin to happen, stand up and raise your heads, because your salvation is near.

Then I saw a new heaven and a new earth... and there was no longer any sea.

(Psalm 46:1-3, GNB; Jeremiah 5:22, GNB; Psalm 66:5-6, GNB; Micah 7:18-19, NIV; Luke 21:25-28, GNB; Revelation 21:1, NIV)

Every day we are made promises. Advertisers promise us cheap peace, translating our wants into needs. A trouble-free existence is ours, for a price. Sometimes preachers, too, promise serenity without strife, tranquillity without turmoil, resurrection without gethsemane or calvary. Whilst we must not let anyone crucify us who cannot resurrect us, Jesus said there is no life except through death. As one mystic put it, the Spirit of God and our own spirits strive together in a storm of love. In this 'strife of love' each spirit is deeply wounded by love. Gethsemane is not a detour. The primal sin of Adam and Eve was to try to get knowledge without working for it, to 'arrive' without the pain of the journey, to attain 'instant godliness'.

God is a sea, says Ruysbroeck. The sea, for the ancient Hebrews, was a turbulent place where danger lurked. (So the Jews did not make good sailors; they left that to the Phoenicians.) Deliverance from the Red Sea was a recurring theme for wonder-full recollection. Apocalyptic writers pictured great beasts coming out of the sea. In heaven there will be 'no more sea'. But the 'second death' is symbolised by a 'lake of fire' (Revelation 19:20, 20:14).

So the sea of love, where we meet God, is sometimes a fearful place. Love is always enhanced by courage and hard work. The objects of temporal love eventually die, so the more we love, the more risks we take. The opposite of love is inertia, doing nothing.

As we begin this journey, sometimes through uncharted, unfamiliar seas, let this text encourage us: 'When you pass through deep waters, I will be with you; your troubles will not overwhelm you... for I am the Lord your God, who saves you' (Isaiah 43:2-3).

Here begins the sea that ends not till the world's end.
  Where we stand,
Could we know the next high sea-mark set beyond
  these waves that gleam,
We should know what never man hath known, nor eye of
  man hath scanned...
Ah, but here man's heart leaps, yearning towards the gloom
  with venturous glee,
From the shore that hath no shore beyond it, set in all
  the sea.

A.C. Swinburne, 'On the Verge', from *A Midsummer Vacation*

The enlightened man shall go out and observe God in his glory with all saints. And he shall behold the rich and generous outflowing of God, with glory, and with himself, and with inconceivable delights towards all the saints, according to the longing of all spirits; and how these flow back, with themselves, and with all that they have received and can achieve, towards that same rich oneness from which all bliss comes forth.

This flowing forth of God always demands a flowing back; for God is a Sea that ebbs and flows, pouring without ceasing into all his beloved according to the need and the merits of each, and ebbing back again with all those who have been thus endowed both in heaven and on earth, with all that they have and all that they can.

Ruysbroeck, quoted in David Walker, *God is a Sea*

The ebbing and flowing of the tide is a continuing phenomenon. Each day the tide comes in and draws out. It is the same with the divine tide. The Father has not simply poured his graces into the hearts of men on an isolated occasion in the past; he continues to do so in the life situation of each person. The divine love floods the universe. Each situation is a graced situation, a sacrament in which the divine is present, open to us, reaching out in love. This ever-present divine love draws us to itself within each situation. The love of the lover draws the beloved to a love of which he alone is not capable.

There are two attitudes with which we can confront this overwhelming truth. We can be like the beach over which the tide flows and ebbs. It is open and unresisting; it receives and it gives; it lets its mood be determined by the tide. On the other hand we could be like the rocks on which the same tide runs but which are hard and stand fast, resisting — even fighting — the tide and refusing to be affected by it. We must imitate the openness and unresisting character of the beach, for it is only then that the divine power within the Father's approach is able to draw us to him... So long as the beach awaits patiently the inflowing of the tide and yields generously to its ebbing, the pattern of nature is fulfilled. In the same way, it is only when the person patiently and humbly opens himself to the divine approach and lets himself be drawn out in response by the divine power within it that the divine plan achieves its fulfilment.

David Walker, *God is a Sea*

Don't let yourself be torn
between yesterday
and tomorrow.
Live always and only
God's today.

Dom Helder Camara, *A Thousand Reasons for Living*

Acknowledging mystery, then, does not prevent authentic 'asking and seeking and knocking', but it does not stop there. It also encourages one to take the best light one has and do what one can to bring glory and not resentment out of any given situations. We do not have to understand perfectly why the waves flood over us to make certain creative responses to them. There is much that can be done with what we do know now that need not wait fuller explanation.

John Claypool, adapted from a sermon
'Absurdity, Causality and Mystery'

God is good... he who gives us our lives not only rules over us but loves us, likes us, is for us and not against us. Out of this realisation comes the ability to receive the events of life with gratitude, not resentment, and to regard them as expressions of mysterious love rather than as acts of hostility. It is amazing the difference a stance of gratitude can make in the way we cope with difficulty. If we begin to look on the things that happen to us as good gifts of a Father, then even the problems take on a different shape. Instead of seeing them as hopeless obstacles to our happiness, we come to see them as the challenges that give life its meaning and excitement. What would our existence be like, really, if no effort were ever called for or no challenges ever posed? Such a levelled-off-existence would be intolerably boring. G.K. Chesterton was right in saying that a positive challenge is a difficulty rightly understood. Problems cease to be overwhelming when we see them as something to be received in gratitude.

John Claypool, *The Light Within You*

Just as it is the nature of the tide to flow in and to draw out again, so it is the nature of the Father not only to reach out in love but also to draw all things to himself. The Father is the fountain and source of all life. He shares that life with his Son and his Spirit in a communion in which what comes forth returns to him. It is this same life which the Father extends through the Son and the Spirit to mankind in a communion in which what comes forth from him is meant to return to him. The Father presents himself as love, openness, self-offering, invitation, sharing, in a way to which every person has the capacity to respond and to find in him his ultimate goal.

David Walker, *God is a Sea*

Accept surprises
that upset your plans,
shatter your dreams,
give a completely
different turn
to your day
and — who knows? —
to your life.
It is not chance.
Leave the Father free
himself to weave
the pattern of your days.

Dom Helder Camara, *A Thousand Reasons for Living*

Lord, I am prone sometimes to imagine that the tides of my life are buffeting me without purpose, tossing me to and fro without meaning, battering me painfully against the hard rocks cruelly. Sometimes the storms really are fierce, the skies are grey, and you seem to be absent. It's just not true that 'my life is all sunshine in the sweetness of the Lord'.

Lord, remind me that you have never promised to deliver from struggle and agony and conflict. In the world we shall have trouble. Your own experience of life among us was a parable of struggle in hope.

But in that struggle you overcame the world. Just as a stone becomes beautifully smooth only in constant friction, so in the mystery of your purposes for us, you create a thing of beauty only in our chastenings. Conflict is the price to be paid for spiritual creativity and growth. That which resists us perfects us.

So Lord, when the waves are huge, and I feel so helpless, let me not move against them in rage, or go under them in helplessness, but flow with them in faith and hope.

'Thou has given so much to us, give us one thing more, a grateful heart; for Christ's sake. Amen' (George Herbert).

May you experience the peace of God in your trouble,
hope when you are tempted to despair,
joy through your pain,
faith and courage, when the heavens seem silent,
and the sure knowledge that the Lord has been through it all too, he understands, he cares, and he loves you, very much.

Lord, may we live by faith, walk in hope, and be renewed in love
until the whole world reflects your glory,
and you are all in all.
Even so, come Lord Jesus. Amen.

WEEK

19

Squeezed dry and then cast aside

My tears have been my food day and night, while men say to me continually, 'Where is your God?'

My thoughts today are resentful, for God's hand is heavy on me in my trouble. If only I knew how to find him, how to enter his court, I would state my case before him and set out my arguments in full; he rubbed my face in the ground and broke my teeth on the gravel. I have forgotten what health and peace and happiness are.

I tell you the truth, unless an ear of wheat falls to the ground and dies, it remains only a single seed. But if it dies, it produces many seeds . . . every branch that does bear fruit he trims clean so that it will be even more fruitful.

We were under great pressure, far beyond our ability to endure, so that we despaired even of life. Indeed, in our hearts we felt the sentence of death. But this happened that we might not rely on ourselves but on God, who raises the dead.

(Psalm 42:3, NIV; Job 23:1-4, NEB; Lamentations 3:16-17, GNB; John 12:24, 15:2 NIV ; 2 Corinthians 1:8-9, NIV)

When misfortune strikes us — illness, unemployment, deep depression, failure in personal relationships — God can seem to be very distant and uncaring and our inner lives begin to wither and die. The ancient Hebrews expressed their feelings in a particular form — that of the lament — often directed to the God whom they no longer experienced!

Today, our tendency, when something goes wrong, is to try to locate the cause of the problem and treat or rectify it. We feel more comfortable looking back over our shoulders than engaging in another common biblical practice, looking in anticipation to the creative work God is going to do up ahead as in John 9:2-3.

Two of the most severe forms of physical pain are giving birth and having kidney stones. Women will willingly become pregnant; but only a masochist would want kidney stones. It makes all the difference when suffering has a desirable, constructive purpose.

Suffering, particularly where it is the result of injustice or where it occurs through no fault of the victim, can lead to anger and bitterness. It can easily block off the flow of practical trust in God. Such pain needs to be expressed if it is to become a resource rather than a liability and achieve its purpose in the fruitful growth of the person or community concerned.

The work of God is built upon the ruins of a man's life.

F. Fénelon, spiritual adviser to Louis XIV of France, source unknown

When building a skyscraper you have to go down before you can go up.

Anonymous

It seems to me that the priest or layman who is not constantly harassed by thorns is underprivileged. His thorns may be in the form of little Hitlers, cynics, critics and professional opposers; or they may be in the form of illness, impediments, scars and disfigurations; or they may be in the form of lost love, betrayal and disillusionment; or they may be in the form of wounded pride, humiliation and ignominy; or they may be in the form of poverty, hunger and destitution; or all of them put together... A thorn usually leads to the cross, and the cross to the confession of sin, and thence to freedom and incomparable strength. But before we can feel the strength of Christ we must know that there is no health in us insofar as our own personal power goes — that of ourselves we can but eventually fail, but in Christ we can know nothing other than final victory.

Austin Pardue, *Why Learn to Pray*

God wounds deeply when he wills to heal.

Herman Kohlbrugge

And my lament
Is cries countless, cries like dead letters sent
to dearest him that lives alas! away.

I am gall, I am heartburn. God's most deep decree
Bitter would have me taste: my taste was me.

Gerard Manley Hopkins, Untitled sonnet

As good go anywhere, they say,
 As to benumme
Both knees and heart in crying night and day,
 Come, come, my God, O come,
 But no hearing.

O that thou shouldst give dust a tongue
 To crie to thee
And then not hear it crying! all day long
 My heart was in my knee
 But no hearing.

George Herbert, *Deniall*

It is not easy, Lord, to follow after you.
While you take the hard road
 with joyous leaps and bounds,
I stumble over every stone
 and slip into every rut.
You calmly weather each storm
 and walk fearlessly through the night.
I am buffeted by the winds,
 and I falter in the darkness.

And you always have answers, Lord,
 for those who confront you.
My tongue is thick and clumsy.
I cannot articulate what I feel
 or what they need to hear.
You have the wisdom and the power
 to meet the needs of men about you.
But I am foolish and ineffective,
 and my brothers turn away from me in disgust.

I have really tried to relate to people about me,
to reach out in love and concern.
I have shared their sorrows and their joys.
I have shelved my ambitions
to respond to their needs.
But when I fail to produce what they want,
or when I am limited by my humanity
and incapacitated by my personal problems
they will have nothing to do with me.
I feel as if I have been used only to be abused.
I am squeezed dry and then cast aside
as if I were of no further value.

Yet I must continue to follow you, O Lord.
It is a hard path to walk,
and I will falter at times.
I long intensely for an occasional oasis
along this journey through wind and sand.
I need desperately your touch of joy and enrichment
as I labour amidst the blood and tears
of this distorted world.
I am empty, Lord.
Enable me to sense your fullness
and grant me the grace and the courage
to be faithful as your son and servant.

Psalm 35 from *Psalms Now* by Leslie Brandt

A Benediction

O God, who knowest us to be set in the midst of so many and great dangers, that by reason of the frailty of our nature we cannot always stand upright; grant to us such strength and protection, as may support us in all dangers, and carry us through all temptations; through Jesus Christ our Lord. Amen.

Book of Common Prayer

WEEK 20

Help Lord, I'm hurting!

Surely our griefs he himself bore, and our sorrows he carried... But he was pierced through for our transgressions, he was crushed for our iniquities; the chastening for our well-being fell upon him, and by his scourging we are healed.

He has sent me to bind up the brokenhearted, to proclaim liberty to the captives, and freedom to prisoners... to comfort... giving a garland... gladness... praise.

He restores my soul.

Therefore my heart is glad, and my soul rejoices; my body also dwells secure.

A wounded spirit who can bear?

I have come in order that you might have life — life in all its fullness.

I am leaving you a gift — peace of mind and heart! And the peace I give isn't fragile like the peace the world gives. So don't be troubled or afraid.

And may the God of peace himself sanctify you through and through... and may your spirit and soul and body be preserved sound and complete.

Why are you angry with me for healing the whole man...?

His wounds have healed ours!

Be transformed by the renewing of your mind.

Forgive your brother from your heart.

Jesus Christ is the same yesterday and today and for ever.

(Isaiah 53:4-5, 61:1-3, NASB; Psalm 23:3, 16:9, RSV; Proverbs 18:14, KJV; John 10:10, GNB; John 14:27, LB; 1 Thessalonians 5:23, AMP; John 7:23, NIV; 1 Peter 2:24, LB; Romans 12:2, NIV; Matthew 18:35, GNB; Hebrews 13:8, NIV)

It happens to every one of us. We have all been hurt deeply, down inside, often through no fault of our own. These hurts of the past influence our lives and the way we act and react today. Transactional Analysts say that some of the condemning 'parent tapes' that have been replaying in our minds since childhood, need to be erased. All things are possible with God, but does he heal past traumatic experiences?

God, our Creator, who tells us that 'even the hairs of your head have all been counted', cares about every aspect of our lives. He, who suffered as one of us, understands our pain, our fears, our hurts. He has compassion on his children as we try to cope with troubled minds, harmful memories, and damaged emotions that still cripple us today.

The same Jesus who came to seek and save the lost, also came to bind up the brokenhearted, to heal, and to give us a life that is full, free and joyous. The same Saviour who died for our sin, also bore our griefs and sorrows. He is willing to bring healing to the whole person.

He waits for us to allow the Holy Spirit to reveal the hurts we have repressed, and to face willingly past painful experiences that we have tried so hard to forget. We can 'become like little children' and invite Jesus to take our hand and go back into every negative situation and visualise his presence there with us. In his love he, who freely gives us all things, will reach out to pour oil into our wounds, bringing healing and peace and enabling us to forgive those who have hurt us.

Walk with me back through the years, Lord,
As I place my hand in thine,
Talk with me about my fears, Lord,
While I travel mem'ry lane.

Speak in my imaginings, Lord,
As I picture Jesus there,
Bring to light the hidden things, Lord,
That I've pressed down year by year.

Heal all that still hurts inside, Lord,
  Until I feel whole and strong,
Until love and peace abide, Lord,
  And forgiveness flows along.

Marj Donellan

Medical science recognises that emotions such as fear, sorrow, envy, resentment and hatred are responsible for the majority of our sicknesses. Estimates vary from 60 per cent to nearly 100 per cent. Emotional stress can cause... serious diseases too numerous to mention.

S.I. McMillen, *None of These Diseases*

Canst thou not minister to a mind diseas'd,
Pluck from the memory a rooted sorrow,
Raze out the written troubles of the brain,
And with some sweet oblivious antidote
Cleanse the stuff'd bosom of that perilous stuff
Which weighs upon the heart?

William Shakespeare, *Macbeth*

God wills healing of the body and mind.

Jamie Buckingham

Somewhere between our sins and our physical ailments lies that part of our lives where we find many of our real failings as human beings — our emotional weaknesses and problems... Christ came to free us from the evil that burdens us... Psychologists have discovered that we are deeply affected not only by what we do, but by what happens to us through the sins of others... if we are denied love... it may affect... our ability to love, and our ability to trust [others] — or God. Inner healing is simply this: Jesus... can take the memories of our past and heal them... and fill with his love all these places in us that have been empty for so long, once they have been healed and drained of the poison of past hurts and resentment.

Francis MacNutt, *Healing*

The study of psychology is helpful in pointing out the roots of our sickness and how the evil in people and in the world twists our personalities. But while psychology is strong on the human analysis of our problems it is not so strong on cure. With the help of Jesus, however, we can get at the childhood wounds that hinder our growth and compel us to act in ways that we know are wrong but can't seem to help... Jesus was a human being like you, and in his humanity suffered in that very area where you need healing so that you might be healed; Jesus can walk back into the past and change its effects upon your present life.

Francis MacNutt, *The Prayer that Heals*

Prayer for inner healing always involves at root a decision to forgive... The purpose of healing... is to restore a person to the original purpose for which he was created, to gift him with the courage to be. It is to set him free from judgment and condemnation and fear about what others think of him.

John and Paula Sandford, *The Transformation of the Inner Man*

When we speak of inner healing, we refer to the experience in which the Holy Spirit restores health to the deepest area of our lives by dealing with the root cause of our hurts and pain... Since Jesus Christ is the same yesterday, today, and tomorrow, he is able to go back into our lives and heal the traumatic episodes. Very often we have suppressed the hurtful occurrences so completely that we are not even aware of their bind upon our hearts. If we let him, the Holy Spirit, who reveals all things, is able to bring to our awareness the situation... he will never overcome our free will but will wait patiently for us to invite him to enter... 'What can the Lord Jesus do to your imagination if you let him in?'

Ruth Carter Stapleton, *The Gift of Inner Healing*

God is not hurried along in the Time-stream of this universe any more than an author is hurried along in the imaginary time of his own novel... You are as much alone with him as if you were the only being he had ever created... His life is not dribbled out moment by moment like ours... If you picture Time as a straight line along which we have to travel, then you must picture God as the whole page on which the line is drawn.

C.S. Lewis, *Mere Christianity*

Our mind functions like a high-fidelity tape recorder, faithfully storing away all that we experience from the time we were born. The recording includes... the feelings, good or bad, desirable or undesirable which accompanied those experiences... Whether they be in our mind at the moment, or are able to be recalled, or now deeply forgotten, [they] have left their mark on us.

Jim Glennon, *Your Healing is Within You*

There are so many adults with fears of water, dogs, cats, heights, elevators, etc. As adults, we try to overcome these fears, we feel embarrassed because of our 'hang-ups'; we try to use our intellect and reason the fears away... Jesus is the only one who can break those chains.

Betty Tapscott, *Inner Healing through Healing of Memories*

I believe that the healing love of Jesus Christ can release our inner child. In fact, I think this is part of the message involved in proclaiming 'liberty to captives' (Luke 4:18) which Jesus announced at the beginning of his ministry. Each of us has experienced traumas which continue to affect our lives... but the child within us never forgets anything.

Barbara Leahy Shlemon, *Healing Prayer*

By going back to memory after memory and turning them over to the Spirit, past hurts will no longer control me; rather, the freeing power of the Spirit will rule.

Dennis Linn and Matthew Linn, *Healing of Memories*

Heavenly Father, my wound is as deep as the sea, who can heal me? No-one is near to comfort me, no-one to restore my spirit, but I will pour out my heart like water in your presence Lord, for great is your faithfulness, you are good to the one who seeks you. You O Lord reign forever, restore me, renew my days as of old.

Lamentations — NIV

Lord, I humbly come to you now and ask you to take my hand and walk with me down those dark corridors of my past. In my mind and my imagination I can picture you now. I see your kind face, your eyes with their yearning love. I feel the

firm but gentle pressure of your hand, so I take courage and walk back:
I see it now, that terrible hurt when I was a small child...
With you I press on and push open one by one the doors of my memory: When no-one would listen to me and I was punished wrongly...
When I felt rejected and unwanted...
The frustration of being totally misunderstood...
Help me now Lord to force open the next door that I've always kept tightly closed, the door of that traumatic experience. I will walk in and look at it in your presence, Lord — I cry out to you as I feel again the terror of it! Jesus, you are there with me, light and love flood the room, and I am not afraid any more...

Thank you, Lord, for the glorious, powerful, caring Father that you are. My heart surges with the warmth and strength of my love for you. Thank you for the healing and wholeness I feel within as your love washes over me. The sting has gone, that dreadful resentment has vanished. It is so good to find that it is easy to freely forgive. I praise you with all my heart.

A Benediction
Stand tall now, knowing that by God's mercy you have been healed and made whole deep within your being. May the compassion of the Father, the sensitive tenderness of the Holy Spirit, and the warm guiding hand of Jesus be with you throughout this day. Amen.

WEEK

21

Hope in time of abandonment

(Jacques Ellul)

What, then, can I hope for, Lord? I put my hope in you. For God alone my soul waits in silence, for my hope is from him. O God of our salvation, who art the hope of all the ends of the earth. Don't stay so far away, O God; my God, hurry to my aid! May those who attack me be defeated and destroyed. May those who try to hurt me be shamed and disgraced. I will always put my hope in you; I will praise you more and more. I will tell of your goodness; all day long I will speak of your salvation, though it is more than I can understand. Remember my affliction and my bitterness, the wormwood and the gall! My soul continually thinks of it and is bowed down within me. But this I call to mind, and therefore I have hope: The steadfast love of the Lord never ceases, his mercies never come to an end; they are new every morning; great is thy faithfulness. 'The Lord is my portion,' says my soul, 'therefore I will hope in him.'

So when God desired to show more convincingly to the heirs of the promise the unchangeable character of his purpose, he interposed with an oath, so that through two unchangeable things, in which it is impossible that God should prove false, we who have fled for refuge might have strong encouragement to seize the hope set before us. We have this as a sure and steadfast anchor of the soul, a hope that enters into the inner shrine behind the curtain, where Jesus has gone as a forerunner on our behalf, having become a high priest for ever after the order of Melchizedek. Let us hold fast the confession of our hope without wavering, for he who promised is faithful.

Blessed be the God and the Father of our Lord Jesus Christ! By his great mercy we have been born anew to a living hope through the resurrection of Jesus Christ from the dead, and to an inheritance which is imperishable, undefiled, and unfading, kept in heaven for you...

Rejoice in hope.

(Psalm 39:7, GNB; Psalm 62:5 and 65:5b, RSV; Psalm 71:12-15, GNB; Lamentations 3:19-24, RSV; Hebrews 6:17-20 and 10:23, RSV; 1 Peter 1:3-4, RSV; Romans 12:12, RSV)

To hope is as human as to love. We were made to face the future just as we were made to face each other. Even in the darkest situations we still hope. Once off the coast of Newfoundland a mini-sub sank. Divers managed to locate it and tapped on the side to see if there was any sign of life. In morse-code a message came back: 'Is there hope?'

'Is there hope?' is a question we all ask, whether in the crises of life — 'Is there hope, doctor?' — or in the daily despair of a difficult marriage, prolonged unemployment or useless employment.

Unlike optimism, Christian hope doesn't opt out when faced with harsh realities. The reason for the realism of Christian hope is the fact that it is cast in the mould of the crucifixion and resurrection of Christ.

Christian hope can face any situation, because it is not based on changeable circumstances, but a settled conviction that nothing can overtake us that Christ hasn't taken care of. It is willing to risk all on the reality of the resurrection. We welcome the future, because it bears the face of Jesus.

Hope springs eternal in the human breast:
Man never *is*, but always *to be* blest.

Alexander Pope

Hope — the uncertain goddess.

Pericles

Hope is the enemy.

Henry Miller, *Tropic of Cancer*

In the subsequent years of ministry in England I have often been asked: 'What is the greatest difficulty you faced in moving from India to England?' I have always answered: *'The disappearance of hope'*. For the elderly and middle-aged there is, for the most part, only the hope of keeping reasonably comfortable amid the disintegration of so many of the familiar values. For very many of the young there is only the terrible spectre of nuclear war, with nothing beyond.

Bishop Lesslie Newbigin, *The Other Side of 1984*

Can true biblical hope serve as a warning against false hope? In a society filled with immanental hope of social engineering, of human potential, of political revolution, we need to hear the great themes of Old Testament hope. Our hope is in the Lord, who is also our salvation; all other hope is hopeless.

David Hubbard, from an article entitled
Hope in the Old Testament

With this third world war which might break out one day, with this wretched gathering which our planet now is, despair returns to tempt me. The idea that we'll never be done with it, that there's no purpose, only petty personal ends for which we fight. We make little revolutions but there's not a human end. Nothing concerning man, only disorders. One can't think such things. They tempt you incessantly, especially if you're old and can think, 'Oh well, anyway, I shall die in five years at the most'. In fact I think ten, but it might well be five. In any case the world seems ugly, bad and without hope. There, that's the cry of despair of an old man who'll die in despair. But that's exactly what I resist, and I know I shall die in hope. But that hope needs a foundation.

Jean-Paul Sartre less than a month before he died in 1980

All utopias of the kingdom of God or of man, all hopeful pictures of the happy life, all revolutions of the future, remain hanging in the air and bear within them the germ of boredom and decay — and for that reason also adopt a militant and extortionate attitude to life — as long as there is no certainty in the face of death and no hope which carries love beyond death.

Jurgen Moltmann, *Theology of Hope*

My hope is built on nothing less
Than Jesus' blood and righteousness,
I dare not trust my sweetest frame,
But wholly lean on Jesus' name,
On Christ the solid Rock I stand,
All other ground is sinking sand.

Edward Mote

Who could believe in a God who will make everything new later if it is in no way apparent from the activity of those who hope in the One who is to come that he is already beginning to make everything new now?

Edward Schillbeeckx, *God the Future of Man*

The hope towards which the Bible moves promises a new creation that radically transcends man's own possibilities. But in promising this it also encourages him to take the steps that are within his power in the direction of this goal, and to refrain from the steps leading in the opposite direction. Anyone who wants to reach the new world across the sea will start off for the port of departure on his own feet and with the means of transport at his disposal in this old world, even though he realises that very different forces will be needed before he can land in the new world and become its citizen. The promise of the hope of God is finding strength to meet a double disappointment: some tell people to put their trust in the next world, and disappoint them by declaring that the present is hopelessly unalterable; others claim that they can realise the heaven of total salvation by their own strength, and disappoint because they ruin the present in a completely inhuman way. On the other hand man, who is of his very nature orientated towards the future, can — trusting in the word of promise — remain radically hopeful within the relativity of 'a step at a time'.

Hans Walter Wolff, *Anthropology of the Old Testament*

To us is given the promise of eternal life — but to us, the dead. A blessed resurrection is proclaimed to us — meantime we are surrounded by decay. We are called righteous — and yet sin lives in us. We hear of ineffable blessedness — but meantime we are oppressed by infinite misery. We are promised abundance of all good things — yet we are rich only in hunger and thirst. What would become of us if we did not take our stand on hope, and if our heart did not hasten beyond the midst of the darkness upon the path illumined by the word and Spirit of God!

John Calvin

Hope leads us into life, into the whole of life. It encourages faith so that it does not degenerate into faintheartedness. It strengthens love so that it does not remain enclosed within itself and with those who are like it. Thus Charles Peguy said:

Hope leads everything.
For faith only sees what *is*.
But hope sees what *will* be.
Charity only loves what *is*.
But hope loves what *will* be —
In time and for all eternity.

Jurgen Moltmann, *The Experiment Hope*

Pardon for sin and a peace everlasting,
your living presence to cheer and to guide;
strength for today, and bright hope for tomorrow —
these are the blessings your love will provide.
Great is your faithfulness...

T.O. Chisolm (1866-1960)

As we grow in faith, love, and hope, help us to understand
that no planning for the future, however necessary,
no programme, no matter how carefully conceived,
can relieve us of the necessity of going forward
into a future that cannot be planned of risk, of danger, of hope
in your incalculable grace.

Lord, be for us the truth on which
life and death are built,
the hope that cannot be destroyed,
the freedom from which love and justice flow
and the joy that has eternity within it.
Amen.

Terry Falla, *Be Our Freedom, Lord*

God of hope, we confess that we have fallen prey to false hopes; hopes of success, prestige, influence; we have invested ourselves emotionally in them only to be disappointed,
We pray for those we see deceived by the illusions of false hope; led by false shepherds, political and psychological messiahs who promise much, but deliver little.
We praise and thank you for our true hope, a sure and certain hope in your Son, and pray that each morning we might rise ready to live each day in the light of the last day. Help us not to be nostalgic for the past nor possessive of the present, but to hold each day open to the future heritage of your Kingdom.
Amen.

A Benediction
And now unto him who is able to keep us from falling and lift us from the dark valley of despair to the bright mountain of hope, from the midnight of desperation to the daybreak of joy; to him be power and authority, for ever and ever. Amen.

Martin Luther King

WEEK

Where is your sting?

(1 Corinthians 15:55)

There in the land of Moab, Moses the servant of Yahweh died as Yahweh decreed; he buried him in the valley opposite Bethpeor; but to this day no one has even found his grave.

Where could I go to escape your spirit? Where could I flee from your presence? If I climb the heavens, you are there; there, too, if I lie in Sheol.

There is a season for everything... A time for giving birth, a time for dying; a time for planting, a time for uprooting... A time for killing, a time for healing... A time for tears, a time for laughter; a time for mourning, a time for dancing.

Where is your plague, Death? Where are your scourges, Sheol?

Happy those who mourn; they shall be comforted.

After Jesus had taken the vinegar he said, 'It is accomplished'; and hanging his head he gave up his spirit.

As they were stoning him, Stephen said in invocation, 'Lord Jesus, receive my spirit.' Then he knelt down and said aloud, 'Lord, do not hold this sin against them'; and with these words he fell asleep.

Now we are seeing a dim reflection in a mirror; but then we shall be seeing face to face. The knowledge that I have now is imperfect; but then I shall know as fully as I am known.

Life to me, of course, is Christ, but then death would bring me something more... I want to be gone and be with Christ, which would be very much the better.

Now, Master, you can let your servant go in peace, just as you promised.

Jesus said, 'I am the resurrection. If anyone believes in me, even though he dies he will live, and whoever lives and believes in me will never die. Do you believe this?'

(Deuteronomy 34:5-6; Psalm 139:7-8; Ecclesiastes 3:1-4; Hosea 13:14; Matthew 5:4; John 19:30; Acts 7:59-60; 1 Corinthians 13:12; Philippians 1:21 and 23; Luke 2:29; John 11:25-26 — all JB)

'Are you prepared to kill?' A recruit to the armed forces was recently put on the spot with this question, to test his commitment to serve. Equally relevant and even more searching would be the question, 'Are you prepared to die?' In an armed encounter, you will not always be the lucky one. Or is death such a bad escape after all? 'Death, where is your sting?'

On the subject of death, the Bible is clear, firm and uncompromising. Moses, David, Simeon, Stephen, Paul and many other biblical characters welcomed its approach. Jesus pointed to a greater life beyond death and offered himself to Martha, Thomas and others, as the 'way' to eternity.

Many Christians today, particularly those engaged in pastoral ministry, live in regular contact with this dying. As a process or an event, it's often shunned in modern Western society. Information is withheld, pretences maintained, farewells foregone. What is the role of the pastor at the deathbed? To be emotionally involved or professionally immune?

Yet he or she is the one person who can inject warmth, truth and hope into the experience of those who are watching, waiting and dying.

We can, of course, learn so much about death and dying from the Two-thirds World. Asians, Africans, Pacific Islanders, mostly live closer to the possibility of death — and so perhaps grasp more fully the meaning and purpose and value of life. Certainly they have less fear!

Death is probably most difficult to accept when it occurs far away, in situations where there can be no watching or waiting or sharing. Grieving at a distance is a hard experience. It drives you back to a sense of utter dependence on the God who 'gives us the victory through our Lord Jesus Christ'.

A doctor said to me recently, 'Having been through the interesting process of dying with so many patients, I can hardly wait to share the experience myself!' Death is an adventure, a vital staging-post, on our pilgrimage. Yes, I am prepared to die!

Nine officers were killed by IRA mortar bombs last week in the worst attack against the Northern Ireland police since the present troubles began. Another officer, a Roman Catholic, was shot dead this week as he was about to enter a church for mass, bringing the total of killings in the province to eighteen in just over two weeks.

The Guardian, March 10, 1985

Death in itself, is nothing; but we fear, to be we know not what, we know not where.

John Dryden

> What's brave, what's noble,
> Let's do it after the high Roman fashion,
> And make death proud to take us.

William Shakespeare, *Antony and Cleopatra*

> No life that breathes with human breath
> Has ever truly longed for death.

Tennyson, *The Two Voices*

Why should man be in love with his fetters, though of gold? Art thou drowned in security? Then I say thou art perfectly dead. For though thou movest, yet thy soul is buried within thee, and thy good angel either forsakes his guard or sleeps. There is nothing under heaven, saving a true friend (who cannot be counted within the number of movables), unto which my heart doth lean. And this dear freedom hath begotten me this peace, that I mourn not for that end which must be, nor spend one wish to have one minute added to the uncertain date of my years. It was no mean apprehension of *Lucian*, who says of *Mennippus*, that in his travels through hell, he knew not the kings of the earth from other men, but only by their louder cryings and tears: which were fostered in them through the remorseful memory of the good days they had seen, and the fruitful havings which they so unwillingly left behind them: he that was well seated, looked back at his portion, and was loth to forsake his farm; and others either minding marriages, pleasures, profit, or preferment, desired to be excused from Death's banquet: they had made an appointment with earth, looking at the blessings, not the hand that enlarged them, forgetting how unclothedly they came hither, or with what naked ornaments they were arrayed.

Francis Bacon, *Essay on Death*

It comes equally to us all, and makes us all equal when it comes. The ashes of an Oak in the Chimney are no Epitaph of the Oak to tell me how high or how large that was. It tells me not what flocks it sheltered while it stood, nor what men it hurt when it fell. The dust of great persons' graves is speechless too, it says nothing, it distinguishes nothing: as soon the dust of a wretch whom thou wouldest not, as of a Prince thou couldest not look upon, will trouble thine eyes, if the wind blow it thither; and when a whirlwind hath blown the dust of the Churchyard into the Church, and the man sweeps out the dust of the Church into the Churchyard, who will undertake to sift those dusts again, and to pronounce, This is the Patrician, this is the noble flower, and this the yeomanly, this the Plebeian bran. So is the death of *Jesabel* (*Jesabel* was a Queen) *expressed; They shall not say, this is Jesabel*; not only not wonder what it is, nor pity that it should be, but they shall not say, they shall not know, This is *Jesabel*.

John Donne, *Death the Leveller*

Should this be found I want these facts recorded. Oates' last thoughts were of his Mother, but immediately before he took pride in thinking that his regiment would be pleased with the bold way in which he met his death. We can testify to his bravery. He has borne intense suffering for weeks without complaint, and to the very last was able and willing to discuss outside subjects. He did not — would not — give up hope till the very end. He was a brave soul. This was the end. He slept through the night before last, hoping not to wake; but he woke in the morning — yesterday. It was blowing a blizzard. He said, 'I am just going outside and may be some time.' He went out into the blizzard and we have not seen him since.

Robert Scott, *Death of Captain Oates*

The disease may, however, be one of those from which there is no certainty that the patient will recover. I am reminded of an old friend, a woman of boundless energy and optimism. One might have wondered if her faith, when she was in good health and engaged in a full and useful life of spiritual service, was only the reflection of her simple and confident nature. I saw her later, immobilised on her bed of pain. In answer to her direct question, her doctor had informed her of the inevitable diagnosis he must make of her condition. She was preparing herself joyfully for death. She was more radiant than ever. Visitors flocked to see her, and found in her a testimony that was more striking than she had given in active life and health.

Paul Tournier, *The Person Reborn*

O Lord Jesus Christ, Son of the Living God, who at this evening hour didst rest in the sepulchre, and didst thereby sanctify the grave to be a bed of hope to thy people; make us so to abound in sorrow for our sins, which were the cause of thy passion, that when our bodies lie in the dust, our souls may live with thee; who livest and reignest with the Father and the Holy Ghost, our God, world without end. Amen.

The Office of Compline

Jesus, confirm my heart's desire
to work and speak and think for thee;
still let me guard the holy fire
and still stir up thy gift in me.

Ready for all thy perfect will,
my acts of faith and love repeat,
till death thy endless mercies seal
and make the sacrifice complete.

Charles Wesley

A Benediction

Go forth upon thy journey, O Christian soul;
in the Name of God the Father, who created thee;
in the Name of Jesus Christ, Son of the living God,
who suffered for thee;

in the Name of God the Holy Ghost, who hath sanctified thee.
May thy portion this day be in peace and thy dwelling in the heavenly Jerusalem.

WEEK

23

Running with angels' laughter

(John Hazelwood)

There is no condemnation for those who are united with Christ Jesus, because in Christ Jesus the life-giving law of the Spirit has set you free from the law of sin and death. I am convinced that there is nothing in death or life, in the realm of spirits or superhuman powers, in the world as it is or the world as it shall be, in the forces of the universe, in heights or depths — nothing in all creation that can separate us from the love of God in Christ Jesus our Lord.

Speak to one another in psalms, hymns and songs; sing and make music in your hearts to the Lord; and in the name of our Lord Jesus Christ give thanks every day for everything to our God and Father.

Don't worry about anything, but in all your prayers ask God for what you need, always asking him with a thankful heart. And God's peace, which is far beyond human understanding, will keep your hearts and minds safe in union with Christ Jesus.

Praise the Lord, my soul!
All my being, praise his holy name!
Praise the Lord, my soul,
And do not forget how kind he is.
He forgives all my sins
and heals all my diseases.

(Romans 8:1, 38-39, NEB; Ephesians 5:18-20, NEB; Philippians 4:6-7, GNB; Psalm 103:1-3, GNB)

The thirteenth of October 1982 was the tenth anniversary of a plane crash in the Andes with forty-five people aboard. Seventeen died immediately. Twelve died in the following days. Seventy days after the crash, sixteen young men who survived were rescued. Twenty-nine-year-old Uruguayan Gustavo Zerbino said on the tenth anniversary: 'The mountains drastically changed our scale of values. I am in society and must be concerned about economic realities. But I try to emphasise the spiritual and human part of life. We lit fires with money in the Andes. Money may help attain goals, but it isn't a goal in itself.' Fernando Parrado, thirty-two, whose mother died in the crash and whose sister agonised for five days in his arms before dying said, 'I'm no preacher. I don't go around telling people to enjoy what they have while they have it, but that is what we learned.'

These two men are not speaking with the same breadth as Paul in his letters but there is a hint of angels' laughter in their approach to life. The shadows of the crash, the deaths, the cold still hang over them. But they are not defeated by the memories nor absorbed by what they now have. They are like Paul in this, that they know the reality of God, as if he were standing astride everything, bearing them up in his arms.

For my purposes I take it that the Caroline Divines are clergymen or bishops of the Church of England who lived, taught and suffered through the years of the reign of James I and Charles I up to 1650... Saints have a resiliency that runs with angels' laughter over the machinations of other men's greed, pride and polity. These saints, enshrined where they are in the dangerous minefields of Stuart and Puritan civil strife and Roman Catholic threat, hold hands with the saints of the fourteenth century in that they see the relationship of God with men shining through the natural world...

John Hazelwood, from the chapter, 'The Spirituality of the Caroline Divines' in *Anglican Spirituality*.

Hurrah for those who never invented anything;
Hurrah for those who never explored anything;
Hurrah for those who never conquered anything;
But who, in awe, gave themselves up to the essence of things,
Ignorant of the shell, but seized by the rhythm of things
Not intent on conquest, but playing the part of the world.

by the Caribbean poet Aime Ceasaire

From the standpoint of the Christian faith, the potential of the world for beauty and squalor, for wonder and terror, for many shades and varieties of meaning, is an authentic potential — as authentic as the potential of radio waves to become sounds. Beauty and squalor and other varieties of meaning are not merely projected upon the world by man's imagination; for the Creator himself has given to the world not only power of being but also power of meaning, not only existence but meaningful existence. So man, in perceiving meaning in the world, perceives what is really there. He sees — no doubt in a distorted or limited way — what God sees: at least he sees the dimension — the dimension of meaning — which God sees. He becomes a point at which God's perception of the world is, as it were, caught in a tiny mirror and projected back to God; so that, if a flight of imagination may be permitted, God sees before him not only the world which he has made in all its depth of meaning but also myriads of points at which something of that depth of meaning is received by human consciousness and reflected back to him. God creates a world which includes among its infinite variety of wonders this culminating wonder — that there are points within it at which, in the consciousness of men, its wonders are received and recognised.

W.H. Vanstone, *The Stature of Waiting*

Some were bearded but no one in that company struck me as being of any particular age. One gets glimpses, even in our country, of that which is ageless — heavy thought in the face of an infant, and frolic childhood in that of a very old man.

C.S. Lewis, in a description of heaven
in *The Great Divorce*

The spring blew trumpets of colour,
  Her green sang in my brain,
I heard a blind man groping
  tap-tap with his cane.

I pitied him his blindness
  but can I say I see?
Perhaps there walks close by a
  spirit that pities me.

A spirit that sees me tapping the
five-sensed cane of time;
Amid such unguess'd glories
that I am worse than blind!

Harry Kemp, 'Blind' in
Great Poems of the English Language

Let then our first act every morning be to make the following resolve for the day: 'I shall not fear anyone on earth. I shall fear only God. I shall not bear ill-will towards anyone. I shall not submit to injustice from anyone. I shall conquer untruth by truth and in resisting untruth, I shall put up with all suffering.'

Mahatma Gandhi

At the beginning of the bus boycott in Montgomery, Alabama, we set up a voluntary car pool to get the people to and from their jobs. For eleven months our car pool functioned extraordinarily well. Then Mayor Gayle introduced a resolution instructing the city's legal department to file such proceedings as it might deem proper to stop the operation of the car pool or any transportation system growing out of the bus boycott. A hearing was set for Tuesday, November 13, 1956.

At our regular weekly mass meeting, scheduled the night before the hearing, I had the responsibility of warning the people that the car pool would probably be enjoined...

When the evening came, I mustered sufficient courage to tell them the truth. I tried, however, to conclude on a note of hope. 'We have moved all of these months,' I said, 'in the daring faith that God is with us in our struggle. The many experiences of days gone by have vindicated that faith in a marvellous way. Tonight we must believe that a way will be made out of no way...'

[Next day] in anxiety and hope, I read these words in the court release: 'The United States Supreme Court today unanimously ruled bus segregation unconstitutional in Montgomery, Alabama.' My heart throbbed with an inexpressible joy. The darkest hour of our struggle had become the first hour of victory. Someone shouted from the back of the courtroom: 'God Almighty has spoken from Washington!'

Martin Luther King, in a sermon
'A Knock at Midnight'

The Prayer of the Goldfish:
O God,
forever I turn in this hard crystal,
so transparent, yet I can find no way out.
Lord,
deliver me from the cramp of this water
and these terrifying things I see through it.
Put me back in the play of your torrents,
in your limpid springs.
Let me no longer be a little goldfish
in its prison of glass,
but a living spark
in the gentleness of your reeds. Amen.

Carmen Bernos de Gasztold, *Prayers of the Ark*

Father, I thank you that Jesus never lost his bright hopefulness even when everything was at its darkest. I remember how he held to you when the devil tempted him in the wilderness, how he cared for children when the disciples impatiently dismissed them, and how he endured the cross because of the joy that was set before him.

Father, help me to live joyfully when today's Pharisaic attitudes threaten to make me doubt your love for all things great and small. Show me how to run with angels' laughter over all arrogance, bigotry, meanness and manipulation — in myself and in others.

A Benediction

The Lord be within you to strengthen you; over and around you to ward off your spiritual foes on every side; under you to hold you up in your goings; behind you to guard you from the assaults of the past; before you to lead you on. Amen.

WEEK

Surprised by joy

(C.S. Lewis)

'I will turn their mourning into gladness; I will give them comfort and joy instead of sorrow. I will satisfy the priests with abundance, and my people will be filled with my bounty,' declares the Lord.

The kingdom of heaven is like treasure hidden in a field. When a man found it, he hid it again, and then in his joy went and sold all he had and bought that field.

Burst into songs of joy together, you ruins of Jerusalem, for the Lord has comforted his people, he has redeemed Jerusalem.

The seventy-two returned with joy and said, 'Lord, even the demons submit to us in your name.'

These things I remember as I pour out my soul: how I used to go with the multitude, leading the procession to the house of God, with shouts of joy and thanksgiving among the festive throng.

How can we thank God enough for you in return for all the joy we have in the presence of our God because of you?

Create in me a pure heart, O God, and renew a steadfast spirit within me... Restore to me the joy of your salvation and grant me a willing spirit, to sustain me.

When your words came, I ate them; they were my joy and my heart's delight, for I bear your name, O Lord God Almighty.

If you obey my commands, you will remain in my love, just as I have obeyed my Father's commands and remain in his love. I have told you this so that my joy may be in you and that your joy may be complete. My command is this: Love each other as I have loved you.

Those who sow in tears will reap with songs of joy. He

who goes out weeping, carrying seed to sow, will return with songs of joy, carrying sheaves with him.

Consider it pure joy, my brothers, whenever you face trials of many kinds, because you know that the testing of your faith develops perseverance. Perseverance must finish its work so that you may be mature and complete, not lacking anything.

Let us fix our eyes on Jesus, the author and perfector of our faith, who for the joy set before him endured the cross, scorning its shame, and sat down at the right hand of the throne of God.

(Jeremiah 31:13-14; Matthew 13:44; Isaiah 52:9; Luke 10:17; Psalm 42:4; 1 Thessalonians 3:9; Psalm 51:10 and 12; Jeremiah 15:16; John 15:10-12; Psalm 126:5-6; James 1:2-4; Hebrews 12:2 — all NIV)

True joy is a rare experience, it seems. We humans are more prone to think in terms of happiness or pleasure than we are of joy, and those who do cast joy a glance often find it illusory or transient. One sceptic, Stanislaw Lec, has cautioned: 'When you jump for joy, beware that no one moves the ground from beneath your feet !' However, joy, the joy that is one of the fruits of the Spirit, is meant to have a central place in the Christian life, enriching not only our own lives but also those around us. As James Packer has said: 'Joy is like jam, you know: it sticks to you as you try to spread it!'

Sometimes it is easy to be joyful. When our daily needs have been amply supplied, when the relationship of family and friends is sweet, when we have seen God working for us and through us, we can fairly readily identify with the psalmist who testified: 'You have made known to me the path of life; you will fill me with joy in your presence' (Psalm 16:11 NIV).

But sometimes, sadly, the experience of joy becomes routine and predictable, hardly distinguishable from ordinary human happiness. Perhaps that is because we focus on the joys of life rather than on the Joy of life; or perhaps it is because we are looking for joy in the wrong places. We have forgotten that, in God's way of doing things, the path to joy is often through obedience and suffering.

So sometimes we are surprised by joy! For joy appears when and where we are not expecting it. When our hearts have been moved to confess sin and our lives have been cleansed and renewed; when our ears have listened to God's word and our wills have been set to obey his commands; when we allow his love to flow through us to others — then we are promised that our joy will be complete. When our hearts are broken by sorrow or persecution; when our faith is stretched to the limit; when our cross is more than we can bear — then we are offered pure joy.

Happiness turns up more or less where you'd expect it to — a good marriage, a rewarding job, a pleasant vacation. Joy, on the other hand, is as notoriously unpredictable as the one who bequeathes it.

Frederick Buechner, *Wishful Thinking*

I'm happy when ev'rything happens to please,
But happiness comes and goes;
While the heart that is stayed on Jesus the Saviour
Ever with joy o'erflows;
Happiness happens, but joy abides,
In the heart that is stayed on Jesus.

Helen Howarth Lemmuel

Different, then, from pleasure and happiness, joy is that abiding beatitude, that deep-down exuberance which comes from God through his Spirit by faith in his Son. Joy is thus supernatural in its source and essence, a foretaste of the face-to-face communion with God that will be rapture for ever.

Vernon C. Grounds, in an article entitled
'Soar with the Eagles, Sing with the Angels'

True joy is the earnest which we have of heaven, it is the treasure of the soul, and therefore should be laid in a safe place, and nothing of this world is safe to place it in.

John Donne, *Sermons, No.28*

Life, of course, is not one big picnic. Something has happened, however, to take the trials and troubles of life and turn their little rivulets of sorrow and sadness into a great stream of gladness and joy.

That stream comes not from mere religion, but from Christ, the Saviour of the world. You might say that life was not very good to Christ . . . Life spat in his face and hung him up to die. Life, however, could not lick Christ. Already ticketed for death, the condemned man entered the city without pretension as a conquering hero. Preparing for death, he organised a victory banquet. His last conversation with the men who had left all to follow him, their hearts now heavy with premonition and apprehension, included this ringing declaration: 'These things have I spoken unto you that my joy might remain in you and that your joy might be full . . .'

Oswald C.J. Hoffmann, in a sermon entitled 'In the Reality of Joy'

Joy, not grit, is the hallmark of holy obedience. We need to be lighthearted in what we do to avoid taking ourselves too seriously. It is a cheerful revolt against self and pride. Our work is jubilant, carefree, merry. Utter abandonment to God is done freely and with celebration. And so I urge you to enjoy this ministry of self-surrender. Don't push too hard. Hold this work lightly, joyfully.

The saints throughout the ages have witnessed to this reality . . . You know, of course, that they are not speaking of a silly, superficial, bubbly kind of joy like that flaunted in modern society. No, this is a deep, resonant joy that has been shaped and tempered by the fires of suffering and sorrow — joy through the cross, joy because of the cross.

Richard Foster, *Freedom of Simplicity*

'The fruit of the Spirit is joy,' Paul said. Joy is a by-product of possessing the Spirit and being possessed by the Spirit. It is the conscious possession of power adequate enough to carry us through every trial, every situation, and it will remain ours to the end . . . In this life, we shall never be free of sorrow. But, then, we shall never be free of joy. And joy is the dominant note. We are in touch with a power that dries all tears, lifts all burdens, satisfies all needs. Our lives are hidden with God in Christ.

John N. Gladstone, in a sermon entitled 'Weeping and Whistling'

So how are we to learn to rejoice in the Lord always? Answer: First, by understanding what the ingredients of Christian joy are, and second (take a deep breath) by choosing it. How does one choose joy? By choosing to practice the art of Christian thinking. By choosing to dwell, over and over, on this fourfold awareness from which the joy flows. Yes, he loves me and accepts me. Yes, my circumstances are sent by God for my good. Yes, I have something supremely worth having: the knowledge of my Saviour. Yes, I am doing something supremely worth doing, in seeking every opportunity to share Jesus Christ with others. As one thinks these things over, joy wells up spontaneously. You choose joy by choosing to think on these things. That is the secret.

J.I. Packer, in a sermon entitled 'Joy'

An orange tree cannot bear fruit in total independence. Sunshine, rain, and soil must play a part if oranges are to be brought forth. So it is with ourselves and joy. We may crave joy and fiercely will to be joyful. But as psychologist Abraham Maslow put it: 'You cannot seek ecstatic moments directly; you must be surprised by joy.' And in saying that, Maslow is endorsing Paul's teaching that joy is a fruit. We cannot directly produce it.

We can, however, cooperate with the fruit-producing forces, and at the same time we can eliminate anything that might blight productivity. An orange-grower prunes his trees, fertilises and waters them, fights insects by spraying, and sometimes, when frost threatens, puts out smudge-pots. Having done his human best, he waits for forces outside himself to produce the desired fruit.

Vernon C. Grounds,
'Soar with the Eagles, Sing with the Angels'

O Joy that seekest me through pain,
I cannot close my heart to Thee:
I trace the rainbow through the rain,
And feel the promise is not vain,
That morn shall tearless be.

George Matheson

You must help me to understand
and to believe, O God,
that while the feelings of your nearness may
dim or diminish,
the fact of your presence is forever secure.

You are always near,
You are with me and you will go before me
even amidst the tragedies and dark crises
that clutter my course through life.
Thank you, O Lord, for surprising me with joy.
May it refresh and recharge
my life and my faith in you.
May it result in a deeper dedication
to your purposes,
and bring some joy to the lives of others
who cross my path.
For the sake of Jesus Christ my Lord. Amen.

Leslie F. Brandt, *A Book of Christian Prayer*

A Benediction

May our God, in whose presence alone is fullness of joy, be so real to us in all the varying circumstances of life, that we can be confident, however dark the night, that joy will come in the morning.

May our Lord Jesus Christ, who, for the joy that was set before him, endured the cross, teach us to pray in his name, that, asking, we will receive, and our joy will be full.

And may the Holy Spirit, through whose power the fruit of joy grows in our lives, give us such motivation and strength to be obedient and faithful servants that we will constantly be surprised by joy.

WEEK

V Day

Stand up to the devil and he will turn and run.

The victory is ours . . . he makes it ours by our Lord Jesus Christ.

The Lord saves not with sword and spear.

Although we live in the world it is no worldly warfare that we are waging.

Fear not, and be not dismayed . . . for the battle is not yours but God's . . . you will not need to fight in this battle; take your position, stand still.

We will go up and fight, just as the Lord our God commanded us . . . And the Lord said . . . 'Do not go up or fight, for I am not in the midst of you.'

Aim at righteousness, godliness, faith, love, steadfastness, gentleness. Fight the good fight of the faith.

. . . be strong — not in yourselves but in the Lord . . . Put on God's complete armour so that you can successfully resist all the devil's methods of attack . . . we are up against . . . spiritual agents from the very headquarters of evil . . . Take your stand then with truth . . . righteousness . . . peace . . . salvation . . . the Word of God . . . faith . . . Pray at all times with every kind of spiritual prayer, keeping alert and persistent.

(James 4:7, NEB; 1 Corinthians 15:57, Moffat; 1 Samuel 17:47, RSV; 2 Corinthians 10:3, Weymouth; 2 Chronicles 20:15-17, RSV; Deuteronomy 1:41-42, RSV; 1 Timothy 6:11-12, RSV; Ephesians 6:10-18, Phillips)

In earthly warfare, both sides normally know when the battle was engaged, when it was over, what it was about, and who won. In Christian experience none of these aspects may be clear to us. Satan's cleverest strategy is deceit.

Deceit about the existence of warfare, so we don't actually expect life to be lived under battle conditions, day in and day out.

Deceit about the onset of each skirmish, to keep us unaware until long after battle has been engaged, and much ground has already been lost.

Deceit about the duration of each skirmish. If we don't resist Satan he won't leave us and flee. The order of events is clear.

Deceit about what constitutes victory. Unless I know what each side is aiming at in the battle how will I be able to work out who has won and when the victory took place?

Deceit about Satan's strategy. Frontal attack is not his style. Look out for something sneaky! He prefers poison to gelignite, debilitating to dynamiting. His greatest success in any given day is to make me just feel 'down' and out-of-sorts, burdened by life.

Deceit about our armoury. God never sends us half-armed into battle — we ourselves launch in ill-equipped.

Deceit about our location in the battle, and therefore about our degree of participation in it. If we think of ourselves as the battle*ground* or battle *spoils* we will see ourselves in a passive location, with God and Satan fighting on us or over us. If we see ourselves as participants but are worried we may get in God's way, we will keep well back and take little or no initiative. Our real location is to be out in front, with God beside us! No known wrong — in our own situation, in any situation for which we have direct responsibility, or even in any other situation within accessible range — is to be left unchallenged. Correct assessment of wrong should always be followed by a strong initiative to bring about change, sometimes by frontal attack but always by some deliberate strategy suited to the sensitivity of the situation. To 'pray about it and leave it to God' can be an unbiblical cop-out. Prayer is not an alternative to battle action: it accompanies battle action. We are to pray and watch at all times.

And everybody praised the Duke
Who this great fight did win
'But what good came of it at last?'
Quoth little Peterkin.

'Why that I cannot tell,' said he
'But 'twas a famous victory . . .
. . . But what they fought each other for
I could not well make out.'

Robert Southey, *Battle of Blenheim*

When the German soldiers went into World War I, most of them shared the popular belief in a nice God who would make everything turn out for the best. Actually, everything worked out for the worst.

Paul Tillich, *The Boundaries of Our Being*

'But sometimes virtue starves, while vice is fed.'
What then? Is the reward of virtue bread?

Alexander Pope, *Essay on Man*

'. . . something else in him had died, something that he had long desired should perish. Was it not what he had once wished to destroy during his ardent years of asceticism? Was it not his Self, his small, fearful and proud Self, with which he had wrestled for so many years, but which had always conquered him again, which appeared each time again and again, which robbed him of happiness and filled him with fear? . . . Too much knowledge had hindered him; too many holy verses, too many sacrificial rites, too much mortification of the flesh, too much doing and striving. He had been full of arrogance; he had always been the cleverest, the most eager — always a step ahead of the others, always the learned and intellectual one, always the priest or the sage. His Self had crawled into his priesthood, into his arrogance, into his intellectuality. It sat there tightly and grew, while he thought he was destroying it by fasting and penitence.'

Herman Hesse, *Siddhartha*

'If the immediate and direct purpose of our life is not suffering then our existence is the most ill-adapted to its purpose in the world: for it is absurd to suppose that the endless affliction of which the world is everywhere full, and which arises out of the need and distress pertaining essentially to life, should be purposeless and purely accidental. Each individual misfortune, to be sure, seems an exceptional occurrence; but misfortune in general is the rule.'

Schopenhauer, *On the Suffering of the World*

'...this, at least, may be maintained, that we do not always find visible happiness in proportion to visible virtue... All that virtue can afford is quietness of conscience, a steady prospect of a happier state; this may enable us to endure calamity with patience; but remember that patience must suppose pain.'

Samuel Johnson, *Rasselas*

It need not surprise us that as an image to convey the nature of Christian living, the Holy Spirit uses that of warfare. No image could be more apt.

John White, *The Fight*

...subject to all manner of tribulations, to troublesome circumstances beyond number, which make us uneven in health, moods and disposition of heart and of behaviour; in a word, people whom God desires to bring low by countless trials and travail as much within as without. We must without doubt believe that it is to our advantage, that it is pleasing to God to sacrifice us to himself...

Brother Lawrence, *The Practice of the Presence of God*

A victory is twice itself when the achiever brings home full numbers... In our last conflict four of his five wits went halting off, and now is the whole man governed by one.

William Shakespeare, *Much Ado About Nothing*

E'en victors are by victories undone.

Epistle to John Dryden

One more such victory, and we are lost.

Pyrrhus

Some Christians are so self-confident that they think they can manage by themselves without the Lord's strength and armour. Others are so self-distrustful that they imagine they have nothing to contribute to their victory in spiritual warfare. Both are mistaken.

John Stott, *God's New Society*

'Much-Afraid,' said the two guides, stooping over her and shaking her by the shoulder gently but firmly. 'Much-Afraid, you know where your help lies. Call for help.' She clung to them and sobbed again. 'I am afraid to call,' she gasped. 'I am so afraid that if I call him, he will tell me that I *must* go that way, that dreadful, dreadful way, and I can't. It's impossible. I can't face it. Oh, what shall I do? Whatever shall I do?'

Hannah Hurnard, *Hind's Feet on High Places*

The Hebrew words for 'salvation' are readily translated 'victory'.

F.F. Bruce, *This is That*

'If the people who run the show are so clever and so powerful, why don't they find something to suit their public? All this poppycock about growing harder so that the grass doesn't hurt our feet . . .'

C.S. Lewis, *The Great Divorce*

From subtle love of softening things,
From easy choices, weakenings,
Not thus are spirits fortified,
Not this way went the Crucified,
From all that dims Thy Calvary,
O Lamb of God, deliver me.

Amy Carmichael of Dohnavur

For yours, Lord, is the kingdom and the power and the glory for ever and ever. I thank you for accepting me into that kingdom and for making me heir to its privileges. Thank you for entrusting me with its keys and for giving me your power to war against the principalities and powers of evil, to bind them, and to loose situations and people in bondage to them.

Thank you that no testing I encounter during the course of today will be beyond your power. Armour me with discernment and the will to win. Help me to be patient in suffering and even to rejoice in it, so long as my own stupidity has not brought it upon me. Keep before me a vision of victory — the victory of the cross — and help me to see each day's events from its perspective.

Thank you for understanding my frailties, the fluctuations of my faith and my utter foolishness in so much that I do. Help me to develop your strength, constancy and wisdom, so that

I may grow up into you in all things and be conformed to your image and likeness. May you be satisfied with the travail of your soul for me.

A Benediction

Bless the Lord! Blessing and honour and glory and might be his for ever and ever. And now be assured of his blessing — his abundant blessing — on all that you seek to do and to be for him. You are his personal investment: he holds you secure in his mighty hand, and he will keep you secure until eternity. You are part of that great multitude that will one day stand before the throne, having come out of great tribulation. God himself will wipe away every tear from your eyes and your crying and pain will be no more. He will shelter you with his presence, and you will rest in his love. So work together with him for good — a peculiar good for a peculiar people — and may the blessing of a loving Father, an understanding Saviour, and the empowering of the Holy Spirit, be with you now and every day. Amen.

Theme: Guidance

'Through the mighty waters' (Psalm 77:19)

Your ways, O God, are holy.
What god is so great as our God?
You are the God who performs miracles;
you display your power among the peoples.
With your mighty arm you redeemed
your people. . .
Your path led through the sea,
your way through the mighty waters,
though your footprints were not seen.

Psalm 77: 13-15a and 19, NIV

WEEK

26

Life's loose ends

'How long are you going to keep us in suspense? Tell us the plain truth: are you the Messiah?'

'Tell us,' they asked Jesus, 'are you the one John said was going to come, or should we expect someone else?'

And about the ninth hour Jesus cried with a loud voice... 'My God, my God, why hast thou forsaken me?'

Now we see only puzzling reflections in a mirror, but then we shall see face to face. My knowledge now is partial; then it will be made whole, like God's knowledge of me.

'I do not know if he is a sinner or not,' the man replied. 'One thing I do know: I was blind and now I see.'

'Do you want us to go and pull up the weeds?' they asked him. 'No,' he answered, 'because as you gather the weeds you might pull up some of the wheat along with them. Let the wheat and the weeds both grow together until harvest.'

I have yet many things to say to you, but you cannot bear them now.

O Lord, how long must I call for help before you listen, before you save us from violence?

I still rebel and complain against God... How I wish I knew where to find him, and knew how to go where he is. I would state my case before him and present all the arguments in my favour. I want to know what he would say and how he would answer me.

(John 10:24, GNB; Matthew 11:3, GNB; Matthew 27:46, RSV; 1 Corinthians 13:12, NEB; John 9:25, GNB; Matthew 13:28-29, GNB; John 16:12, RSV; Habakkuk 1:2, GNB; Job 23:1-5, GNB)

We all live in a world of loose ends. It seems that God is not very tidy, any more than nature is neat and tidy. He leaves us with many questions unanswered, and they are the deep and important questions. It is perhaps one of the sure signs that we have left infancy and childhood behind that we not only recognise but are also grateful that this is so. This is part of our growth as persons.

There is something in most of us that would like to have everything tied up in neat parcels, and tucked away in appropriate pigeon-holes, so that these matters no longer perplex us, or compel us to think about them any more. But this is not how God works. How comforting and safe it would be if we were always told what to do, particularly in the field of ethics, but God does not absolve us from the responsibilities of the freedom he has given us, compelling us to make our own decisions, and live by faith rather than sight. There is no infallible guidance for fallible men and women which will ensure that we always know the right course to take.

It would seem clear from a reading of the gospels that our hankering for plain, straightforward and authoritative answers to our religious questions and perplexities would not commend itself to Jesus. He sometimes declined to give any such simple and direct answer. Instead he referred people to his teaching as a whole, to his whole attitude and manner of life, and then sent the question down again to the court of their own judgment for a verdict.

It is not that we are reduced to struggling through life on a balance of probabilities. Chesterton reminded us that the only virtue of having an open mind is that, like an open mouth, you can close it on something. We come as close to the certainty we crave as we are ever likely to do at the point of our commitment to Christ, when we can say, 'One thing I know: I was blind and I can see — however dimly,' and trust him for the rest.

Man has an inveterate habit of what I should call a premature tidiness. He is a little previous, strapping up the luggage of his mind before he has everything in, summing up and pronouncing judgment before he has heard all the evidence, dabbing on labels without noting the contents of the parcels. We classify too hurriedly; it saves the bother of tedious discrimination — tares, wheat, sheep, goats, those who are right, those who are wrong.

A.E. Whitham, *The Pastures of His Presence*

In recent years the magnificent pinetrees in Kensington Park... have been dying. Experts say there can be little doubt that this is due to the misdirected tidiness of the gardeners, who swept up the old dead pine-needles and left the roots without natural comfort and protection.

Old newspaper cutting

Never get things too clear. Religion can't be clear. In this mixed-up life there is always an element of unclearness... If I could understand religion as I understand that two and two make four, it would not be worth understanding. Religion can't be clear if it is worth having. To me, if I can see things through, I get uneasy — I feel it's a fake, I know I have left something out, I've made a mistake.

Baron von Hugel, in Introduction to
Letters from Baron Friedrick von Hugel to a Niece

I went to the theatre
With the author of a successful play.
He insisted on explaining everything;
Told me what to watch;
The details of directions,
The errors of the property man,
The foibles of the star.
He anticipated all my surprises
And ruined the evening.
Never again! And mark you,
The greatest author of all
Made no such mistake.

Christopher Morley, *No Coaching*

Coherency is God's gift; he gives it freely but it can only be received by those who preserve an untidiness of mind. The tidy mind is not the truthful mind; the utterance that leaves no room for doubt or place for question is the fruit of a mind that is full of unwarranted conclusions. To think truly, and to speak and act truthfully... a minister of the Word must deliberately preserve an untidy mind. This untidiness of mind will irritate him; he will often be weary of living in what seems a mental muddle... Generally his respite consists in the realisation that to bear the burden of this muddle is the true way of preserving real knowledge.

R.E.C. Browne, *The Ministry of the Word*

But all that seems to make nonsense of the world, all the irrationalities and defeats, the waste, the sheer negation and futility which makes life seem like a tale told by an idiot, are concentrated in the cross of Christ. That was utter, irrational meaninglessness, the apparent denial of any faith in God, any confidence in truth or goodness.

It is no use asking, What sense does it make? The whole point is, surely, that *Jesus made sense of it,* working negatively and non-meaning into the ultimate pattern of God's purpose.

F.R. Barry, *Asking the Right Questions*

Job never found an answer to the problem of unmerited suffering. The problem remained insoluble, but in it he met God. That is where man always meets God. That is where man most frequently meets his fellows. For he is so constituted that he needs problems more than solutions. His soul thrives on questions, but grows sickly on answers — especially answers served up by others and, most of all, answers laid down by authority.

John V. Taylor, *The Go-Between God*

Whenever we are confronted by a crossroads, whenever we are in doubt, whenever our mind sees two alternatives, instead of saying, 'Oh God, make me blind, Oh God, help me not to see, Oh God, give me loyalty to what I now know to be untrue,' we should say, 'God is casting a ray of light which is a ray of reality on something I have outgrown — the smallness of my original vision. I have come to a point where I can see more and deeper, thanks be to God.' That is not perplexity, it is not bewilderment, it is not the anguished doubt of the believer who hides his head and hopes that he will be able to revert to the age of eight.

Metropolitan Anthony, *God and Man*

It must be acknowledged that this is an ambiguous world. If atheism is improbable there are times when theism does not seem very probable either. In the face of suffering, waste, and apparent aimlessness it is hard to have faith in God... and obviously it is harder for some people than for others... Although I have said that theism is the more reasonable of the two beliefs, I do not think the arguments have ever been conclusive; by its very nature faith falls short of certitude and has its own vulnerability. The world remains ambiguous, and it is part of what it means to be a finite creature that we have to take our stand in this world and decide for faith or against it, without knowing in advance the answers to all our questions. Only in the end, the Christian believes, will faith be changed to sight.

John Macquarrie, *God and Secularity*

We are not in a rigid and static universe, but one that is dynamic and growing; the important thing is not to have correct information about God but to be susceptible to God's spirit, to be growingly aware of his pressures upon our life . . . we are travellers, always on the road, and rejoicing to be on the road, for there, as on the Emmaus Road, Christ reveals himself, not in absolute information, but in the burning heart.

W.B.J. Martin, *Five Minutes to Twelve*

To these questions (the ambiguities of life) only two answers are possible. The first is, 'I do not know', and the second 'I believe'.God is ambiguous even in his Son. He is so concerned that we should love light rather than darkness that he creates a world in which the two are not to be distinguished, save by the fact that one is *light*, and the other is *darkness*.

E.L. Allen, *Thou Must Venture*

We can do worse than remember a principle which both gives us a firm Rock and leaves us the maximum flexibility for our minds. The principle: Hold to Christ, and for the rest be totally uncommitted.

Herbert Butterfield, *Christianity and History*

Thank you, Lord, for the times when I sought a clear word from you and received it. Help me to thank you even more for the times when I did not. Help me to understand what you are saying to me when you are silent. Help me especially, if I am something of a perfectionist who likes to have everything neat and tidy, to accept that this does not seem to be the way you work. Let me remember always, with a wholesome check on my dogmatism, that there is a wide sweep to your purposes that defies my little calculations.

Give me the courage to act on my own insights, without needing to be told what to do, and not to pretend to certainties I do not have. Above all, make me sure of Jesus, who passed this way before me and made sense of it all. And when I crave for more light on the way I travel, let me be honest enough to ask myself if I am true to the light I already have.

Make me more patient and understanding with those people who keep asking, 'Why?' Forgive me because I often try to fit people into neat categories, hang precise labels on them, and dismiss those who don't readily fit into my little scheme of things.

Thank you for the opportunities you give me to grow according to the gracious design you have for my life, and for the assurance that one day I shall truly see.

A Benediction

Now the God of peace, who brought back from the dead that great shepherd of the sheep, our Lord Jesus, by the blood of the everlasting agreement, equip you thoroughly for the doing of his will! May he effect in you everything that pleases him, through Jesus Christ, to whom be glory for ever and ever. Amen.

WEEK

27

Not fare well, But fare forward, voyagers

(T.S. Eliot)

The Lord said to Abram, 'Leave your native land, your relatives, and your father's home, and go to a country which I am going to show you.'

Abraham believed God, and it was reckoned to him as righteousness.

The Lord said to Moses, 'Leave this place, you and the people you have brought out of Egypt, and go to the land that I promised to give Abraham, Isaac, and Jacob and to their descendants.'

'. . .be sure that you do everything that the Lord your God has commanded you. . . so that everything will go well with you and so that you will continue to live in the land that you are going to occupy.'

The Lord will keep your going out and your coming in: from this time forth and for evermore.

He gives me new strength. He guides me in the right paths, as he has promised.

Examine me, O God, and know my mind; test me and discover my thoughts. Find out if there is any evil in me and guide me in the everlasting way.

'Whoever does not take up his cross and follow in my steps is not fit to be my disciple.'

. . .the younger son gathered all he had and took his journey into a far country, and there he squandered his property in loose living . . .when he came to himself he said. . . 'I will arise and go to my father. . .'

That very day two of them were going to a village. . . Jesus himself drew near and went with them. . . he went in to stay with them . . . And their eyes were opened.

Jesus said, 'I am the way, and the truth, and the life.'

(Genesis 12:1, GNB; Romans 4:3, RSV; Exodus 33:1, GNB; Deuteronomy 5:32-33, GNB; Psalm 121:8, RSV; Psalm 23:3, GNB; Psalm 139:23-24, GNB; Matthew 10:38, GNB; Luke 15:13,17-18, RSV; Luke 24:13,15,29,31, RSV; John 14:6, RSV)

'Cheshire-Puss,' [Alice] began, rather timidly . . . 'Would you tell me please which way I ought to go from here?' 'That depends a good deal on where you want to get to,' said the Cat. 'I don't much care where . . .', said Alice. 'Then it doesn't matter which way you go,' said the Cat.

Lewis Carroll, *Alice in Wonderland*

Of course, it *does* matter which way we go, whom we encounter, how open we are to the experience of God along the way. The prodigal son's journey took him astray, until, in dire straits, he 'came to his senses' (Luke 15:13ff). The two men on the road to Emmaus (Luke 24:13ff) had an experience, but could have missed the meaning: their journey was a spiritual search as much as a walk to Emmaus, as Jesus encountered them, conversed with them, encouraged them, recalled for them God's larger story, and patiently waited for them to come to their own understanding. Then at that liminal, fantastic moment of the breaking of bread together, the two 'came to see' Jesus for who he was, and were impelled to witness to what they now *knew* to be true — Christ was risen indeed! A powerful allegory for those whose soundings are in Christian waters.

'Journey' is a common metaphor for living, but purpose and destination is implied. In the life-long pilgrimage which is the spiritual life, there is no 'holy moment' isolated from the rest, but growth and struggle, dark times and bright, sorrows and joys. It is a journey in which God is loving us toward wholeness, seeking to overcome the disunity within and between us. It calls for growing self-discernment and discipline of lifestyle, for a covenantal relationship with God and a self-giving relationship with neighbour. It is not a journey we can undertake alone, but rather only within a worshipping, serving, reflective and healing community. At base, we can assert that the creative spiritual journey is really just *growing in faith* — all else is so much commentary in the rhythms of brokenness and reconciliation, judgment and grace, death and resurrection.

But, 'like the development of a child's drawings, faith becomes progressively more detailed and connected in form and force, and more fluent and free in its execution' (Jerome W. Berryman).

In the thirteenth century the Franciscan, Bonaventure, wrote *The soul's journey into God* in which he identified three stages of the journey: the rectification of one's fallen state, the exercise of the gifts of the Holy Spirit, and the affective union with God characterised by joy and repose. He saw the crucified Christ as the beginning, means, and final consummation of the journey. In this century, psycho-analyst Carl Jung's concept of 'individuation' has helped some understand the process of bringing consciousness and the unconscious into a working relationship. In Jung's understanding of this life-long process, the 'first half of life is given over to differentiating and bringing into consciousness the problems of life that come to the fore at that time: the sex drive and the power drive . . . The second half of life then involves the task of reintegration (recognising as an aspect of the self) that which we had not chosen' (Wallace B. Clift). Somewhere in the overlap between Bonadventure's mystical union in love, and Jung's union of opposites in the psyche, lies the largely uncharted territory of your and my growth in the faith, our profound moments of encounter with the divine, and the joy of knowing that God calls us to fully tap the resources of the Spirit in even the most mundane experiences of life.

Recent popular writings on the 'mid-life crisis' point us to pilgrimages as old as the Aeneid and the Odyssey: the one pointing life in a new direction, the other affirming in a new way one's original calling. Outer journeys can express or create the context for the real, interior journey. Alternatively, the urge to fresh goals and deeper meaning can be subordinated to contentment with past achievements. Whenever and however the *krisis* comes, it is a true time of judgment, a God-given opening to be seized with courage, entered in faith, and pursued with passion. But beware the dragon that sits by the side of the road, lest he devour you —

'we go to the Father of Souls, but it is necessary to pass by the dragon' (St Cyril of Jerusalem).

I am a part of all that I have met;
Yet all experience is an arch where-thro'
Gleams that untravell'd world, whose margin fades
For ever and for ever when I move.
How dull it is to pause, to make an end,
To rust unburnish'd, not to shine in use!

Alfred, Lord Tennyson, *Ulysses*

We shall not cease from exploration
And the end of all our exploring
Will be to arrive where we started
And know the place for the first time.

T.S. Eliot, 'Little Gidding', *Four Quartets*

Does the road wind up-hill all the way?
Yes, to the very end.
Will the day's journey take the whole long day?
From morn to night, my friend.

Christina Georgina Rosetti, *Uphill*

To quote Carl Jung, '...we cannot live the afternoon of life according to the programme of life's morning: for what in the morning was true will at evening have become a lie. A person in the second half of life... no longer needs to educate his conscious will, but experience his own inner being.'

Quoted in Jacobi and Hull, editors, *Psychological reflections*

Where am I now? Is this the love and care
Of Jesus for the men that pilgrims are?
Thus to provide that I should be forgiven!
And dwell already the next door to heaven!

There's no discouragement
Shall make him once relent
His first avowed intent
  To be a pilgrim...

He knows he at the end

Shall life inherit . . .
He'll labour night and day
To be a pilgrim.

John Bunyan, *Pilgrim's Progress*

Two roads diverged in a wood, and I —
I took the one less travelled by,
And that has made all the difference.

Robert Frost, *The road not taken*

Thy way, not mine, O Lord,
However dark it be!
Lead me by Thine own hand,
Choose out the path for me.

Horatius Bonar, *Thy way, not mine*

Lead, kindly light, amid the encircling gloom;
lead thou me on.
The night is dark, and I am far from home;
lead thou me on.
Keep thou my feet; I do not ask to see
The distant scene — one step enough for me.

It was not ever thus, nor prayed that thou
Should'st lead me on.
I loved to choose and see my path; but now
lead thou me on.

John Henry Newman

I shall walk with thee through the valley, and thou shalt fear no shadow. Hold to My promises. They are given to thee as a chart is given to ship, and a compass to the hunter. Thou mayest set Thy course by My promises. They will lead thee and guide thee in places where there is no trodden path.

Frances J. Roberts, *Come Away My Beloved*

Keep my mind open to the newness of your gospel.
Keep me always growing to maturity, growing into union with you.
Keep me from ever thinking that I am there.

'Old and new' (Mark 2:21-22)
Rex Chapman, *A kind of praying*

Lord God, I thank you for the call to journey with you through this introduction to life eternal. I thank you for the familiar territory I have already traversed; for the more taxing climb beyond the plains into the spiritual foothills; for the timely strength to make my way through the undergrowth of personal and family cares, across the deep valleys of national conflicts, and up the increasingly steep and rock-strewn mountainsides of international un-peace.

I am grateful for those you chose to accompany me on this expedition — some I would not have picked myself, but you knew in advance what personal resources and strength of character, what skills and perceptions would be needed, and I marvel at some of the special companions you've recruited.

Each day, Lord, has its routines and its challenges. It is refreshing-exhausting work toiling into your mountains, at times precarious, at times frustratingly slow, at times exhilarating as I catch a glimpse of panoramic views of the soul's route between distant peaks. At critical points your engineers have come to my aid, and constructed bridges across a valley, formed rough tracks around a peak or across some marshy area.

There is always the day's march to be done, new challenges in the new day, the temptation of reverting to a familiar, safe route, and the impetus to try a new one — however hesitantly. I realise even now how much you've kept up the supplies; what I find on the path meets my daily necessities for sustenance and abundantly so. I've been amazed too, Lord, at the coherence of my company: different individuals, we find a common bond of purpose, interdependence, trust and love, despite our seeming diversity.

Thank you.

And so it is with a sense of excitement and anticipation that I set off each day, wondering what this *day will bring, what new vistas and challenges. There may well be bruises and scrapes, an occasional fall, but a sense of purpose and shared adventure can then break-in and pervade our journey together. The new range of peaks beyond call us on; what could have frustrated us as a barrier seems to have a magnetism to draw us further.*

There is enough in each day to reward us, yet a sense that the journey has barely begun; so much more lies ahead — higher ranges, new companions on the way, others whose paths touch for a time then diverge . . .

Thank you Lord.

You, who are the Way, show me your way. Amen.

A Benediction

May the God who created this wonderful world, with its myriad paths and challenging crossroads, grant you his firm direction. May the Son, who brings light to the darkest valley, heal your hurts and share your burdens. May the Holy Spirit, who has always breathed life and hope where there is chaos and despair, renew you in soul and spirit for the day to come. Amen.

WEEK

28

That steersman we call God

(Robert Louis Stevenson)

Now when Pharoah let the people go, God did not guide them by the road towards the Philistines, although that was the shortest; for he said, 'The people may change their minds when they see war before them, and turn back to Egypt.' So God made them go round by way of the wilderness towards the Red Sea; and the fifth generation of Israelites departed from Egypt. Moses took the bones of Joseph with him, because Joseph had exacted an oath from the Israelites: 'Some day,' he said, 'God will show his care for you, and then, as you go, you must take my bones with you.' They set out from Succoth and encamped at Etham on the edge of the wilderness. And all the time the Lord went before them, by day a pillar of cloud to guide them on their journey, by night a pillar of fire to give them light, so that they could travel night and day. The pillar of cloud never left its place in front of the people by day, nor the pillar of fire by night.

He went into a cave and spent the night. And the word of the Lord came to him, 'What are you doing here, Elijah?' He replied, 'I have been very zealous for the Lord God Almighty. The Israelites have rejected your covenant, broken down your altars, and put your prophets to death with the sword. I am the only one left and now they are trying to kill me too.' The Lord said, 'Go out and stand on the mountain in the presence of the Lord, for the Lord is about to pass by.' Then a great and powerful wind tore the mountains apart and shattered the rocks before the Lord, but the Lord was not in the wind. After the wind there was an earthquake, but the Lord was not in the earthquake. After the earthquake came a fire, but the Lord was not in the fire. And after the fire came a gentle whisper. When Elijah heard it, he pulled his cloak over his face and went out and stood at the mouth of the cave. Then a voice came to him, 'What are you doing here, Elijah?'

But when the Spirit of truth comes he will lead you to the complete truth, since he will not be speaking as from himself but will say only what he has learnt; and he will tell you of the things to come.

(Exodus 13:17-22, NEB; 1 Kings 19:9-13, NIV; John 16:13, JB)

Imagine Elijah out in the wilderness. See him standing there. He would have felt the powerful elements as God acted. The wind probably whipped his hair around his face, the earthquake would have shaken his very being and the fire seared his face. Certainly enough to shake up the most dismal servant of God who had doubts about God's power to direct a life. These three elements — wind, earthquake and fire — broadcast the coming of God. This was not the first time he had produced smoke on a mountain in order to direct his people. Exodus 19:16,18 records a similar event. Similarly when David was in distress and called on God, he heard God answering through earthquake and fire (Psalm 18:6-13).

God has always supplied signs for people prepared to read them. His presence has continued through the ages. He has never been really away from his people. There are times when God has stepped back; times when people have ignored the guidance of their Creator but we cannot blame him for such times. Ours the rebellion, the stubborn ways, the refusal to accept guidance. When Christ came, he promised to guide his church and he promised his powerful presence when he said with force: 'And surely I will be with you always, to the very end of the age' (Matthew 28:20, NIV). God has given us the scriptures which provide broad principles by which we are to live. He never takes the cloud of his Spirit away from us no matter how much we may fear this could happen. Provided we sincerely desire his will he will always be present.

There is something else to remember. Take one step at a time, even if it's only a small step. Take the next step. Always the next step. Questions may flood your mind but always take the next step.

I came about like a well-handled ship. There stood at the wheel that steersman whom we call God.

Robert Louis Stevenson

God is able and willing to guide us far more than the hesitant faith of many of his children has yet made possible. The poverty of our spiritual lives; our unwillingness to put a fence around some definite portion of our day and keep it for him; our unbelief concerning his voice in the soul — all these have hampered him. It is not denied that with all our blindness he has been able to guide us in some degree. But how much more effectively could he counsel and direct us if faith was really expectant and we listened as well as prayed.

W.E. Sangster, *God Does Guide Us*

God, our sovereign and immutable Master, openly declares that life is no will o' the wisp encounter with luck. His determined will is being accomplished free of frustration. The plan is comprehensive in scope and complete down to the tiniest detail. And it is all for his glory. Rather than causing us to fear, this truth is designed to put us at ease and calm our anxieties... What should be the Christian's attitude toward the determined will of God? He should recognise it as a reality — clearly taught in the Word of God. Rest in it as good, because that's what God says about it — he causes all things to work together for good to those who love him (Romans 8:28). Beyond that, don't worry about it and don't try to figure it out, because his ways are unfathomable (Romans 11:33).

Charles R. Swindoll, *God's Will*

There is an experience which becomes more and more familiar to everyone who is trying to follow Christ — a feeling of the growing loneliness of his Christian life. It comes from a sense of the peculiarly personal interest which Christ takes in him, which sometimes seems so strong as almost to make him feel that his life is being detached from all the other lives around him, that it is being drawn out of the crowd of humanity, as if an unseen arm linked in his were taking him aside for a nearer intimacy and a deeper and more private fellowship. It is not, indeed, that the great family of God are to be left in the shade for him, or that he is in any way the favourite of heaven;

but it is the sanctifying and, in the truest sense, humbling realisation that God makes himself as real to each poor unit as if he were the whole; so that even as in coming to Christ at first he felt himself the only lost, so now in staying with Christ he feels himself the only found.

Henry Drummond, *The Will of God*

You see, even Jesus did not say, 'I have explained the world.' What he did say was, 'I have overcome the world.' And if we can only trust where we cannot see, walking in the light we have, which is often very much like hanging on in the dark; if we do faithfully that which we see to be the will of God in the circumstances which evil thrusts upon us, we can rest our minds in the assurance that circumstances which God allows, reacted to in faith and trust and courage, can never defeat purposes which God ultimately wills. So doing, we shall wrestle from life something big and splendid. We shall find peace in our own hearts. We shall achieve integration in our own minds. We shall be able to serve our fellows with courage and joy, and then one day — for this has been promised — we shall look up into his face and understand. Now we see in a mirror, darkly. But then, face to face. Frankly, hard though it be to say so, it is a lack of faith not to be able to bear the thought of anything which God allows.

Leslie D. Weatherhead, *The Will of God*

Father, forgive my doubting your power to guide me whatever the circumstances. Help me to trust you even through the darkest night when it seems from my viewpoint that all hope is gone. Give me the faith to conquer my fears and faith to hold on when there is only what seems to me a slender hope that you will see my plight. Listen to my prayer and guide me in the way I should go.

Loving Lord, help me to believe that you know all about my life from start to finish and that you are fully prepared to lead me step by step, day by day along the path of your choosing. Give me I pray the wisdom to choose your way and to keep walking in your way.

Great God of wonders, lift me out of myself, I pray, to the lofty heights of belief so that I may soar like an eagle high above my cares and anxiety, confidently knowing you are able to show me how to deal with the barriers I put up that prevent me finding your will.

A Benediction

Lord God, help me to leave this topic of guidance with a far greater confidence than I started when I began reading this meditation. Through your grace, send me on my way confident in your guiding power. Amen.

WEEK

And I am black, but O! my soul is white

(William Blake)

'I am the light of the world,' he said. 'Whoever follows me will have the light of life and will never walk in darkness.'

The light shines in the darkness, and the darkness has never put it out.

God is light and there is no darkness at all in him. If then, we say that we have fellowship with him, yet at the same time live in the darkness, we are lying both in our words and in our actions.

Whoever loves his brother lives in the light, and so there is nothing in him that will cause someone else to sin.

You are the world's light — a city on a hill, glowing in the night for all to see.

Let your light so shine before men, that they may see your good works and give glory to your Father who is in heaven.

God was always with me then and gave me light as I walked through the darkness.

Let us then cast off the works of darkness and put on the armour of light.

When Moses went down from Mount Sinai carrying the Ten Commandments, his face was shining because he had been speaking with the Lord.

We Christians . . . can be mirrors that brightly reflect the glory of the Lord and as the Spirit of the Lord works within us, we become more and more like him.

(John 8:12, GNB; John 1:5, GNB; 1 John 1:5-6, GNB; 1 John 1:10, GNB; Matthew 5:14, LB; Matthew 5:16, RSV; Job 29:3, GNB; Romans 13:12, RSV; Exodus 34:29, GNB; 2 Corinthians 3:18, LB)

As one of today's 'civilised' people, I hardly know what it is like to be in the dark. Electricity effortlessly sets my house ablaze with light as bright as the noonday sun, and I take it all so much for granted. Darkness is really a stranger to me, but certainly more friend than foe. I have to imagine the sense of relief a needed light must have brought in the blackness of a moonless night. But even as physical darkness may have retreated to the edge of civilised man's existence, emotional and spiritual darkness has not. They are greater realities than ever in our world.

My mother bore me in the southern wild,
And I am black, but O! my soul is white.
White as an angel is the English child,
But I am black, as if bereav'd of light.

William Blake, 'The Little Black Boy', *Songs of Innocence*

There was a time when meadow, grove, and stream,
The earth, and every common sight
To me did seem
Apparelled in celestial light,
The glory and the freshness of a dream.
It is not now as it hath been of yore; —
Turn whatsoe'r I may,
By night or day,
The things which I have seen I now can see no more.

William Wordsworth, 'Ode: Intimations of Immortality'

Part 1
Weary,
So weary,
My heart cries out in weariness.
Just to lie here, lie here, Lord,
For a day, a week, a month, a year, a lifetime.

I yearn for rest,
Rest in the blackness,
Not to have to move, think, plan, communicate;
My life is so busy,
My life is a treadmill,
Oh, to have nothing to do!

Lying,
Lying in the blackness,
Lying exhausted in the darkness,
My soul turns Godwards,
My soul turns towards the light.

Part 2
'I came into men's lives, little one,
To heal, restore, to make you whole.
I am the light, shining in the darkness,
Burning in the darkness to guide your way.
The path is not a treadmill,
A ceaseless, inescapable treadmill
But an exciting, wondrous, upward path,
Where shadows and pitfalls are illumined by me.

'If you travel with me,
I make all plain.
Little by little,
I show you the way;
Travelling in the blackness,
You rushed into sorrows,
You pushed into emptiness,
Your feet are all sore from blindly stumbling,
Your heart is weary with meaningless rush.

'Travelling with me,
Is a joyous experience.
If your life is not joyful,
You're not travelling by me.
Come, travel a mile with me,
Travel the while with me,
Walk with me, talk with me.
In all, we will share.'

Part 3
Where is my weariness?
Was life once meaningless?
Father, how beautiful is life, all through!
You soften the ugliness,
Illumine the loveliness,
Living is ecstasy,
Travelling with you!

Bronwyn Pryor, 'Illumination'

What is perhaps the most incredible common element in the accounts [of human survival of biological death] I have studied, and is certainly the element which has the most profound effect upon the individual, is the encounter with a very bright light... not one person has expressed any doubt whatsoever that it was a being, a being of light. Not only that, it is a personal being. It has a very definite personality. The love and the warmth which emanate from this being to the dying person are utterly beyond words, and he feels completely surrounded by it and taken up in it, completely at ease and accepted in the presence of this being. He senses an irresistible magnetic attraction to this light.

Raymond A. Moody, *Life after Life*

The oldest of all stories about creation tells us that God created light before he created the sun and the earth... It is not impossible at all. For nowadays we know that light is a form of energy and all created things are made of energy... we are therefore made not of solid and impenetrable matter, but of energy... This being so, it is not strange at all that when we establish a closer connection with God in prayer we... receive more abundant life — an increased flow of energy. We are the electric light bulbs through whom the light of God reaches the world... Knowing then that we are part of God, that his life within us is an active energy... we can speed up the natural healing forces of the body... While love is the wiring that connects our souls with his, faith is the switch that turns on the power... Therefore we need not hesitate to give thanks for each adjustment, however great or small, that we would like his loving care to make in us... 'I rejoice that this moment thy healing light is removing all pain from the spine and filling the back with new vigour and life.' What if we practice this system and fail? Shall we doubt God? Edison did not doubt electricity when his experiments with the light bulb failed. Instead of that, he doubted the wires that he had used... For more than 6,000 times he tried again... If we are sensible, we will not doubt God, we will doubt our world and we will doubt ourselves.

Agnes Sanford, *The Healing Light*

At the moment when the blackness seemed darker than ever, I cried out, 'Lord, I don't care what happens or how miserable I am, I thank you for this entire experience. I know you are going to bring something good out of it.' Instantly, the darkness of the hospital room was shattered by a brilliant white light, brighter than the sun. It was as bright as the light I'd seen in a vision several years before... As I lay on my bed in the hospital room, my entire body flooded by that wonderful, brilliant light, I suddenly realised that what had once been a vision, now was a reality. The years I had walked by faith, believing that God was using my pain for good, were years climbing [the ladder of praise] through the cloud of darkness and uncertainty. Without the cloud, I would never have learned to let go of my reliance on my senses and feelings. Now I could wholeheartedly thank God for every circumstance of my life that added to the dark cloud. How else could I have learned to utterly trust in him? How else could I have come to experience this beautiful saturation of light and joy [above the cloud layer]?... There is nothing haphazard about God's plan for our lives. Nothing, absolutely nothing, however strange, inconsistent, or evil it may seem to us, happens without God's specific consent.

Merlin Carothers, *Power in Praise*

So long as we stay in the light we're safe because Satan cannot endure light and will not come near it. A true incident has become an unforgettable symbol of this for me... On both sides the attraction was intensifying... Mary didn't ask her caller to sit down. She remained standing in the centre of the room bathed in a cone of light from the electrical fixture overhead. As she concentrated on Jesus as represented by that light, she felt herself becoming less aware of John and more aware of the enveloping light of God all around her... Mary did not follow John into the darkness of the adjoining bedroom... As long as she stood in the light, the values she really cared about — her marriage, the home she and Bill had made together, their children — would be safe... At last, reluctantly, he left... Mary had found for herself the reality of the 'armour of light'.

Catherine Marshall, *Something More*

Lord, light of my life, I praise you and thank you for coming into my being and scattering the darkness of disbelief, doubt and despair.

Your light within has brought such joy, such beauty and such life.

When I look at others, help me to see beneath their skin, however 'black' it may appear, to the white purity of their inner soul. And, finding your light there, lay aside all my negative judgments and criticisms over their outward appearance, stance or situation, however different from mine.

Fan your flame within me by the breath of your Holy Spirit, so that it glows ever brighter like a lamp whose wick is turned up. For I would be filled with your light.

I give you permission to turn your searchlight onto all the dark corners within me that I prefer to keep hidden, a secret to myself alone — past guilts; present self-indulgences; the stunted future expectations I hold for my life. I give you permission to melt my will and make it yours, so that together, we can bring those ghosts out into the light of your love to be transformed.

You want this far more than I, Lord, so I trust you, that you are doing it, even as I sit here with my eyes upon you. I won't trust my feelings, but rather I trust your promises.

I know, Lord, that all the dark days of my life have been part of your perfect plan, to bring me to where I am today. Without them, I would probably be far from desiring your light. So I praise you for them. Bless this day through which I am about to walk. I trust you for guidance and inspiration for today's tasks, for the protection of your armour of light, and pray that you will use me this day to shed your radiance on all I meet.

A Benediction

The blessing of God's light be upon you as you go, unclouded, into this day. As the light of the sun never ceases to shine for you, neither does the love of God. Relax and enjoy being a reflector, knowing you are being used even as you merely keep turned towards the light. Amen.

WEEK

30

It is better to be faithful than famous

(Theodore Roosevelt)

Daniel made up his mind not to let himself become ritually unclean by eating the food and drinking the wine of the royal court, so he asked Ashpenaz to help him, and God made Ashpenaz sympathetic to Daniel.

Shadrach, Meshach and Abednego replied to the king, 'O Nebuchadnezzar, we do not need to defend ourselves before you in this matter. If we are thrown into the blazing furnace, the God we serve is able to save us from it, and he will rescue us from your hand, O king. But even if he does not, we want you to know, O king, that we will not serve your gods or worship the image of gold you have set up.'

Then the other supervisors and the governors tried to find something wrong with the way Daniel administered the empire, but they couldn't, because Daniel was reliable and did not do anything wrong or dishonest. They said to one another, 'We are not going to find anything of which to accuse Daniel unless it is something in connection with his religion.'

Anyone who starts to plough and then keeps looking back is of no use to the kingdom of God.

Be faithful to me, even if it means death, and I will give you life as your prize of victory.

Your conduct among the surrounding peoples in your different countries should always be good and right, so that although they may in the usual way slander you as evil-doers, yet when disasters come they may glorify God when they see how well you conduct yourselves.

My footsteps have followed close in him, I have walked in his way without swerving.

But I reckon my own life to be worth nothing to me; I

only want to complete my mission and finish the work that the Lord Jesus gave me to do, which is to declare the Good News about the grace of God.

(Daniel 1:8-9, GNB; Daniel 3:16-18, NIV; 6:4-5, GNB; Luke 9:62, GNB; Revelation 2:10b, GNB; 1 Peter 2:12, J.B. Phillips; Job 23:11, JB; Acts 20:24, GNB)

Those Sunday School pictures of Daniel must be wrong. The ones showing a virile, macho 30-year-old in the lion pit. Either they are misleading or my calculations are awry. Or the dates are not meant to dovetail.

Let's assume that Daniel was, at the age of seventeen, a member of the transporation contingent of 605 BC. Then let's assume that the lion pit episode occurred at the beginning of the rule of Cyrus/Darius in 538 BC. That makes Daniel eighty-four! At an age when many of us can no longer walk at all, he is still treading on hot coals!

All the indications are that he had delivered exceptional service to Babylon. Early promise and outstanding college results led to promotions, responsibility and authority.

More importantly he combined astute public service with loyal divine service. For seventy years Daniel had been loyal to his real King — the Lord of Heaven.

His courageous faithfulness was part of a well-rounded godly lifestyle: his gracious courtesy, his commitment to solidarity with his friends and to disciplined prayerfulness, his willingness to participate fully in the life of Babylon, his patient caring for Nebuchadnezzar during the king's dark humiliation, his squeaky-clean reputation in civil life.

But above all his unswerving loyalty to God placed patriotism, ambition, job security and even his life on the line.

What an inspiration to the hard-pressed Jews during the centuries that followed. What an example today to Christians in public life, in a secular environment or under an alien regime.

We are pilgrim people, a people who have decided never to arrive, a people who live by hope, energised not by what we already possess but by that which is promised: 'Behold, I create new heavens and a new earth.'

Sure, it's tiring; and it's tough. Imagination comes harder than memory, and faithfulness is more demanding than success. But so what if we fail? Remember, we are not required to finish the task — any more than we are allowed to put it aside.

William Sloane Coffin, *The Courage to Love*

What will it mean in practice for me to put God first? This much, at least. All the 101 things I have to do each day, and the 101 demands on me which I know I must try to meet, will all be approached as ventures of loving service to him, and I shall do the best I can in everything for his sake — which attitude, as George Herbert quaintly said, 'makes drudgery divine; who sweeps a room, as for thy laws, makes that and th' action fine.'

And then I shall find that, through the secret work of the Spirit which is known by its effects, my very purpose of pleasing God gives me new energy for all these tasks and relationships, energy which otherwise I could not have had. 'I could not love thee, dear, so much, loved I not honor more,' said the poet. Put 'God' for 'honor', and you have the deepest truth about the Christian's love of his neighbour. Self-absorbed resentments dissolve, the zest for life, happiness in doing things, and love for others all grow great when God comes first.

J.I. Packer, *I Want to be a Christian*

'I *was* going to say I wished we'd never come. But I don't, I don't, I don't. Even if we *are* killed. I'd rather be killed fighting for Narnia than grow old and stupid at home and perhaps go about in a bath-chair and then die in the end just the same.'

Jill in *The Last Battle* by C.S. Lewis

When we are called to follow Christ, we are summoned to an exclusive attachment to his person. The grace of his call bursts all the bonds of legalism. It is a gracious call, a gracious commandment. It transcends the difference between the law and the gospel. Christ calls, the disciple follows; that is grace and commandment in one. 'I will walk at liberty, for I seek thy commandments' (Psalm 119:45).

Dietrich Bonhoeffer, *The Cost of Discipleship*

It is helpful to remember that some of God's greatest saints and responsible leaders have not always been clear what to do, and because actions and decisions could no longer be delayed, they have had to move forward in the dark, hardly knowing whether the Lord was with them or not. Both Hudson Taylor and D.E. Hoste had such experiences in their leadership of the China Inland Mission.

The more I became involved in increasing responsibilities in Christian service, the less I found myself thinking of guidance and the more of duty.

John Laird, *No Mere Chance*

But it was precisely this persistent loyalty to the old ways of Judah, this constant refusal to cut himself loose from 'Jerusalem', this repeated claim that the truth and salvation for the world lay there and nowhere else, that made many powerful people in Babylon hate Daniel. They hated him not merely because he was a foreigner and stranger, not merely because they were jealous of his extraordinary ability, but mainly because, in spite of the fact that he was so impeccably loyal and helpful to Babylon, the whole orientation of his outstanding life tended to point not to Babylon but to Zion.

Too often he stood simply for what Jerusalem alone stood for. Too clearly his talk and his way of life bore witness to his strange belief that salvation for mankind could come only from the God who had chosen Zion as his dwelling place.

Ronald Wallace, *The Lord is King*

Christ has many services to be done; some are easy, others are difficult; some bring honour, others bring reproach; some are suitable to our natural inclinations and temporal interests, others are contrary to both. In some we may please Christ and please ourselves, in others we cannot please Christ except by denying ourselves. Yet the power to do all these things is assuredly given us in Christ, who strengthens us.

I am no longer my own, but Thine. Put me to what Thou wilt, rank me with whom Thou wilt; put me to doing, put me to suffering; let me be employed for Thee or laid aside for Thee, exalted for Thee or brought low for Thee; let me be full, let me be empty; let me have all things, let me have nothing; I freely and heartily yield all things to Thy pleasure and disposal.

John Wesley,
from the Covenant Service of the Methodist Church

'Eighty and six years have I served him, and he hath done me no wrong; how then can I blaspheme my king who saved me?'

Bishop Polycarp, when urged to 'curse the Christ'.
He was subsequently burnt at the stake.

We have each day to be faithful for the one short day, and long years and a long life will take care of themselves without the sense of their length or their weight ever being a burden.

Andrew Murray

And believing must lead to obedience. Christians have constantly been in trouble for defying human authorities and challenging consensuses. Peter would not stop evangelising when told to (Acts 4:19f; 5:27ff) and was in and out of prison as a result. Christians risked persecution in the early days by refusing the formalities of Roman state religion, just as latter-day African Christians have courted martyrdom by rejecting tribal rites. Athanasius sentenced himself to exile by standing against the Arian world. Luther jeopardised his life by refusing to recant at Worms.

Christians today make themselves unpopular by opposing such social realities as the pornography trade and such social conveniences as abortion on demand. These are samples of the costly nonconformity which Christians have practised down the ages.

Why do they behave so awkwardly? Because standing under God's authority, they are sure that his revelation requires them to act as they do at whatever personal cost. Luther said at Worms, 'My conscience is captive to the Word of God; to go against conscience is neither right nor safe; here I stand, there is nothing else I can do; God help me; amen.' The privilege of knowing God's truth with certainty and precision carries with it the responsibility of obeying that truth with equal precision. Christianity is no armchair faith, but a call to action.

J.I. Packer, *Freedom, Authority and Scripture*

The ploughman who looks back is the would-be disciple whose mind is still partly on the life he left to follow Jesus. The work of the kingdom of God requires singleness of purpose.

F.F. Bruce, commenting on Luke 9:62
in *The Hard Sayings of Jesus*

Beloved, it is morn!
A redder berry on the thorn,
A deeper yellow on the corn,
For this good day new-born:
Pray, Sweet, for me
That I may be
Faithful to God and thee.

Emily Henrietta Hickey, 'Beloved, it is Morn'

Who would true valour see,
Let him come hither;
One here will constant be,
Come wind, come weather;
There's no discouragement
Shall make him once relent
His first avowed intent
To be a pilgrim.

John Bunyan

'You haven't got it *right*!' says the exasperated piano teacher. Junior is holding his hands the way he's been told. His fingering is unexceptionable. He has memorised the piece perfectly. He has hit all the proper notes with deadly accuracy. But his heart's not in it, only his fingers. What he's playing is a sort of music but nothing that will start voices singing or feet tapping. He has succeeded in boring everybody to death including himself.

Jesus said to his disciples, 'Unless your righteousness exceeds that of the scribes and Pharisees, you will never enter the kingdom of heaven' (Matthew 5:20). The scribes and Pharisees were playing it by the Book. They didn't slip up on a single do or don't. But they were getting it all wrong.

Righteousness is getting it all *right*. If you play it the way it's supposed to be played, there shouldn't be a still foot in the house.

Frederick Buechner, *Wishful Thinking*

Lord, when I place myself in Daniel's shoes I wonder how I would have reacted. Knowing me, I would have rationalised each situation and looked for a 'both/and' rather than the 'either/or' option.

I find the example of Daniel inspiring. It's good to have a hero figure even though I'm not very heroic myself. I feel the let-down of knowing I don't perform consistently as a Christian. When I do manage to stand up or stand firm for you, I end up seeming stand-offish and pompous. That only makes things worse. I begin to feel that lifelong loyalty to you is an impossible dream. How can I ever imagine that I will be able to look back at the end of the journey and feel satisfied?

Save me from being depressed about yesterday's lapses. Reassure me of your forgiveness and acceptance. Make me wiser today.Help me to see the way through, which will bring honour to you.

Teach me that the only step I should be concerned about is the next step.

Help me to wake up each day with a heartfelt gratitude for your many mercies and a deep desire to please you above all others.

Grow courtesy, warmth and gentleness in me so that unnecessary confrontation can be avoided. But, when it's clear that fidelity to you demands a dangerous, unpopular or embarrassing path, help me to tread it with gracious courage.

A Benediction

Go forward in the sure knowledge that such qualities as faithfulness, patience and self-control are gifts of the Holy Spirit. Keep your eyes fixed on Jesus, the author and perfector of our faith. Keep running; do not lose heart! Amen.

WEEK

31

As you worship, so you serve

(Calvin Coolidge)

Shout for joy to the Lord, all the earth. Serve the Lord with gladness; come before him with joyful songs. Know that the Lord is God. It is he who made us, and we are his; . . . we are his people, the sheep of his pasture. Enter his gates with thanksgiving and his courts with praise; give thanks to him and praise his name. For the Lord is good and his love endures for ever; his faithfulness continues through all generations.

Bless Yahweh, my soul, bless his holy name, all that is in me! Bless Yahweh, my soul, and remember all his kindnesses . . . Yahweh has fixed his throne in the heavens, his empire is over all. Bless Yahweh, all his angels, heroes mighty to enforce his word, attentive to his word of command. Bless Yahweh all his armies, servants to enforce his will. Bless Yahweh, all his creatures in every part of his empire! Bless Yahweh, my soul.

And what is faith? Faith gives substance to our hopes, and makes us certain of realities we do not see. It is for their faith that the men of old stand on record. By faith we perceive that the universe was fashioned by the word of God, so that the visible came forth from the invisible. By faith Abel offered a sacrifice greater than Cain's, and through faith his goodness was attested, for his offerings had God's approval; and through faith he continued to speak after his death. By faith Enoch was carried away to another life without passing through death; he was not to be found, because God had taken him. For it is the testimony of Scripture that before he was taken he had pleased God, and without faith it is impossible to please him; for anyone who comes to God must believe that he exists and that he rewards those who search for him.

(Psalm 100, NIV; Psalm 103, 1-2, 21-22, JB; Hebrews 11:1-6, NEB)

From ancient times people have sought another being before whom to bow in honour. There has been a constant searching for an object to worship. The Bible records many ways in which people have sought their gods. People have made gods of almost anything.

For Christians, basic ideas of worship come from the Jews' traditions of worship. They believed in one supreme being they called Yahweh. So awed were they by this supreme being they would never utter his name.

The Jews knew they were before the Almighty when they worshipped. They knew he was aware of exactly what was happening at such times. God was the witness of their worship and upon this historical foundation our present-day worship is laid. If we wish to worship in sincerity and truth, we need to recognise exactly who God is. Once his role is clear, our role becomes clear. If we fail to understand these things, while we may appear to worship we will not be worshipping. For our public worship to be in order, our private worship must be meaningful.

Alas, in regard to things spiritual, the foolishness of many is this, that they in the secular sense look upon the speaker as an actor, and the listeners as theatregoers who are to pass judgment upon the artist. But the speaker is not the actor — not in the remotest sense. No, the speaker is the prompter. There are no mere theatregoers present, for each listener will be looking into his own heart. The stage is eternity, and the listener, if he is the true listener (and if he is not he is at fault), stands before God during the talk.

Soren Kierkegaard, *Purity of Heart*

In worship we retell and act out a story. The story has to do with what God has done for us and what our response is to his work. It is an enactment of the event that gives meaning and purpose to life. It aligns the believer with the Christ-event and with the community of the faithful throughout history.

Therefore when worship is acted out in faith, the believer experiences again the refreshment of his or her relationship to God and spontaneously experiences the joy of salvation.

Robert E. Webber, *Worship Old and New*

You tell me nothing new: you are not the only one that is troubled with wandering thoughts. Our mind is extremely roving; but as the will is mistress of all our faculties, she must recall them, and carry them to God, as their last end. When the mind, for want of being sufficiently reduced by recollection at our first engaging in devotion, has contracted certain bad habits of wandering and dissipation, they are difficult to overcome, and commonly draw us, even against our wills, to the things of the earth. I believe one remedy for this is to confess our faults, and to humble ourselves before God. I do not advise you to use multiplicity of words in prayer; many words and long discourses being often the occasions of wandering: hold yourself in prayer before God, like a dumb or paralytic beggar at a rich man's gate: let it be your business to keep your mind in the presence of the Lord.

Brother Lawrence, *The Practice of the Presence of God*

Instead of complaining that God has hidden himself, you will give him thanks for having revealed himself so fully; and you will give him thanks also for not having revealed himself to proud scholars, who are not worthy to know so holy a God. Two sorts of person know him; those who have a humble heart and love lowliness, whatever their degree of intellect, high or low; and those who have enough understanding to see the truth, whatever objections they may have against it.

B. Pascal, *The Pensees*

The great fact of life is the human soul confronting the transcendent holiness of God. No person is ever left alone without God. An individual may try to ignore God but he cannot have peace without him; he may deny or reject him but not without a consciousness of judgment. God claims every creature. Worship is the loving response of the creature to his Creator. There is no sovereign right but God's... Christian worship is God-centred. God took the initiative in worship by creating man for fellowship with himself. As the ground of being, he is the source and sustainer of life. As sovereign ruler, God confronts us. He comes to us as the one worthy of worship, and because he is worthy he stands in judgment over us and makes demands upon us. As we respond in worship God allows us to experience new manifestations of his goodness and his love.

Franklin M. Segler, *Christian Worship*

First, let us fling wide the doors and windows of our minds and make some attempt to appreciate the 'size' of God. He must not be limited to 'religious' matters or even to the 'religious' interpretation of life. He must not be confined to one particular section of time nor must we imagine him as the local God of this planet or even only of the universe that astronomers have so far 'discovered'. It is not, of course, physical size that we are trying to establish in our minds. (Physical size is not important. By any reasonable scheme of values a human being is of vastly greater worth than a mountain ten million times his physical size.) It is rather to see the immensely broad sweep of the Creator's activity, the astonishing complexity of his mental processes which science laboriously uncovers, the vast sea of what we can only call 'God' in a small corner of which man lives and moves and has his being.

J.B. Phillips, *Your God is Too Small*

Most holy God, Maker of heaven and earth, I acknowledge that you alone are worthy of worship. May your Holy Spirit make my worship more meaningful. Lift me out of my selfish ways, lift me up until like Isaiah I see the Lord 'seated on a throne, high and exalted'. Then may I exclaim like Isaiah, 'Holy, holy, holy is the Lord Almighty; the whole earth is full of his glory.'

Heavenly Father, help me to keep the focus of my personal worship away from self and on Christ as the one who has revealed God to me and through whom I am able to celebrate your glory. Make me wise in my worship so that I may shun anything which will distract me and turn my thoughts away from you.

A Benediction

Gracious Father, help me to take with me a sense of your powerful presence, knowing that wherever I go you will be there ahead of me, that whenever I need your strength it will be available to me through the tremendous power of your mighty Spirit and that I can live boldly in your name every moment of the day ahead of me. Amen.

WEEK

32

Stealing in the Lord's name

Let the thief no longer steal, but rather let him labour, doing honest work with his hands, so that he may be able to give to those in need. But you yourselves wrong and defraud, and that even your own brethren. You then who teach others, will you not teach yourself? While you preach against stealing do you steal?

They made me the keeper of the vineyards, but, my own vineyard I have not kept!

A good man leaves an inheritance to his children's children.

A righteous man walks in his integrity — blessed are his sons after him!

You husbands must conduct your married life with understanding.

If. . . any of you does not know how to meet any particular problem he has only to ask God — who gives generously to all men without making them feel foolish or guilty — and he may be quite sure that the necessary wisdom will be given him.

In Christ, you were. . . set free from the sins of the flesh. . . and in him are sharing the miracle of rising again to new life — and all this because you have faith in the tremendous power of God, who raised Christ from the dead. . . . God has now made [you] to share in the very life of Christ.

(Ephesians 4:28, RSV; 1 Corinthians 6:8, RSV; Romans 2:21, RSV; The Song of Solomon 1:6, RSV; Proverbs 13:22, RSV; Proverbs 20:7, RSV; James 1:5, Phillips; Colossians 2:11-13, Phillips)

God got my attention in an unexpected way while on a three-day retreat with a small group of fellow clergy.

We participated together in a relational Bible study based on the parable of the Good Samaritan, and, drawing from the data of the biblical record, background studies and our own imagination, we explored together many aspects of the characters in the story. The priest, levite, injured traveller and the Samaritan were all carefully analysed with the purpose of enabling us to identify fully or partially with one or more of them and relate the parable to our own lives.

However, although as a group we had overlooked considering the robbers, I found myself identifying with these who had selfishly and ruthlessly hurt and stolen from the innocent traveller. I came under deep conviction concerning the many people whom I had robbed of my time and love over the years.

After that group meeting I spent three hours in solitude in the retreat chapel letting God address me. I listed the names of those from whom I had stolen my quality time and my care and concern. Heading the list was my wife and then my family. My notes of the ways I had taken from them what was their right included: quality time to listen, to talk, to commune, to pray, to enjoy each other, to do those things they wanted to do. So often I have offered them the fag-end of my energy instead of my freshness, alertness, enthusiasm and joy.

My reflection led me to the disturbing awareness that all this failure to make significant space for those dearest to me brought into serious question my motives for my ministry. Was this neglect due to living in obedience to God's will or was I acting out of motives to satisfy my own needs for self-actualisation or selfish egocentric drives?

In that chapel I had a solemn encounter with God which led to confession, acceptance of forgiveness and a renewal of my covenant with God.

That evening I wrote a long letter to my wife listing the hurts I had caused her and asking forgiveness. Later that letter made a profound impression on her. She said, 'Only the Holy Spirit could have revealed these things to you.' There was forgiveness and the beginning of healing and enrichment of our love. Later I wrote to my eldest son — and there was a similar work of grace.

If you really want to gauge the quality of your spiritual life, check your love dimensions. Not how often you read the Bible, or how much scripture you have memorised... but whether the people with whom you are living regard you as a lover — a person reflecting the love of Christ which he sheds into our heart.

Howard Hendricks, in *The Work of An Evangelist*

When the family of the Christian leader, especially if he has to be away from home a lot, knows that they matter enormously to him, then the Gospel he talks about begins to become good news at home. Children need to be loved, and loved, and loved. Loved without strings attached. Loved if they don't go to church. Loved when they are a pain in the neck. Only in that way can they understand at gut level about the love of the Father which pursues them undiminished whether they hear or whether they forbear (Ezekiel 2:5)... Each of us will have our own different ways of expressing love and care for the family. But unless that is a high priority, we will find that we may gain the whole world and lose our own children.

Michael Green, in *The Work of an Evangelist*

I opened Thomas Kelly's *Testament of Devotion*... He caught my attention by describing perfectly my condition and the condition of many I knew: 'We feel honestly the pull of many obligations and try to fulfil them all. And we are unhappy, uneasy, strained, oppressed and fearful we shall be shallow... We have hints that there is a way of life vastly richer and deeper than all this hurried existence, a life of unhurried serenity and peace and power. If only we could slip over into that Centre!... We have seen and known some people who seem to have found this deep Centre of living, where the fretful calls of life are integrated, where No as well as Yes can be said with confidence. This ability to say Yes and No out of the divine Centre was foreign to me... To say Yes to pleas for help or opportunities to serve usually carried an aura of spirituality and sacrifice. I could say Yes easily, but I did not have the ability to say No. What would people think of me if I refused?... As we yield to the Centre everything about us becomes focused, synoptic. This yielding is nothing more than the experience of the great commandment to love God with all our being. A French Christian, Marie of the Incarnation, wrote in 1628, 'My spirit was more and more being simplified... In the depths of my soul... these words were continual: "Ah!

My Love, my Well-Beloved! Be blessed O my God!"... And since that time my soul has remained in its centre which is God.'

Richard Foster, *Freedom of Simplicity*

Faulty values and choices in the past have closed many options in the present and the future... The central reason for reappraising your lifestyle and values is not the fear of having a heart attack or suffering some other disaster. Rather it is to make sure that you are on the road you really want to travel — the road that will allow you to use the years ahead creatively, productively, and joyfully, whatever life brings. A better future is more likely to occur by choice than by chance.

Howard Clinebell, *Growth Counseling for Mid-Years Couples*

One day I was working at a boring job and a friend came to join me. He loitered about for nearly an hour, perched on the edge of the table, smoking a cigarette and talking occasionally of nothing in particular. When he had gone I was filled with a special joy because I realised that he had deliberately wasted an hour with me; it was not that we were discussing something of importance or that I needed consoling: it was a pure and unsolicited gift of time. If we think about it, for busy people time is often the most precious thing they have to give. Doctors, priests, those who counsel, will always 'spend' time with those in need. They may sit up all night with someone who is distressed; they may pass long hours in listening to problems, or in giving advice; but this is all time deliberately spent. We only deliberately waste time with those we love — it is the purest sign that we love someone if we choose to spend time idly in their presence when we could be doing something more 'constructive'.

Sheila Cassidy, *Prayer for Pilgrims*

In a world full of strangers, estranged from their past culture and country, from their neighbours, friends and family, from their deepest self and their God, we witness a painful search for a hospitable place where life can be lived without fear and where community can be found... The term hospitality... should not be limited to its literal sense of receiving a stranger in our house... but as a fundamental attitude towards our fellow human being, which can be expressed in a great variety of ways. Hospitality... means primarily the creation of a free space where the stranger can enter and become a friend instead of an enemy. Hospitality is not to change people but to offer them space where change can take place.

Empty space tends to create fear. As long as our minds, hearts and hands are occupied we can avoid confronting the painful questions to which we never give much attention and which we do not want to surface. Occupation and not empty space is what most of us are looking for... Being busy, active and on the move has nearly become part of our constitution... Preoccupation is in fact a greater stumbling-block than occupation... We indeed have become very pre-occupied people, afraid of unnameable emptiness and silent solitude... Preoccupations are our fearful ways of keeping things the same, and it often seems that we prefer a bad certainty to a good uncertainty. Our preoccupations help us to maintain the personal world we have created over the years and block the way to revolutionary change.

So we can see that creating space is far from easy in our occupied and preoccupied society. And still, if we expect any salvation, redemption, healing and new life, the first thing we need is an open receptive place where something can happen to us. Hospitality, therefore, is such an important attitude. We cannot change the world by a new plan, project or idea. We cannot even change other people by our convictions, stories, advice and proposals, but we can offer a space where people are encouraged to disarm themselves, to lay aside their occupations and preoccupations and to listen with attention and care to the voices speaking in their own centre.

Henri Nouwen, *Reaching Out*

O Love that wilt not let me go,
I rest my weary soul in thee:
I give thee back the life I owe,
that in thine ocean depths its flow
may richer, fuller be.

George Matheson, *The Australian Hymn Book*

My God, you are immortal, invisible, incomprehensible in your greatness, and mysterious in your almighty power. But because you are my Father, I am not afraid. I bow in awe before you but I speak with confidence and familiarity as child to parent.

I confess I have, somehow, not yet brought into balance all the elements clamouring to be ordered in my complicated existence. My life has become an unlikely plot, a conspiracy I helped begin but do not, any longer, hardly control at all.

Give me grace to find the space to allow you to get my undivided attention, then to listen unhurriedly and follow your guidance willingly.

Fill me anew with your Spirit so that I may experience an intimate connection between my spiritual life and my temporal needs.

Enable me to keep adequate space for all who enter my life this day, especially those who walk closest with me.

Take this day into your own keeping. Control, direct, instruct and sustain me. Totally transform me by your Spirit of love. May each life I touch be blessed because you are the secret centre of my life. Amen.

A Benediction

May your spiritual experience become richer as you see more and more fully God's great secret, Christ himself! Now to him who is able to keep you from falling and to present you before his glory without fault and with unspeakable joy, to the only God, our saviour, be glory and majesty, power and authority, through Jesus Christ our Lord... Amen (Colossians 2:2,; Jude 24,25, Phillips).

WEEK

33

The holidays have begun

(C.S. Lewis)

Love not the world neither the things that are in the world... For the world passeth away, and the lust thereof; but he that doeth the will of God abideth for ever.

Eye hath not seen, nor ear heard, neither have entered into the heart of man, the things which God hath prepared for them that love him.

As for me, I know that my Redeemer lives, and that he will stand upon the earth at last. And I know that after this body has decayed, this body shall see God! Then he will be on my side. Yes! I shall see him, not as a stranger, but as a friend. What a glorious hope!

For our homeland is in heaven where our Saviour the Lord Jesus Christ is.

We know that when Christ appears we shall be like him for we shall see him as he really is.

I heard a loud voice speaking from the throne: 'Now God's home is with mankind! He will live with them and they shall be his people. God himself will be with them and he will be their God. He will wipe away all tears from their eyes. There will be no more death, no more grief or crying or pain. The old things have disappeared.' Then the one who sits on the throne said, 'And now I make all things new!'

(1 John 2:15,17, KJV; 1 Corinthians 2:9, KJV; Job 19:25-26, LB; Philippians 3:20, LB; 1 John 3:2, GNB; Revelation 21:3-5, GNB)

When I was young the idea of heaven didn't appeal to me much. When I looked at artists' impressions of the biblical imagery they seemed artificial and unsatisfying. Streets of gold and pearly gates seemed a poor substitute for blue skies and snowy mountains and crashing waves. And I could not get excited about an endlessly extended church service, however glorious the surroundings. Heaven might be very pleasant but on the whole I preferred to stay at home.

I first began to explore new ideas about heaven when I failed in sports. I was always the duffer in the team and I felt the humiliation deeply. Perhaps in heaven, I pondered, I might be able to play netball without falling over or dropping the ball. I could imagine Jesus standing on the sidelines cheering and saying, 'Well done!' As a teenager I rejected these childish notions and returned to the vision of an eternal mass meeting. Yet I feared even the Hallelujah Chorus might wear thin after a century or so.

It was years before I discovered that other people shared my feelings. We would all dutifully agree that heaven must be great but our hearts were not in it. Then one day I got the mumps. In the enforced break from routine I began to read books which challenged my stereotyped ideas. New thoughts overturned my previous imaginations.

What would it be like, I wondered, to live outside the limits of time and space? No sense of waiting, no boredom, no monotony, no sequence of passing years. Instead there will be just one great joyful 'now'.

What will it mean to be eternally 'like Christ'? We certainly won't be clones or robots, for he is eternally unique. Rather we shall still be ourselves yet sharing the qualities of his life. At last we shall be exactly the way God planned us — with all our possibilities realised. Maybe I might even get to play netball.

When God creates his new kingdom surely it will be no less splendid or original than this world of ours? He isn't impressed with gold or pearl or rubies. His handiwork is perfect in detail and beautiful beyond belief. Probably the new world will be like ours, only more real, more natural, more breathtaking.

Will we know one another there? Probably we will, not by our outward appearance but through a spiritual intuition. This means there'll be no pretence, no dishonesty, no misunderstanding. Nor shall we be idle. God knows how much we need satisfying activity.

For the first time I began to get excited about heaven.

Sometimes I even feel homesick for that unseen country and its King.

But Stephen, full of the Holy Spirit, looked up to heaven and saw God's glory and Jesus standing at the right hand side of God. 'Look,' he said, 'I see heaven opened and the Son of Man standing at the right hand side of God!'

Acts 7:55-56

Now you must note that the City stood upon a mighty hill; but the pilgrims went up that hill with ease, because they had these two men to lead them up by the arms; also they had left their mortal garments behind them in the river; for though they went in with them, they came out without them. They therefore went up here with much agility and speed though the foundation upon which the city was framed was higher than the clouds.

John Bunyan, *Pilgrim's Progress*

Thy years neither come nor go; whereas ours both come and go. Thy years stand together, because they do stand; nor are departing thrust out by coming years, for they pass not away; but ours shall all be when they shall be no more. Thy years are one day; and thy day is not daily, but Today, seeing thy Today gives not place unto tomorrow, neither doth it replace yesterday. Thy Today is Eternity.

St Augustine, *Confessions XI*

In that blessed city there shall be this great blessing, that no inferior shall envy superior, as now the archangels are not envied by the angels, because no-one will wish to be what he has not received... And thus along with his gift, greater or less, each shall receive this further gift of contentment, to desire no more than he has.

Neither are we to suppose that because sin shall have no power to delight them, free will must be withdrawn. It will on the contrary be all the more truly free, because set free from delight in sinning to take unfailing delight in not sinning.

St Augustine, *The City of God XXII*

I rekindled me with a new vision, such as no light is so pure that my eyes could not have withstood it. And I saw light in the form of a river glowing with effulgence, between two banks painted with marvellous spring. From this stream were issuing living sparks, and on every side were setting themselves in the flowers like rubies which the gold encompasses. Then as if inebriated by the odours, they plunged again into the wonderful flood and, as one was entering, another was issuing forth.

O splendour of God, through which I saw the high triumph of the true kingdom, give me power to tell how I saw it!

Dante, *The Divine Comedy*

Flesh fade, and mortal trash
Fall to the residuary worm; world's wildfire, leave but ash:
  In a flash, at a trumpet crash,
I am all at once what Christ is, since He was what I am, and
This Jack, joke, poor potsherd, patch, matchwood,
  immortal diamond,
  Is immortal diamond.

G.M. Hopkins

Nature is not done away but is perfected by glory.

Thomas Aquinas, *Summa Theologica*

The difference between the old Narnia and the new Narnia was like that. The new one was a deeper country; every rock and flower and blade of grass looked as it if meant more. I can't describe it any better than that: if ever you get there you will know what I mean.

It was the Unicorn who summed up what everyone was feeling. He stamped his right forehoof on the ground and neighed and then cried: 'I have come home at last! This is my real country! I belong here. This is the land I have been looking for all my life, though I never knew it till now. The reason why we loved the old Narnia is that it sometimes looked a little like this.'

C.S. Lewis, *The Last Battle*

In heaven we will live and live more fully and satisfyingly than ever before. And that life will involve all the really important elements of what we know as life: relationships, development, knowledge, communication... We shall recognise our loved ones but more by who they are than by what they look like.

But better than that, we shall know them with a depth and insight and love unimaginable in our present human existence.

David Winter, *Hereafter*

That is our destiny in heaven — to be like Christ: not Christ limited, as he was on earth, to the confines of time and flesh, but Christ risen, the great, free, timeless Christ of Easter morning.

David Winter, *Hereafter*

You!
Never seen before
Yet I have known you all my life.

You were there in that vague and misty face
That o'er my cradle focussed into love.
You in the noise and clamour of the place
That taught my mind to think and act and move.

You, in the frank and warring friends of youth
Whose loyalty persisted to the grave.
It was your beauty, your appeal, your truth,
When teenage hero-worship held me slave.

You were there that dazzling morning when serene
Contentment was reflected in his smile,
Whose love has held me all the years between,
Who mourns yet, now that I am gone awhile.

In all I could achieve, imagine, prize,
All that could stimulate my thought and wit.
Those mischief-calculating infant eyes
That dared my wrath and made a game of it.

You even there!

And now, Familiar Stranger, we have met
And joys of earth are caught in joys above.
For you were there, you *were* the joy —
Whom, never seen before, I truly love.

Lorna Jenkins

'You do not look as happy as I meant you to be.'

Lucy said, 'We're so afraid of being sent away, Aslan. And you have sent us back to our own world so often.'

'No fear of that,' said Aslan. 'Have you not guessed?'

Their hearts leapt and a wild hope rose within them.

'There was a *real* railway accident,' said Aslan softly. 'Your father and mother and all of you are — as you used to call it in the Shadowlands — dead. The term is over: the holidays have begun. The dream is ended: this is the morning.'

C.S. Lewis, *The Last Battle*

Lord, I have to admit that many times I find this present world of mine more dear than the world you have promised in the future. For all its difficulties and frustrations, this is the world I know and I cannot imagine what life with you will be like.

Help me to believe that a God who can create giraffes and snowflakes will inhabit a world where there is still beauty and humour, as well as the sublime.

Help me to love you so well and to desire your companionship so much, that when I come into your presence it will be a joyous reunion of old friends.

Help me to live each day so completely that if you called me tonight I would go without reluctance or regrets.

Help me to see this world through the perspective of the kingdom of heaven so that I may be able to distinguish which are the really important things and which are insignificant in the long view.

Lord, when I enter your final kingdom there will be many things that you will need to correct in me. Some of my attitudes would find no place there. Some of my ideas are warped and twisted. There are people I've rejected or misunderstood. Help me to submit my life into your hands now so that your purifying work can begin at once. For I will not be able to bear the joy of your presence until sin has no place in me and I do not want to delay the judgment of my sin until I am in your presence.

Rather, O Lord, I long to come to you with eager expectation, grateful for the life you have already given, ready to undertake whatever plan you have for me in the future.

A Benediction

Now to God Almighty, whose plans for us do not end in death, to our Lord Jesus Christ, who entered our world so that we might enter his, and to the Holy Spirit, who works in our hearts constantly preparing us for that great day, be all our praise and love until we meet him face to face. Amen.

WEEK

34

The king is coming

For as the lightning comes from the east and flashes to the west, so will be the coming of the Son of Man.

'Men of Galilee,' they said, 'why do you stand here looking into the sky? This same Jesus, who has been taken from you into heaven, will come back in the same way you have seen him go into heaven.'

Be patient, then, brothers, until the Lord's coming. See how the farmer waits for the land to yield its valuable crop and how patient he is for the autumn and spring rains. You too, be patient and stand firm, because the Lord's coming is near.

The Lord is not slow in keeping his promise, as some understand slowness. He is patient with you, not wanting anyone to perish, but everyone to come to repentance. But the day of the Lord will come like a thief. The heavens will disappear with a roar; the elements will be destroyed by fire, and the earth and everything in it will be laid bare. Since everything will be destroyed in this way, what kind of people ought you to be? You ought to live holy and godly lives as you look forward to the day of God and speed its coming... But in keeping with his promise we are looking forward to a new heaven and a new earth, the home of righteousness. So then, dear friends, since you are looking forward to this, make every effort to be found spotless, blameless and at peace with him.

Dear friends, now we are children of God, and what we will be has not yet been made known. But we know that when he appears, we shall be like him, for we shall see him as he is. Everyone who has this hope in him purifies himself, just as he is pure.

And now, dear children, continue in him, so that when he appears we may be confident and unashamed before him at his coming.

(Matthew 24:27; Acts 1:11; James 5:7-8; 2 Peter 3:9-12a and 13-14; 1 John 3:2-3; 1 John 2:28 — NIV.)

The world may end tonight or earth could be attacked by aliens. Whatever happens, only one man can save us. Buck Rogers in the 25th Century. 7.30 tonight.

Television Commercial

Dr Margaret Mead, the late anthropologist, has asked the question: 'Are we going to survive?' She said, 'The major struggle of marriage is not who takes out the garbage. Does it matter who takes it out if we are not going to be here?' She asks again, 'Are we going to be here? It is very doubtful. The whole world is in terrible danger. We could go tonight.'

Ray Stedman, from a printed sermon entitled 'Are These the Last Days?'

Why is God landing in this enemy-occupied world in disguise and starting a sort of secret society to undermine the devil? Why is he not landing in force, invading it? Is it that he is not strong enough? Well, Christians think he is going to land in force; we do not know when. But we can guess why he is delaying. He wants to give us the chance of joining his side freely. I do not suppose you and I would have thought much of a Frenchman who waited till the Allies were marching into Germany and then announced he was on our side. God will invade. But I wonder whether people who ask God to interfere openly and directly in our world quite realise what it will be like when he does. When that happens, it is the end of the world. When the author walks onto the stage, the play is over. God is going to invade, all right: but what is the good of saying you are on his side then, when you see the whole natural universe melting away like a dream and something else — something it never entered your head to conceive — comes crashing in; something so beautiful to some of us and so terrible to others that none of us will have any choice left? For this time it will be God without disguise; something so overwhelming that it will strike either irresistible love or irresistible horror into every creature. It will be too late then to choose your side. There is no use saying you choose to lie down when it has become impossible to stand up. That will not be the time for choosing: it will be the time when we discover which side we really have chosen, whether we realised it before or not. Now, today, this moment, is our chance to choose the right side. God is holding back to give us that chance. It will not last for ever. We must take it or leave it.

C.S. Lewis, *Mere Christianity*

Strange to say there are four very evident attitudes manifested in the professing church towards this blessed hope: aggressive hostility, listless apathy, fearful apprehension and loving expectancy. Some hate it; some are totally ignorant of it; some are afraid of it; and some love it.

Ruth Paxson, *Life on the Highest Plane*

The centring of the Christian hope on the personal return of the Lord Jesus Christ needs to be underlined. It is possible to become so involved in the intricacies of prophetic fulfilment or with a study of the accompanying events that we can miss the central event... the Christian hope for the future is not a timetable of events. It is not concerned finally with a series of impersonal happenings. Its heart is nothing other than the expectation of the personal appearing of the Lord. If we find our interest in the last things is centred elsewhere than in the Lord himself, then we are already out of step with scripture.

Bruce Milne, *The End of the World*

An ocean liner leaves New York bound for Liverpool. Its destination has been determined by proper authorities. Nothing can change it. This is at least a faint picture of sovereignty. On board the liner are several scores of passengers. They are not in chains, neither are their activities determined for them by decree. They are completely free to move about as they will. They eat, sleep, play, lounge about on the deck, read, talk altogether as they please; but all the while the great liner is carrying them steadily onward toward a predetermined port... The mighty liner of God's sovereign design keeps its steady course over the sea of history. God moves undisturbed and unhindered toward the fulfilment of those eternal purposes which he purposed in Jesus Christ before the world began.

A.W. Tozer, *The Knowledge of the Holy*

An eleven-year-old boy, engrossed in an adventure book, protested when told to go to bed. He pleaded to no avail that he must find out whether the hero would escape from an impossible situation and would rescue the heroine from the clutches of the villain. Later, with the aid of a flashlight beneath the bedcovers, he read the final chapter of the book. Sure enough, the hero rescued the heroine, and the villain was captured and put in jail. However, because he could not imagine how such a turnabout had happened, he began reading again at the place he had been forced to stop. Each time the villain did something wrong the boy said, 'If you knew what I know, you wouldn't be acting like you are.'

Avery Willis Jr., *Biblical Basis of Missions*

When the drama of history is over, Jesus Christ will stand alone on the stage. All the great figures of history, Pharoah, Alexander the Great, Charlemagne, Churchill, Stalin, Johnson, Mao Tse Tung — will realise that they have been but actors in a drama produced by another.

Helmut Thielecke, *The Waiting Father*

J. Hudson Taylor, founder of the China Inland Mission wrote: 'Well do I remember the effect when God was pleased to open my heart to the great truth that the Lord Jesus was coming again, and might come at any time. Since he might come any day, it is well to be ready every day. I do not know of any truth that has been a greater blessing to me through life than this.'

J. Oswald Sanders, *The Incomparable Christ*

D.G. Barnhouse was once asked what he would do if he knew Christ was returning tomorrow. He replied that he would do what he had planned. He knew he was doing God's will and that's all that mattered.

(Unknown)

Finish then thy new creation:
Pure and spotless let us be;
Let us see thy great salvation,
Perfectly restored in thee,
Changed from glory into glory,
Till in heaven we take our place,
Till we cast our crowns before thee,
Lost in wonder, love and praise.

Charles Wesley

Lift up your heads
to the coming king.
Bow before him and adore him, sing.
To his majesty
let your praises be
pure and holy, giving glory
to the king of kings.

Steven L. Fry

At the name of Jesus every knee shall bow
Every tongue confess him king of glory now;
'Tis the Father's pleasure we should call him Lord,
Who from the beginning was the mighty word.

Caroline M. Noel (Philippians 2:10-11)

Thank you, Lord, for the days in which we live. What exciting, what frightening days they are. Thank you for the assurance that you are still in charge, that we do not determine our own destiny nor set our own schedule.

Thank you that you are working out the events of earth according to your own programme and nothing can stay your hand.

Thank you for letting me live in these days.

Help me to keep sane and sober,
alert and watchful,
expectant and hopeful,
labouring while it is still day
in the fullness and power of the Spirit
to accomplish your purposes for a time such as this.

Lord, the first time you came so quietly;
The next time there will be shouting and the trumpet of God.
The first time you came in poverty and humiliation;
The next time you will come in glory.
The first time you came in weakness;
The next time you will come in power.
The first time you came to loneliness;
The next time you will be accompanied by the heavenly hosts.
I get a little nervous when I really think about it.
After all, you're the king and I'm not exactly court material.
And I'm going to be like you, for I shall see you as you are.
Therefore Lord, will you accept the adoration of my heart and the devotion of my life in order that I might always live for that which is eternal and be found faithful.
Until you come again
In your name, Amen.

A Benediction

And now may the dying Saviour's love
the risen Saviour's power
the ascended Saviour's blessing
and the returning Saviour's glory
Be the joy and comfort of your hearts
Now and forever. Amen.

Theme: Refining

'Through fire and water' (Psalm 66:12)

For you, O God, tested us;
you refined us like silver.
You brought us into prison
and laid burdens on our backs.
You let men ride over our heads;
we went through fire and water,
but you brought us to a
place of abundance.

Psalm 66: 10–12, NIV

WEEK

35

Christ's law of life

For whoever would save his life, will lose it; and whoever loses his life for my sake and the gospel's will save it.

Master... I was afraid, and I went and hid your talent in the ground.

A grain of wheat remains a solitary grain unless it falls into the ground and dies; but if it dies, it bears a rich harvest.

So do not start worrying: 'Where will my food come from, or my drink, or my clothes? (These are the things the pagans are always concerned about)... Instead, be concerned above everything else with the kingdom of God and with what he requires of you, and he will provide you with all these other things.

I have been crucified with Christ; it is no longer I who live, but Christ who lives in me.

The fruit of the Spirit is love, joy, peace, patience, kindness, goodness, faithfulness, gentleness, self-control; against such there is no law.

If one of you wants to be great, he must be the servant of the rest; and if one of you wants to be first, he must be the slave of all. For when I am weak, then I am strong.

(Mark 8:35, RSV; Matthew 25:24-25, RSV; John 12:24, NEB; Matthew 6:31-33, GNB; Galatians 2:20, RSV; Galatians 5:22-23, RSV; Mark 19:43-44, GNB; 2 Corinthians 12:10, RSV)

The various forms of our first Bible sentence (Mark 8:35) occur often enough in the gospels for us to regard it as expressing Jesus' basic law of living. The other sentences group themselves around two aspects of that profound saying.

The primary meaning is the folly of trying to 'play it safe' in the face of Christ's call to a radical adventure of faith, in which we risk losing what we most want to preserve. Second, there are many things we seek which do not seem to yield to a direct approach, one that is self-defeating. They are, rather, a kind of by-product of something else altogether.

This latter is a principle of very wide application. Its relevance to many human quests is well-known, such as happiness, security, freedom, peace and so on, but its operation in other areas may not be so well recognised. Personal influence, for example. The harder we try to accomplish this, the less we succeed. Few things get our hackles up more quickly than the suspicion that somebody is trying to set us a good example.

Another example is the common quest for ecstatic spiritual experiences for their own sake. This so easily becomes a form of self-indulgence, and is subject to the law of diminishing returns. The truly great moments come unbidden, and are unpredictable.

The cultivation of personal character by means of devotional exercises is another example. Character, in our use of the word, is not really a biblical word at all. Goodness is not the aim, but the result of our dedication to God's will. 'Man's chief end is to glorify God, and enjoy him forever,' and goodness is a by-product of that.

It could be a valuable devotional exercise to try to identify other areas where this principle applies.

The man, says Jesus, who is always trying to 'save' his life, to ensure security, material, intellectual, spiritual, to keep his personality sheltered from the risks and hardships which are an essential part of the discipline of life, will find at the end that he has lost it: there is nothing there to save, nothing but a handful of dust, the dust of withered opportunities. The man who sees the truth of this eternal law of life . . . and is therefore ready to take risks, to throw away security and hazard life itself, will find that he has discovered its secret, and entered into the fulfilment of it.

F.A. Cockin, in *The Christian Faith*

The more a man goes out from himself, or goes beyond himself, the more the spiritual dimension of his life is deepened, the more he becomes truly man, the more he grows in likeness to God, who is Spirit. On the other hand, the more he turns inward and loses himself in self-interest, the less human does he become. This is the strange paradox of spiritual being — that precisely by going out and spending itself, it realises itself. It grows not weaker, but stronger, for it is not a quantifiable thing.

John Macquarrie, *Paths in Spirituality*

I cannot emphasise the element of risk too strongly. To embark on a change of milieu, a change of habit, always feels like a 'little death'. Every step forth into a new dimension of life is a kind of dying. It must have been that, quite literally, for birds that lost their forest feeding-grounds, and ventured into the edge of the lake, initiating a habit that was to launch a new species of spoonbill. Certainly for us who are so much more *conscious* of the choices we make and the habits we change, real advance never seems like self-fulfilment, though that is what it is; it is always experienced first of all as self-surrender.

John V. Taylor, *The Go-Between God*

Friendship can only occur when we give ourself to the other, and to offer ourself to someone else is the most risky of all human endeavours.

Andrew M. Greeley, *The Friendship Game*

War knows no power; safe shall be my going,
Secretly armed against all death's endeavours;
Safe, though all safety's lost, safe where men fall;
And if these poor limbs die, safest of all.

Rupert Brooke

True attention is an involuntary self-surrender to the object of attention. The child who is absorbed is utterly relaxed. The adult mind, also, must be unstriving, receptive, expectant, before there can be any creative insight. Again and again this is the state of mind in which new truth dawns. We do not work it out or think it out; rather, we have the sense of waiting for the disclosure of something that is already there.

John V. Taylor, *The Go-Between God*

. . . truth, like love and sleep, resents
Approaches that are too intense.

W.H. Auden, *New Year Letter*

Writers on ethics have often spoken of 'the paradox of hedonism' — the fact that the quest for happiness defeats itself. But they have not so often noticed what I call 'the paradox of moralism' — the fact that the quest for goodness defeats itself.

D.M. Baillie, *God Was in Christ*

This whole concern about our own effort, moreover, is hostile to the spirit of peace. The faith which does not rely wholly upon God, but partly on exciting or disciplining its own soul, lives in valetudinarian anxiety about its spiritual health. To be perpetually feeling our own pulse is the surest way to rob ourselves of the self-forgetting vigour in which health is displayed.

John Oman, *Grace and Personality*

Only those who are generous to the limits of self-loss can hope to be channels of the generosity of God. In that crisis the I, the separate self, with its loves and hates, its personal preoccupations, is sacrificed and left behind. And out of this most true and active death to self, the spirit is reborn into the new life: not in some transcendental world, but in this world, among those who love us and those we love.

Evelyn Underhill, *The School of Charity*

In his poem (*Song of a Man Who Has Come Through*), Lawrence has deliberately used biblical imagery to suggest the mysterious depths of human life: the irresistible wind, the bubbling inner fountain, a knock on the door in the night. We can, if we give ourselves in surrender to God and our fellows, travel fast without movement; reap what we never sowed; be refreshed from the deep fountain welling up from the heart; find our deepest friend in the one who frightens us by coming in out of the night. And all this, provided we do not say to Christ, the Spirit-bearer: 'Ask of me and you will not receive; seek and you will not find; knock and I will not open the door.'

Peter de Rosa, *Not I, not I, but the wind that blows through me*

Seeking and losing life belong together so closely that any one prudently trying to save his life might as well be intent on losing it. But, turned around, the connection between losing one's life and actually saving it breaks apart on the words, 'For my sake and the gospel's.' Whatever else these words may mean, they certainly direct a man's whole intention and attention toward another goal than in the end saving his own life.

Paul Ramsay, *Basic Christian Ethics*

Show me, Lord, what all this has to do with me, and the service I am trying to render in your world. Am I too much of an activist? Am I trying to take over in areas where you are trying to say to me, 'Move over, and let me be God'?

Keep me from becoming obsessed with what I see as success, and to be more concerned with doing your will as I discover it; and from being too discouraged by what seems to me failure, knowing how ambiguous these two words are in Christian affairs. Save me from the fear of losing what I prize, not realising that by giving it to you I gain and enhance it.

Help me truly to understand the paradox of 'I, yet not I'. I seem to drive myself too much towards certain goals, overlooking the fact that they are the fruits of the surrender of my will to you and your purposes in the world. Help me to understand what is happening when what I want most seems to elude me at every turn, and what I have surrendered comes my way unbidden, and strangely enriched.

So many of your words seem a little hard to understand, but, if I am to be quite honest, my confusion often arises not from my lack of understanding but from my lack of willingness. Remind me of what I so easily allow myself to forget: that this world is full of situations which call for courage and the taking of risks. Let me know the joy, the 'creative ecstasy' of really losing myself for your sake in some enterprise for the help and liberation of others.

A Benediction

May the grace of Christ uphold you,
And the love of God enfold you;
May the Holy Spirit guide you,
And all joy and peace betide you,
Now and always. Amen.

WEEK

36

Honey from dead lions

Jacob was left alone; and a man wrestled with him until daybreak. When the man saw that he did not prevail against Jacob, he touched the hollow of his thigh; and Jacob's thigh was put out of joint as he wrestled with him. Then he said, 'Let me go for the day is breaking.' But Jacob said, 'I will not let you go, unless you bless me...' And there he blessed him. So Jacob called the place 'The face of God', ...'for I have seen God face to face and yet my life has been preserved.'

We do not want you to be ignorant, brethren, of the affliction we experienced in Asia; for we were so utterly, unbearably crushed that we despaired of life itself. Why, we felt that we had received the sentence of death; but that was to make us rely not on ourselves but on God who raises the dead; he delivered us from so deadly a peril, and he will deliver us; on him we have set our hope that he will deliver us again.

Yet it was the Lord's good plan to bruise him and fill him with grief. But when his soul has been made an offering for sin, then he shall have a multitude of children, many heirs. He shall live again and God's programme shall prosper in his hands. And when he sees all that is accomplished by the anguish of his soul, he shall be satisfied; and because of what he has experienced, my righteous Servant shall make many to be accounted righteous before God, for he shall bear all their sins. Blows and bruises tell for good; they go deep into the very soul.

But I have this treasure (i.e. this shining light) in a mere earthen jar, to show that its amazing power belongs to God and not to me. I am hard pressed on every side, but never cut off: perplexed, but not driven to despair; routed, but not abandoned; struck down, but not destroyed; never free from the danger of being put to death like Jesus, so that in my body the life of Jesus may also be seen. For every day I live, I am being given up to death for Jesus' sake, so that the life of Jesus may be visible in my mortal nature.

For us it is plain justice; we are paying the price for our misdeeds; but this man has done nothing wrong. . . Jesus, remember me. . .

(Genesis 32:24-26, 29-30, RSV; 2 Corinthians 1:8-10, RSV; Isaiah 53:10-11, LB; Proverbs 20:30, Moffatt; 2 Corinthians 4:7-11, Goodspeed; Luke 23:41-42, NEB)

We wrestle, in our service for God, with the failures we have in changing people. We know that this is the work of the Holy Spirit, that our contribution, though it take every part of us, is a modest one. Yet our hearts are hungry for such a valued seal of God's approval. Looking within, our hearts show that *we* are not much changed, either. This compounds our dissatisfaction. So much that we know sits on us cumbrously like Saul's armour.

In God's economy, self-knowledge comes mostly through adversity. When we fall and break the pretty image we have of ourselves, we see through to God. The process is usually a lengthy one, even though the failure, shame, collapse and dismay may seem to come in a matter of a few days, or a few hours. We experience something like the desolation of Jeremiah when fair Zion was 'eaten by uglies'. People who imagined that we were immune, impregnable, incorruptible are saddened — though some may breathe more freely. In our darkness, in our brokenness we taste the bitterness of being wholly wrong, only to find the consolation of God's love at a deeper level. We have become one of the poor and learn that we are blessed. When Christians become poor, they acquire a new respect for the poor everywhere. They begin to perceive people as they are: lost, dismayed, flawed, much as they see themselves to have been — but also loved by the same patient, waiting Father. They learn not to make judgments upon other people's wretchedness, but to look within to the creatureliness that is God's handiwork. And, having themselves found hope in darkness, sweetness in the taste of defeat, joy in being wholly in the wrong with God, they become hopeful for others, for all the others whom God sends to cross their path.

The poor are with us, everywhere — sent by God in all the images of their plight. They become neighbours. ('Neighbours are nearby and far away.') They may appear as intruders upon our contented domesticity, with their silent cry that they too are human, creatures of God, who have known the joy of family. The sacred indignity of their dying puts us in their debt. They have claims on our caring, upon the churches' and nations' resources and the whole family of man. In them does not God seek to make another breaking of our self-image, as persons and as communities of the Spirit? We are those who are caught up in a worldwide movement of living well upon the poverty of the poor. We look often to the crucified, for pardon and orientation; so are we to look upon the poor.

But 'tis the poor who make the loving words.
Slowly they stoop; it is a sacrament:
The poor can feed the birds.

The feat of love, the love that is the cure
For all indignities — it reigns, it calls,
It chains us to the pure.

Shaw Neilson, 'The Poor Can Feed the Birds'

At some point early in his life Watchman had learned the lesson of 'brokenness', whereby the Christian, being once touched by God as to his own strength and permanently crippled there (as was Jacob at Jabbok) discovers in that experience the ever new strength of God.

Angus Kinnear commenting on Watchman Nee's life
in *Against the Tide*

The ease with which the Adversary wounded Jacob makes us suspect that he could have won the struggle at any time. The meaning of the encounter was to change and test Jacob, not to destroy him. The wound Jacob received is the mark a person carries who encounters spiritual reality as deeply as did Jacob . . . The experience is indelible and changes us forever. It becomes like a wound, constantly reminding us of the spiritual reality we have known . . .

John A. Sanford, *The Man who wrestled with God*

The cross is the one totally realistic dialogue between the man God made us and the man we make ourselves.

Sebastian Moore, *The Crucified is No Stranger*

We shall always be learners, but at some point we shall learn that fundamental lesson, after which nothing can be the same again. There is now no way of not being a cripple. From that point begins a knowledge of God beyond anything we have ever dreamed... To what are we consecrated? Not to Christian work, but to the will of God, to be and to do whatever he pleases.

Watchman Nee, *Against the Tide*

While the Saviour of the world is moaning 'My God, my God, why hast thou forsaken me?' — at the same time the thief is preaching by the Saviour's side, as becomes a preacher, first and foremost to his own edification... 'It is as a guilty man I suffer'.

Soren Kierkegaard, *The Gospel of Sufferings*

The greater the grief the greater the creative energy to which it gives rise. I am sure that is so in my own case. (Since my wife's death seven years ago) I am nearer to those who suffer and I understand them better.

Paul Tournier, *Creative Suffering*

Batter my heart, three-person'd God, for you
As yet but knock, breathe, shine, and seek to mend;
That I may rise, and stand, o'erthrow me, and bend
Your force, to break, blow, burn and make me new.
I, like an usurp'd town, to another due,
Labour to admit you, but Oh, to no end,
Reason your viceroy in me, me should defend,
But is captiv'd and proves weak or untrue.
Yet dearly I love you, and would be loved fain,
But I am betroth'd unto your enemy:
Divorce me, untie, or break that knot again,
Take me to you, imprison me, for I
Except you enthrall me, never shall be free,
Nor ever chaste, except you ravish me.

John Donne, 'Holy Sonnet 14'

When a man before God always suffers as a guilty one (Luke 23:41) then at every moment, no matter what may happen, it is guaranteed that God is love, or to be more precise, at every moment he is prevented from entering into doubt, by the sense of guilt asserting itself upon him . . .

The thought that God is love holds within itself all joy.

Soren Kierkegaard, *The Gospel of Sufferings*

Father, I have many things in my past life to be embarrassed about, to be ashamed of. And perhaps tomorrow . . . I fed myself on egotism and folly and I mixed it with religion. To give to others I preached the cross yet wished desperately to live, to succeed in the esteem of others, my peers. But now, Father, now that your blessing has come to me in the struggling darkness, I know the light. You are without shadow!

Father, I observe that now it is easier to be with people, it is very often a joy, this labour of loving. I'm pleased and grateful to be hopeful for them and encouraging to them. So much bread comes back! I feel I belong to them — though it sounds grand to say it — to this whole human race, especially those you send across my path and heart. You have certainly blessed my way with many angels, threatening to make me richer than I could have understood. Because I've been thus humbled I have to pray: keep me in that place, take me along the road of your choosing. You have my full permission, even though I'm occasionally surprised that you take me so literally and respond so speedily.

Thank you for the gifts of all the Christian women and men I know. Prosper them. Thank you that we may do something for the poor whose gift it is often to be so generous as to make us appear unspontaneous, calculating. Bless all those who encourage others, who serve the poor. Blessed are the poor in spirit . . .

A Benediction

Riches I heed not, nor man's empty praise;
thou mine inheritance, now and always;
thou and thou only the first in my heart;
high King of heaven my treasure thou art.

High King of heaven, after victory won,
may I reach heaven's joys, O bright Heaven's sun;
Heart of my own heart, whatever befall,
still be my vision, O ruler of all.

(Irish, about eighth century)

WEEK

37

Accepted... and celebrating

One of the Pharisees asked him to eat with him, and he went into the Pharisee's house, and sat at table. And behold, a woman of the city, who was a sinner, when she learned that he was sitting at table in the Pharisee's house, brought an alabaster flask of ointment, and standing behind him at his feet, weeping, she began to wet his feet with her tears, and wiped them with the hair of her head, and kissed his feet, and anointed them with the ointment. Now when the Pharisee who had invited him saw it, he said to himself, 'If this man were a prophet, he would have known who and what sort of woman this is who is touching him, for she is a sinner.'

And he said to the woman, 'Your faith has saved you; go in peace.'

Rejoice in the Lord always.

Where the Spirit of the Lord is, there is freedom.

Welcome one another, therefore, as Christ has welcomed you, for the glory of God.

(Luke 7:36-39; Luke 7:50; Philippians 4:4; 2 Corinthians 3:17; Romans 15:7 — all RSV)

The Woman

'A woman of the city... a sinner' did not have a home in suburbia. Her life was rough; she did not always have a lock on her door. Her body was her asset, and sex paid better than a kitchen. She was admired in a fashion, as a body with a price. Sometimes she was used and not paid and that was a double blow to her diminished sense of self-worth.

She tried not to think of her past — the aches and the cold and the acquaintances who never quite became friends. There was no point in thinking of the future for days never went as planned.

Jesus was different. He did not size her up. He did not expect her to perform. He did not condemn her. He accepted her as she was.

She gave herself totally to him; not a giving as she gave to the men who paid her. She wept. No barriers. A release of feeling, of anger, of frustration, of joy poured over his feet. And she wiped his feet with her hair, not pausing to consider — for to expose your hair like that then would be like removing your bra and using that as a towel now. She made full use of her body, but in such a different way.

Where did she get that expensive flask of ointment? Best not to ask. A whole flask. No token action, but all she had. As always, she traded past and future for the present.

Her confession was total. Not in words, for in her experience words were empty. But in action, with her whole life — tears, hair, ointment.

But doesn't forgiveness depend on repentance? And what did she say that showed faith? The depth of her turning was that she staked everything on his acceptance; for even her city reputation now would be tarnished. Her fragmented self at last was touched in a way that began a healing, and she could go in peace.

Grace strikes us when we are in great pain and restlessness. It strikes us when we walk through the dark valley of a meaningless and empty life. It strikes us when we feel that our separation is deeper than usual.

Paul Tillich, *The Shaking of the Foundations*

In a non-threatening atmosphere where there is warmth and acceptance and someone to receive what we have to give, creativity begins to flow.

Elizabeth O'Connor, *Eighth Day of Creation*

You touched me and I burned for your peace.

Augustine, *Confessions*

It is *not* the love of the woman that brings her forgiveness, but it is the forgiveness she has received that creates her love. By her love she shows that much has been forgiven her, while the lack of love of the Pharisee shows that little has been forgiven him.

Paul Tillich, *The New Being*

Simon the Pharisee

Simon was an educated man with a home and a sound position in the established order. He was interested in Jesus — only professionally, of course. Really a favour to have such an itinerant teacher home for lunch.

Could have interviewed him at the office, but sometimes the home atmosphere can put these types at ease. Amazing how a feed and a few glasses can loosen the tongue. Don't overdo it though; no washing the feet or kiss of peace as a real guest might expect. Show my hospitality and my broadmindedness and pick up ideas he might have.

Then this prostitute came in. I was embarrassed, but Jesus did not mind at all. He just let her go on and on. I thought, 'You're a lecher or a fool. No prophet would let her get close and allow her to carry on like that.' he tried to carry it off with an aphorism or two, but now I had his measure.

In the traditional Christian view, the Pharisees have become representatives of everything evil, but in their time they were the pious and morally zealous ones. Their conflict with Jesus was not simply a conflict between right and wrong; it was, above all, the conflict between an old and sacred tradition and a new reality which was breaking into it and depriving it of ultimate significance.

Paul Tillich, *The New Being*

The burden he [Jesus] wants to take from us is the burden of religion. It is the yoke of the law, imposed on the people of his time by the religious teachers. . .

Paul Tillich, *The Shaking of the Foundations*

We withdrew after the rector of the day declared it sinful to guess the number of beans in a jar at the annual church fete.

Patrick White, describing why he left
a church in *Flaws in the Glass*

Jesus

Jesus accepted Simon's invitation. He noticed the social snubs and observed how Simon did not want to meet him in a personal fashion but sized him up — role 'A' assessing exhibit 'B'. He knew well enough how the woman felt on that score.

As she reached towards him in a desperate, awkward, overdone, extravagant and total bid for recognition as a person, he allowed her — and freed her — to do so.

The Pharisee was offended, bottled up. So Jesus dealt with him gently and verbally. Simon had too much to lose to respond from within and so he replied cautiously. Concerned primarily about a theological point, Simon and his colleagues missed completely one of the warmest and deepest turnings to God.

What may appear as indifference to religion in our culture may, in fact, represent a concern to get at a more basic Christianity.

Veronica Brady, *A Crucible of Prophets*

Jesus did not seem to be the person they had told me about. He was more ironic for one thing; ruder for another. He appeared to have a major preoccupation; he did not like people who thought they knew what life and love was all about, but he liked the ones who had made a mess of things, who had given up the struggle and just did the best they could. Goodness was not what he went for. Brokenness was.

Laura's impression on reading the Gospels,
in Monica Furlong's novel, *Cousins*

The church should be celebrating and giving so much that it draws people to him [Jesus]. I think the church should be an example and not a judgment seat.

Noel Paul Stookey, interviewed in *On Being*

No matter what danger enthusiasm may have brought to the church, the final defeat of enthusiasm has always signalised the sleeping church, even the busiest one . . . There is no Christian freedom without a dose of enthusiasm; and today, after long abstention, that dose ought to be generous rather than meagre, even if the result should be slight intoxication.

Ernst Kasemann, *Jesus Means Freedom*

The community which is filled with different energies of Christ's liberating power is therefore not an exclusive community of the saved, but the initial and inclusive materialisation of the world freed by the risen Christ.

Jurgen Moltmann, *The Church in the Power of the Spirit*

Father, I see in Jesus someone different. Centred in you. He drew out all the woman was wanting to give and he gently probed Simon's brittle veneer. A centre in you; that is your gift. I sense it sometimes, at least in part. You give good gifts and I should like more of that one, a gift that somehow enables others also to share in the gift.

Lord Jesus, I am under pressure to be sound and orderly and a company person. I get strokes for that. And it's safe, secure. But something inside me shrivels. You never operated that way, and your people never have thrived that way. I push away the turmoil; help me to accept it. I try to plan; help me to accept the people and events that tumble in, and to know the wholeness that is your peace.

You are here with me, Spirit of the living God. You encourage me to live in the freedom that is the logo of your presence. There are no 'proper' ways to celebrate your freedom. Your freedom area is large and inviting, so I'll celebrate in the ways you open to me.

A Benediction
'Peace I leave with you; my peace I give to you; not as the world gives do I give to you. Let not your hearts be troubled, neither let them be afraid,' said Jesus (John 14:27, RSV).

WEEK

38

Blessed destitution

Blessed are the poor in spirit, for theirs is the kingdom of heaven.

To some who were confident of their own righteousness and looked down on everybody else, Jesus told this parable: Two men went up to the temple to pray, one a Pharisee and the other a tax collector. The Pharisee stood up and prayed about himself: 'God, I thank you that I am not like all other men — robbers, evildoers, adulterers — or even like this tax collector. I fast twice a week and give a tenth of all I get.' But the tax collector stood at a distance. He would not even look up to heaven, but beat his breast and said, 'God, have mercy on me, a sinner.' I tell you that this man, rather than the other, went home justified before God. For everyone who exalts himself will be humbled, and he who humbles himself will be exalted.

God opposes the proud but gives grace to the humble. Submit yourselves, then, to God. Resist the devil, and he will flee from you. Come near to God and he will come near to you. Wash your hands, you sinners, and purify your hearts, you double-minded. Grieve, mourn and wail. Change your laughter to mourning and your joy to gloom. Humble yourselves before the Lord, and he will lift you up.

(Matthew 5:3; Luke 18:9-14; James 4:6b-10 — all NIV)

The desire to procure and accumulate securities and assets is one of the fundamental impulses in human experience. Fulfilment and satisfaction are sought by progressively increasing our ability to control and manipulate our environment. Success comes to those who learn quickly how to stack the cards in their own favour. This acquisition of power is manifested in a great variety of ways in different cultures, individuals and groups.

In his proclamation of the kingdom of God Jesus exposed the futility and deception of seeking fulfilment in this way. 'What does it profit a man to gain the whole world and forfeit his life?' Jesus taught that the blessedness of God is to be found in 'poverty of spirit'. When we begin to appreciate our finitude we become liberated from the paralysis of self-concern. Jesus lived in total reliance upon God, demonstrating the freedom which comes from recognising our ultimate dependence upon the one who made us in his image.

When our lives are dominated by the desire to become secure through the attainment of assets, we live in bondage to powers which destroy and distort life rather than those that lead to fulfilment and satisfaction. It does not matter if it is money or property, position or privilege, qualifications or expertise. All these things, useful in themselves, become forces of destruction when seen as ends in themselves. To live in total abandonment to God and his kingdom is to begin to experience authentic human life — life as it is meant to be.

One of the primary characteristics of 'spiritual poverty' is the freedom to live our lives for others. Liberated from the oppressive bondage of self-centredness, we become free to discover the presence of God in the life of others. No longer concerned to establish our own worthiness we become free to confess our failures and experience God's forgiveness. No longer threatened by others and their abilities we are free to love our neighbours, and even our enemies.

Jesus knew the freedom of 'blessed destitution'. He calls us to live our lives in constant recognition of our 'littleness' and our 'powerlessness', and thereby discover the way to authentic human existence.

The poor are all the people who have to put up with violence and injustice without being able to defend themselves. The poor are all the people who have to exist on the very fringe of death, with nothing to live from and nothing to live for. But in Jesus' message the poor are surely all of us too, since we have nothing to offer the coming God except the burden of our guilt and the rags of our exile — like the Prodigal Son.

Jurgen Moltmann, *The Power of the Powerless*

What does Jesus mean by 'poor in spirit'? In Luke's account it is simply 'you poor'. What kind of poverty is he talking about? If you have a lot of money, you'll probably say spiritual poverty. If you have little or no money, you'll probably say physical poverty. The rich will thank God for Matthew; the poor will thank God for Luke. Both will say, 'He blessed me!' Well, then, who really did get the blessing? Chances are, neither one. For it is exactly this attitude of self-praise and self-justification and self-satisfaction that robs men of a sense of great need for the kingdom and its blessings. When one says, 'I don't need to be poor in things; I'm poor in spirit,' and another says, 'I don't need to be poor in spirit; I'm poor in things,' both are justifying themselves as they are, and are saying in unison, 'I don't need'. With that cry on his lips, no man can repent.

Clarence Jordan, *The Sermon on the Mount*

Authentic abandonment or poverty in spirit realises that God is not 'out there'. God is 'with us', inviting us to work actively as co-creators, totally dedicating our lives to accomplish the divine plan in that part of history entrusted to us by the span of our life. This invitation requests merely the giving of ourselves. We are totally at the service of our Maker who has inaugurated the plan. We are to submit to its ethic in our life and proclaim it to our world. This kind of abandonment finds us freely choosing to live under the authority of this power of God within us to accomplish God's purposes in our society. In this way we become poor in spirit, anointed with God's favour. We can bring good news to the poor of our world... Realising our own needs and our powerlessness, we respond in God's power to care about other powerless brothers and sisters whom we see in need. As God has seen us in need and not left us helpless, so we too exist, by our nature, to respond in care to those we see in need.

Michael Crosby, *The Spirituality of the Beatitudes*

Privation is the lot of the disciples in every sphere of their lives. They are 'poor'. They have no security, no possessions to call their own, not even a foot of earth to call their home, no earthly society to claim their absolute allegiance. Nay more, they have no spiritual power, experience or knowledge to afford them consolation or security. For his sake they have lost all. In following him they lost even their own selves, and everything that could make them rich. Now they are poor — so inexperienced, so stupid, that they have no other hope but him who called them.

Dietrich Bonhoeffer, *The Cost of Discipleship*

May God create in us a true poverty of spirit so that we may be fully at God's disposal, free from the ambitions, options, power, and prestige of this world which make us feel so poor and little by comparison. Such people our Lord calls blessed. May we be liberated from that stifling and overwhelming sense of poverty that destroys personhood, and may we be freed from the contemporary illusions of life and death. May we then find resurrection life in the midst of what appears to be certain death, and the riches of our Lord's grace to the little ones in the midst of what appears to be hopeless poverty.

Gene Beerens, in *Sojourners* Magazine

In poverty of spirit man learns to accept himself as someone who does not belong to himself. It is not a virtue which man 'acquires'; as such it could easily turn into a personal possession that would challenge our authentic poverty. Man truly 'possesses' this radical poverty only when he forgets himself and looks the other way... To be able to surrender oneself and become 'poor' is, in biblical theology, to be with God, to find one's hidden nature in God; in short, it is 'heaven'... To become a man as Christ did is to practise poverty of spirit, to obediently accept our innate poverty as human beings.

Johannes Baptist Metz, *Poverty of Spirit*

Liberate me, Father, from my self-centredness. Help me to see clearly the futility of trying to establish myself as worthy before you. Help me to see others as people to love, rather than people to compete with, envy, or criticise. Grant to me the freedom which comes from knowing that you come to me in my frailty and fallenness.

When I turn from the path which you have called me to walk, confront me with my poverty and the futility of my strivings.

When I try to achieve my goals by an illegitimate use of power or position;
when I put someone down or question their worthiness;
when I seek security anywhere but in your care;
show me the blessedness of my destitution, and give me the courage to live precariously, trusting only in you.

A Benediction
Go forward into life with confidence in one thing alone — the blessedness which comes to those who abandon themselves in the presence of God. Accept your 'spiritual poverty' as a gift from God and rejoice in the freedom of destitution.

WEEK

39

Words! Words! Words!

Were not our hearts burning within us while he talked with us on the road and opened the scriptures to us?

The words I have spoken to you are spirit and they are life.

Man does not live on bread alone, but on every word that comes from the mouth of God.

My message and my preaching were not with wise and persuasive words, but with a demonstration of the Spirit's power.

Our gospel came to you not simply with words, but also with power, with the Holy Spirit and with deep conviction.

His worshippers must worship in spirit and in truth.

(Luke 24:32; John 6:63; Matthew 4:4; 1 Corinthians 2:4; 1 Thessalonians 1:5; John 4:24 — all NIV)

'Words! Words! Words! I'm so sick of words!' cried Liza Doolittle in *My Fair Lady*, impatient with reluctant suitors. Liza spoke for modern humanity — for us the very concept of words has been devalued. Why this indifference to words, if not mistrust of them? There are many reasons: post-Watergate political cynicism; saturation by television advertisements; the breakdown of trustworthy promises in business and marriage, and even the failure of Christians to show their faith by their works. More subtle influences in the decline of words have been linguistic and communication theories. For the church, the most tragic feature is the profusion of verbose, ambiguous and unbiblical kinds of theology that confuse everybody.

Words have *power*. Think of the positive, sustaining effect of Churchill's speeches, or the negative impact of slander or gossip. On the divine level, the one thing necessary to recover lost ground for the credibility of words is *the union of Word and Spirit*. This alone will rescue preaching from the deadness of mechanical formality. Instead of being dimmed by repetition and weathered by familiarity, our messages then will regain that vibrant, first-hand authority that sets them apart from the dusty scribe, and makes their words throb with pulsating earnestness.

J.B. Phillips has reported the awesome impression that the translation of the New Testament made upon him: like that of a house whose power mains cannot be turned off while an electrician rewires the whole building. That little-tapped potential must energise our handling of God's Word, or else we will end up with a 'form of godliness, but lacking the power thereof'.

Orthodoxy is essential, but it is not enough. We need the authentication that only the Holy Spirit can give.

D.M. Lloyd-Jones, Letter, 1969

Preaching is theology coming through a person who is on fire... What is the chief end of preaching? I like to think it is this. It is to give men and women a sense of God and his presence.

D.M. Lloyd-Jones, *Preaching and Preachers*

Alice Maynell, the Catholic poet, was once talking with a friend about the mass in the Roman Catholic church. This friend spoke of her inability to understand how Mrs Maynell could accept the doctrine of the Real Presence of God in the sacraments. 'Yes,' said Mrs Maynell, 'it may be difficult, but you Protestants have something worse than the Real Presence — you have *the Real Absence*.' It was an acute and penetrating comment on much of our Protestant worship, but it has a wider application. It applies to a minister's own inner life, from which any reality in what he says must find its source. We can never bring the real presence of God to other lives if we have the real absence in ourselves.

H.E. Luccock, 'Reality in Preaching'

John Calvin emphasised this marriage of Word and Spirit, when he defined preaching as that public exposition of scripture 'in which God himself is present in judgment and in grace, as if God himself came in person solemnly to summon us.'

T.H.L. Parker, *The Oracles of God*

It ought not to be so, but it has often happened that the student in college has gathered *fuel*, but lost *the fire* which is to kindle it. It will be to our everlasting disgrace if we bury our flame beneath the faggots which are intended to sustain it.

C.H. Spurgeon, *Lectures to My Students*

I preached what I did feel, what I did smartingly feel.

Spiritual Riches of John Bunyan

What was said was deep and memorable and arresting. But always that kept opening vistas, down which one's own mind could catch glimpses of endless truths that crowded in on one. This preacher was like a diviner, in whose subtle hand the hazel wand twisted and turned and pointed. And parched, desperate people had but to drive their spades into the hot, dry, arid sand, and there was living water in abundance.

A.J. Gossip

Let us see that our knowledge of Christ be not a powerless, barren and impractical knowledge: O that in its passage from our understanding to our life, it might powerfully melt, sweeten and ravish our hearts.

John Flavel, *Works*

Unction in the preacher puts God in the gospel.

E.M. Bounds, *Power through Prayer*

The living interest of Christ and of the Holy Spirit is not breadth, but it is depth... A gospel deep enough has all the breadth of the world in its heart. If we are only deep enough the breadth will take care of itself. I would ten times rather have one man who was burning deep, even though he wanted to burn for my modern theology, than I would have a broad, hospitable, and thin theologian who was willing to take me in and a nondescript crowd of others in a sheet let down from heaven, but who had no depth, no fire, no skill to search, and no power to break. For the deep Christianity is that which not only searches us, but breaks us.

P.T. Forsyth, *The Work of Christ*

When W.E. Sangster of London was on the edge of a serious breakdown, he was asked to attend a certain Christian meeting. Reluctant and exhausted, he went, and found from the second sentence of the preacher that God was ravishing his heart and renewing his mind through the words. He was staggered also that others were not as enriched as he had been. The experience of meeting God then blessed him through subsequent years, and confirmed his commitment to preaching. This is his conviction: 'I often go to speak at meetings with that memory in mind. I find myself praying that somebody's awful extremity may be met. I whisper to God out of my unworthiness: "Do it again, Father!" '

When your words came, I ate them; they were my joy and my heart's delight, for I bear your name, O Lord God Almighty.

Jeremiah 15:16, NIV

This is my comfort in my affliction: for thy word has quickened me.

Psalm 119:50 AV

O Lord, grant me a warm heart!

George Whitefield

My heart I give you, Lord, eagerly and entirely.

John Calvin, personal motto

What fire is this that so warms my heart? What light is this that so enlightens my soul? O fire! that always burns, and never goes out, kindle me. O light! which ever shines, and is never darkened, illuminate me. O that I had my heat from you, most holy fire! How sweetly you burn! How secretly you shine! How powerfully do you inflame me!

St Augustine, Soliloquies, chapter 34 free translation

A Benediction

Now may Spirit and Word be forever married in our experience; may the heat of joy and the light of truth burn in our hearts, and may we, who with unveiled faces behold his glory, become increasingly transformed into his likeness with ever-increasing glory, which comes from the Lord, who is the Spirit. Amen.

WEEK

Love without limits

You have learnt how it was said 'Eye for eye and tooth for tooth'. But I say this to you: offer the wicked man no resistance. On the contrary, if anyone hits you on the right cheek, offer him the other as well; if a man takes you to law and would have your tunic, let him have your cloak as well.

Surely he has borne our griefs and carried our sorrows; yet we esteemed him stricken, smitten by God, and afflicted. But he was wounded for our transgressions, he was bruised for our iniquities; upon him was the chastisement that made us whole. And with his stripes we are healed.

You have learnt how it was said 'you must love your neighbour and hate your enemy'. But I say this to you: love your enemies and pray for those who persecute you.

For Christ suffered for you and left you a personal example, and wants you to follow in his steps. He was guilty of no sin, nor of the slightest prevarication. Yet when he was insulted he offered no insult in return. When he suffered he made no threats of revenge.

Father, forgive them; they do not know what they are doing.

(Matthew 5:38-40, JB; Isaiah 53:4-5, RSV; Matthew 5:43-44, JB; 1 Peter 2:21-23, Phillips; Luke 23:34, NEB)

Should we permit the behaviour of others towards us to change our standards, ideals and behaviour?

In fact, the behaviour of others towards us does evoke changes within us. If we respond to our highest ideals and insights, we try to act patiently, tolerantly and lovingly. But when we receive in return nothing but misunderstanding, indifference, accusations of insincerity, and hostility, then we begin to change. We lose patience, we become defensive. Like Peter, we think it's a big deal to forgive up to seven times. But seventy times seven? No way.

The change in us is the consequence of our allowing the attitudes and actions of another to gain power over us.

We may even rationalise. We argue that it is in *their* interests that we do not allow them to get away with it.

We may also argue that whilst Jesus' teaching is ideal, we've got to be practical and realistic.

Jesus' prayer, 'Father, forgive them, they don't know what they're doing,' exemplifies his characteristic reaction to hostility and violence throughout his life. He dared to stake his whole being on the veracity and ultimate power of love. He refused at any point to allow the abuse and attacks of others to change one whit his attitudes or reaction towards them.

Never once did he change his nature — which was to save those who reviled him — to accommodate or adjust himself to others.

The cross is foolish not only to the unbelieving world. In his personal life the Christian also has a struggle with the foolishness of the cross — the symbol of the uncompromising and unconditional love demonstrated by Jesus and demanded of his disciple.

Yet it is the way the Master went. And a cross-less Christianity is a distortion and a travesty.

An old man in India sat down in the shade of an ancient banyan tree whose roots disappeared far away in a swamp. Presently he discerned a commotion where the roots entered the water. Concentrating his attention, he saw that a scorpion had become helplessly entangled in the roots. Pulling himself to his feet, he made his way carefully along the tops of the roots to the place where the scorpion was trapped. He reached down to extricate it. But each time he touched the scorpion, it lashed his hand with its tail, stinging him painfully. Finally his hand was so swollen he could no longer close his fingers, so he withdrew to the shade of the tree to wait for the swelling to go down. As he arrived at the trunk, he saw a young man standing above him on the road laughing at him. 'You're a fool,' said the young man, 'wasting your time trying to help a scorpion that can only do you harm.' The old man replied, 'Simply because it is in the nature of the scorpion to sting, should I change my nature, which is to save?'

William Sloane Coffin, *The Courage to Love*

Love will conquer hate.

Mohandas Gandhi

Forgiveness does not mean ignoring what has been done, or putting a false label on an evil act. It means rather that the evil act no longer remains as a barrier to the relationship. Forgiveness is a catalyst which creates the atmosphere necessary for a new beginning. *Agape* is sheer unqualified, creative and redemptive goodwill for all people. Love alone is capable of transforming with redemptive power.

I have lived with the conviction that unearned suffering is redemptive. There are some who still find the cross a stumbling block, others consider it foolishness. But I am more convinced than ever that it is the power of God to social and individual salvation.

Martin Luther King, *Strength to Love*

The meek only inherit abuse!

Unknown

The spirit of self-denial and the spirit of service coming together produce a new being: the most formidable being on earth — the Terrible Meek! They are terrible in that they demand nothing, and hence cannot be bought or tempted, and that there are no lengths they are not prepared to go for others. Christ in the presence of Pilate is a picture of the terrible meek. He could not be bullied — he could not be changed. Nothing could make him love less. He wanted nothing, except to give his life for the very people who were crucifying him. The future of the world will be in the hands of those who serve the world, suffer for the world, and so save the world.

E. Stanley Jones, *The Christ of the Mount*

Lord, in my head, and deep in my heart, I know that the way of Jesus is unquestionably right. The purity of his love leaves me wondering. But, Lord, you also know, better than I understand it, the struggle I have inside. The sheer practicalities of daily human interaction all tell me it won't work. I want to save myself. But then, didn't Jesus? The difference between us is that his final choices — not to save himself — were always the right ones. Mine almost never are. My natural impulse, Lord, is to defend myself, to protect myself, to refuse to become vulnerable to the hostility of others.

The cross is so much heavier than I thought. In the first flush of discipleship, and the glow of my young faith, I picked it up readily. But now? I've discovered that the cross is not a comfortable symbol. It impinges on almost every decision I have to make — even the small ones. I want to choose against the path of pain, involvement, personal cost. I can easily love my friends — and forgive them when necessary. But my enemies? Those who hurt me? Every day I let the attitudes of others determine my reactions.

Lord, I see all this. And I know that your way, not mine, is right. Please help me, however stumblingly, to pick up the cross — in little things and big — until, by your grace, I become a little more like Jesus. Please help me. Amen.

O Holy Spirit, who so deeply disturbs our peace,continue, we pray, your probings and promptings and goad us until we go your way, to our own greater blessing and deeper peace. In Jesus Christ our Lord.

George Appleton, *Journey for a Soul*

A Benediction

May the grace of our Lord Jesus Christ
make us gracious,
The love of God our Father
make us loving
And the fellowship and power of the Holy Spirit
fill and empower us
Until we show, in our lives,
more of the spirit and the marks of Jesus Christ.
Amen.

WEEK

A faith that *does* justice

What to me is the multitude of your sacrifices? says the Lord; I have had enough of burnt offerings of rams and the fat of fed beasts; I do not delight in the blood of bulls, or of lambs, or of he-goats. When you come to appear before me, who requires of you this trampling of my courts? Bring no more vain offerings; incense is an abomination to me. New moon and sabbath and the calling of assemblies — I cannot endure iniquity and solemn assembly. Your new moons and your appointed feasts my soul hates; they have become a burden to me, I am weary of bearing them. When you spread forth your hands, I will hide my eyes from you; even though you make many prayers, I will not listen; your hands are full of blood. Wash yourselves; make yourselves clean; remove the evil of your doings from before my eyes; cease to do evil, learn to do good; seek justice, correct oppression; defend the fatherless, plead for the widow.

But now the righteousness of God has been manifested apart from law, although the law and the prophets bear witness to it, the righteousness of God through faith in Jesus Christ for all who believe. For there is no distinction; since all have sinned and fall short of the glory of God, they are justified by his grace as a gift, through the redemption which is in Christ Jesus, whom God put forward as an expiation by his blood, to be received by faith. This was to show God's righteousness, because in his divine forbearance he had passed over former sins; it was to prove at the present time that he himself is righteous and that he justifies him who has faith in Jesus.

(Isaiah 1:11-17; Romans 3:21-26 — both RSV)

Many Christians are puzzled about the implications of the gospel of Christ for their society. Where the Old Testament speaks so clearly about social justice, and denounces oppression and alienation, the New Testament seems to be not so outspoken.

Yet increasingly, Christians are becoming active in social and political concerns, especially in democratic nations where they have the freedom to do so. This freedom is in stark contrast to the Christians in many countries under totalitarian or Marxist regimes who suffer not only personal hardship but also great restriction in living out the gospel. Out of this contrast comes a desire for many Christians in free countries to engage in authentic social action. But how to do it?

In Isaiah's time it is perfectly clear that God was not willing to accept the sacrifices of his people, or listen to their prayers, unless they brought their community life into line with God's laws of righteousness. They had to turn away from evil, create justice in the community, and support the weak.

Behind this of course is the assumption that God was in touch with his people, and that they were in a relationship with him. In fact, to know the Lord is to do justice and show compassion, because we automatically reflect his character in our behaviour. So the Lord says to Jeremiah: 'Did not your father have food and drink? He did what was right and just, so all went well with him. He defended the cause of the poor and needy, and so all went well. Is that not what it means to know me?' declares the Lord (Jeremiah 22:15-16).

To know the Lord Jesus is likewise to reflect his character in our world. For God the Father justifies the person who has faith in Jesus, and this demonstrates his own character of justice and righteousness. The New Testament compulsion to social action and social justice is no less than the Old Testament obligation.

The Old Testament reveals a God who has a *passion* for justice, while Jesus blesses those who hunger and thirst to see right prevail. For the Christian, a passion for justice cannot therefore be dismissed as 'the politics of envy' if it is seeking to establish what is right, fair and good.

Brian Wren, *Education for Justice*

Old Testament justice topples over on behalf of those in direct need. This justice is not the same as fairness, as though everyone started from the same line. It is not portrayed by the blind-eyed goddess of justice. We owe that picture of justice to the Greeks. The blind goddess properly stands over the law courts. She does not look to see if the plaintiff or the defendant has the greatest needs; she is blind. She dispenses evenhanded justice. She assumes that she is settling a dispute between equals. In the Bible the righteous God is not blind; his eyes are wide open. Because he is against sin, which distorts relationships between his children, he pushes away the oppressor and is active on behalf of those in special need. He sees the need of widows, orphans, foreigners, the oppressed and he acts for them.

David Sheppard, *Bias to the Poor*

The Christian pursuit of justice will be action rooted in solidarity with all persons, especially the poor. It will be action conformed to the demands of mutuality and reciprocal interdependence expressed in the norms of social justice. It will be action which acknowledges the claim of every unique individual to those material and social goods necessary for the satisfaction of basic human needs: food, clothing, housing, health care, social security, decent working conditions, etc.

David Hollenbach SJ, *The Faith that does Justice*

In the life, death and resurrection of Jesus Christ, the world experienced a new redemptive action by God. It was a free act of God, an act of grace offered to all, the perfect sacrifice to overcome sin. It is a new and perfect demonstration of the justice of God which triumphs over the powers of evil. We are invited to respond with faith in Christ as Lord and with just relationships with our neighbours.

Changing Australia

Lord, we sit in the comfort of our homes
where we have space, and warmth and peace,
and often we don't want to know about the problems of others.

We put down the newspaper and turn off the television
when we see uncomfortable facts we'd rather not know.
Forgive us our lack of care and help us to understand
the real problems of those who have no proper home of their own...
or no family to belong to... or no friend to turn to.
Help us to move through understanding to action
so that we shall continually look for ways
by which we can help to bring about your kingdom on earth.
Help us to use our time, our minds, our energies, our money,
through work, through friendship and through community action,
to help those in this nation and elsewhere who are without food or shelter or clothes
and therefore without hope.
And as we go about caring
may they find the God who is the source of all caring. Amen.

A Benediction

Eternal God and Father, by whose power we are created and by whose love we are redeemed: guide and strengthen us by your Spirit, that we may give ourselves to your service, and live this day in love to one another and to you; through Jesus Christ your Son our Lord. Amen.

Australian Prayer Book

WEEK

The moving finger writes...

(Edward Fitzgerald)

Enoch walked with God.
Moses, whom the Lord knew face to face.
Israel served the Lord all the days of Joshua, and all the days of the elders who outlived Joshua.
Saul and Jonathan, beloved and lovely!
Jeroboam the son of Nebat, who made Israel to sin.
Before him (Josiah) there was no king like him, who turned to the Lord with all his heart and with all his soul and with all his might... nor did any like him arise after him.
Johoram... departed with no one's regret.
Abraham, my friend.
Abraham... was called the friend of God.
Antipas my witness, my faithful one.

(Genesis 5:24; Deuteronomy 34:10; Joshua 24:31; 2 Samuel 1:23; 1 Kings 22:52; 2 Kings 23:25; 2 Chronicles 21:16,20; Isaiah 41:8; James 2:23; Revelation 2:13 — all RSV)

Browsing through cemeteries and studying the epitaphs on tombstones might be considered a rather morbid pursuit, although occasionally one might discover a delightful example of unconscious humour, such as this inscription in an English churchyard:

> Erected to the memory of Adam Abrahams, drowned in the Severn by a few affectionate friends.

Here the bad grammar occasions the humour, whereas the head-board of a grave in the Sparta Diggings, California, compounds bad spelling and grammar with extraneous detail:

In memory OV
JOHN SMITH, who met
wierlent death neer this spot,
18 hundred and 40 too. He was shot
by his own pistill;
It was not one of the new kind,
but a old-fashioned
brass barrel, and of such is the
Kingdom of heaven.

More often than not there is a genuine appreciation of the person who has died, sometimes shading out into extravagance, although, even here, a bitterness developed through long experience sometimes emerges, as in this epitaph at Grey Friars, Edinburgh, Scotland:

Here snug in grave my wife doth lie;
Now she's at rest and so am I.

Very rarely there may be found an objective thought which rises above fulsome praise or barbed criticism. In Caermathern Churchyard, in Wales, for instance, there is an inscription:

Praises on tombs are trifles vainly spent.
A man's good name is his best monument.

It is the duty of man so to live that he leaves behind a pleasant memory of himself.

Thomas Carlyle

This *is* important. What is said of us when we depart this life reflects the overall impression for good or evil which we make upon others by our multiplied words and actions during our lifetime. But the title of this meditation hints at a higher, more comprehensive and final judgment:

The Moving Finger writes; and having writ,
Moves on; not all thy Piety nor Wit
Shall lure it back to cancel half a line,
Nor all thy Tears wash out a Word of it.

Edward Fitzgerald, *Omar Khayyam*

Scripture underlines and personalises this weightier responsibility: Let your light so shine before men, that they may see your good works and give glory to your Father who is in heaven.

Matthew 5:16

Man's judgment is necessarily imperfect, subjective and prone to change, but God's verdict on our lives is absolute and unchangeable. Hence the challenge which comes to us as we meditate upon the many 'epitaphs' in the Bible. Granted that the foundation of our acceptance by God is our faith in the completed work of his Son, Jesus Christ, what are we building, day by day, on that foundation?

For no other foundation can one lay than that which is laid, which is Jesus Christ. Now if any one builds on the foundation with gold, silver, precious stones, wood, hay stubble — each man's work will become manifest; for the Day will disclose it, because it will be revealed with fire, and the fire will test what sort of work each has done.

1 Corinthians 3:11-13

The divine testimony is that Enoch, Moses and Abraham had the closest possible relationship with God; that Joshua's influence was so decisive that it influenced the succeeding generation, as well as his own; that Josiah was unique amongst the kings of Judah for his unswerving commitment and loyalty to God. David's reference to Saul might seem gratuitous but there was no doubt about the loveliness and pleasantness in Jonathan's life.

In stark contrast, who would welcome a verdict like that on Jeroboam, the first king of the northern tribes after the disruption which followed the death of Solomon? Almost every subsequent reference concerning him highlights the fact that he was largely responsible for leading Israel into sin. Perhaps even sadder is the verdict on King Jehoram, who 'departed with no one's regret', which is paralleled in an inscription on a tombstone at Painswick, in Gloucestershire, England:

My wife is dead, and here she lies;
Nobody laughs and nobody cries;
Where she is gone to, or how she fares,
Nobody knows, and *nobody cares*.

Jehoram lived unloved and died unlamented; there was nothing in his life which invited respect or remembrance.

What will others think and say of me? What will God's all-comprehending and absolutely just verdict be? I am reminded that the unit is not the life but the moment; that the ultimate judgment will be based upon the multitude of impulses, thoughts, words and actions that make up each day; that there is a *now* when I can resolutely set my will to honour God by my filial love, loyalty and total obedience; a *now* when I can serve my fellows with a sacrificial love and commitment which mirrors Christ's own self-giving. The children's hymn expresses these truths simply, yet meaningfully:

Growing every day in awe,
For thy Name is holy;
Learning every day to love
With a love more lowly.

Walking every day more close
To our Elder Brother;
Growing every day more true
Unto one another.

Leaving every day behind
Something which might hinder;
Running swifter every day,
Growing purer, kinder.

Lord, so pray we every day
Hear us in thy pity;
That we enter in at last
To the Holy City.

Mary Butler

God's 'Well done, good and faithful servant' will be given not for isolated flashes of brilliance or occasional successes, however stupendous, but for that daily constancy of life which results in steadily increasing Christ-likeness. This is possible for the humble, one-talented believer as well as for the multitalented. At Ataikola, in what is now Bangladesh, there is a monument erected to the memory of a pioneer Baptist missionary, Miss Ellen Arnold, with an inscription which sums up this attitude:

> Jesus said, 'I am the Way, the Truth and the Life'.
> Miss Arnold walked that Way, taught that Truth and lived that Life.

Father, help me to realise that this day brings with it priceless opportunities of fellowship with yourself, of growing in grace and in the knowledge of your Son and of coming alongside other people to help, encourage and strengthen them.

Grant me the grace to open myself completely to your Holy Spirit, that he may lead me into all truth; the truth of your Word and the truth of a daily life which glorifies you. May no-one be caused to stumble by any word or action of mine; may no-one be the poorer because of my neglect or thoughtlessness. Touch my mind so that I may think for you; touch my eyes that I may see my fellows as you see them; touch my lips so that my words might comfort, encourage or rebuke as necessary; touch my hands so that all tasks might be performed well; touch my heart, my innermost being, so that your love might control me.

Help me, dear Lord, so to live this day that with truth I may be able to say, with the One whom I seek to follow, 'I have finished the work you gave me to do'. And guard me from the spiritual pride which can so easily follow work done successfully in your name and strength, for to you I owe everything, including the will to desire and the strength to achieve.

A Benediction

Lord, go with us into this day and grant us, moment by moment, the enjoyment of your presence, a sensitivity to the promptings of your Holy Spirit and an awareness of the rich provision you have made for us to live victoriously, this and every day. Amen.

WEEK

43

A dreadful prospect, a desirable end

God is a righteous judge, a God who expresses his wrath every day... He who is pregnant with evil and conceives trouble gives birth to disillusionment. He who digs a hole and scoops it out falls into the pit he has made. The trouble he causes recoils on him; his violence comes down on his own head.

Though grace is shown to the wicked, they do not learn righteousness; even in a land of uprightness they go on doing evil and regard not the majesty of the Lord. O Lord, your hand is lifted high, and they do not see it. Let them see your zeal for your people and be put to shame; let the fire reserved for your enemies consume them.

The Lord... is righteous; he does no wrong. Morning by morning he dispenses his justice, and every new day he does not fail, yet the unrighteous know no shame... 'Therefore wait for me,' declares the Lord, 'for the day I will stand up to testify. I have decided to assemble the nations, to gather the kingdoms and to pour out my wrath on them — all my fierce anger. The whole world will be consumed by the fire of my jealous anger.'

Do not fear those who kill the body and after that have nothing more they can do. I will warn you whom to fear; fear him who, after he has killed, has authority to cast into hell.

...our Lord Jesus Christ is revealed from heaven with his mighty angels in blazing fire... he will do justice upon those who refuse to acknowledge God and upon those who will not obey the gospel of our Lord Jesus. They will suffer the punishment of eternal ruin, cut off from the presence of the Lord... Destroyed they shall be, because they did not open their minds to love of the truth, so as to find salvation.

Therefore God puts them under a delusion, which works upon them to believe the lie, so that they may all be brought to judgment, all who do not believe the truth but make sinfulness their deliberate choice.

. . . there were loud voices in heaven, which said: 'The kingdom of the world has become the kingdom of our Lord and of his Christ, and he will reign for ever and ever.' And the twenty-four elders, who were seated on their thrones before God, fell on their faces and worshipped God, saying: 'We give thanks to you, Lord God Almighty, who is and who was, because you have taken your great power and have begun to reign. The nations were angry; and your wrath has come. The time has come for judging the dead, and for rewarding your servants the prophets and your saints and those who reverence your name, both small and great — and for destroying those who destroy the earth.'

(Psalm 7:11,14-16, NIV; Isaiah 26:10-11, NIV; Zephaniah 3:5,8, NIV; Luke 12:4-5, NEB; 2 Thessalonians 1:7b-9; 2:10b-12, NEB; Revelation 11:15-18, NIV)

The prospect of a judgment that is final and a condemnation that is irrevocable causes distress to all sensitive persons. The understandable recoil of mind and emotion has led many to ignore or deny these teachings. Yet for those whose knowledge of God and of final reality are derived from divine speaking rather than human speculating, there is no possibility of denying judgment and hell, which are all too clearly attested in the teaching of Jesus and of scripture generally. Moreover, they are not found there as an extraneous or unassimilated extra, but as an integral part of the whole biblical portrayal of the nature of God and of the reality he has made and is making. Seen in this light, some of our distress at the prospect of judgment is a measure of the discrepancy between the biblical revelation of the character of God and our own more sentimental notions. Here, as in so many other things, the revealed reality of God cuts across our preferences.

Yet there is a distress at the inevitability of judgment that is both valid and necessary (see, for example, Luke 19:41-44). Such pain is both an index of the momentous, even awesome character of human choice and responsibility and a measure of the horror of grace spurned and destruction embraced.

In the Bible the certainty of judgment to come evokes joy as well as tears. Most honest readers of the Bible would have to feel dismayed by the way in which some passages rejoice in this prospect. Yet closer inspection shows that the authors are not motivated by the almost ghoulish pleasure at the terrors of judgment that has been evident all too often in Christian history. Rather, their joy is the result of a passionate devotion to the honour of God and a zeal for the triumph of his purposes. His judgment is prayed for and rejoiced in because it means both the vindication of his truth and holiness in the face of all that is false and wicked, and also the renewal and restoration of the creation, eliminating all that is rebellious and fully implementing his righteous rule. They know that the alternative to judgment is a creation which becomes a labyrinth of evil, in which all fixed points are finally obscured by layer upon layer of duplicity or wiped away in the escalating spiral of violence. (Any good spy novel will provide you with a glimpse into such a world.)

It is no light thing, therefore, to pray regularly for the coming of God's kingdom, for to do so is to pray for the execution of final judgment. The believer faces this prospect with tears and yet greets it with joy.

It is no light thing, either, to relate daily to persons who are being prepared for glory or who are preparing themselves for destruction!

There are only two kinds of people in the end: those who say to God, 'Thy will be done,' and those to whom God says, in the end, '*Thy* will be done.'

C.S. Lewis, *The Great Divorce*

The love of God, with arms extended on a cross, bars the way to hell. But if that love is ignored, rejected and finally refused, there comes a time when love can only weep while man pushes past into the self-chosen alienation which Christ went to the cross to avert.

Michael Green, *The Empty Cross of Jesus*

Hell is not like a gaol where prisoners are longing to be free but like a sit-in where the protesters have barricaded themselves in.

Hugh Silvester, *Arguing with God*

The agents of hell disappear, the human, they shrink and
dissolve
Into dust on the wind, forgotten, unmemorable; only is here
The white flat face of Death, God's silent servant,
And behind the face of Death and Judgment
And behind the Judgment the Void, more horrid than active
shapes of hell;
Emptiness, absence, separation from God;
The horror of the effortless journey, to the empty land
Which is no land, only emptiness, absence, the Void,
Where those who were men can no longer turn the mind
To distraction, delusion, escape into dream, pretence,
Where the soul is no longer deceived, for there are no objects,
no tones,
No colours, no forms to distract, to divert the soul
From seeing itself, foully united forever, nothing with nothing,
Not what we call death, but what beyond death is not death,
We fear, we fear.

T.S. Eliot, *Murder in the Cathedral*

...God's judgments alone stand between us and a universal tyranny. If the effects of original sin were allowed to work themselves out unchecked, man's inhumanity to man would know no bounds. Such elements of stability, freedom, mercy and goodness we enjoy, we owe to the operation of God's righteous judgments among us.

J.W. Wenham, *The Goodness of God*

Heaven and its happiness are wrongly conceived as immunity from judgment instead of joy in the consummation of judgment in righteousness and holiness for ever.

P.T. Forsyth, *The Work of Christ*

It is a serious thing to live in a society of possible gods and goddesses, to remember that the dullest and most uninteresting person you can talk to may one day be a creature which, if you saw it now, you would be strongly tempted to worship, or else a horror and a corruption such as you now meet, if at all, only in a nightmare. All day long we are, in some degree, helping each other to one or other of these destinations.

C.S. Lewis, *Screwtape Proposes a Toast*

Lord, have I over-reacted? Have I been so conscious of the 'so heavenly-minded, no earthly use' danger that I have lived too much as though there were no deadline and destination ahead of us all? You know how hard I have to fight in my work against the 'tyranny of the urgent', seeking to prevent the immediate from crowding out the important. Have I, in the midst of all this, succumbed to the same tyranny in another way by now allowing the immediate to shape the ultimate? Have I been so concerned to distance myself from ghastly caricatures of biblical teaching that the reality and finality of judgment have no real place in my working theology? Have I related to individuals only in terms of the day and its needs, and not also in the light of the eternal destiny to which we are moving? I have tried hard not to allow my capacity for compassion and grief to be dulled by constant exposure to news and pictures of human suffering. Have I, in the midst of all this, allowed my capacity for grief and outrage to be dulled by constant exposure to the human wickedness that slights the honour of your name, spurns your grace, and rebels against your wise and righteous rule? Do I long for the end of physical evil more than I long for the end of moral evil? Lord, you know me. Give me grace to know myself.

Lord, correct me. Restore the balance and perspective I need, not so that I may pride myself on my neat, orderly theology, but so that I may live in line with your truth, allowing each day to be shaped in the right way by the last Day.

Lord, renew me. Give me a new sense of awe at the burning purity of your holiness, and a fresh sense of zeal for the honour of your name.

Lord, use me. Help me to live and serve in a way that alerts people to the reality and finality of the ultimate horizons by which all our lives are bounded. Give me grace, where there is opportunity, to give bold but gracious testimony to the One who rescues us from the coming wrath.

A Benediction

May God himself direct and protect you this day. Approach your work this day in such a way that the last Day will show that you did not run or labour in vain. Approach your decisions this day as someone who is to appear before the judgment seat of Christ. Approach your relationships as one who is dealing with those who will be 'immortal horrors or everlasting splendours'. Above all, approach the throne of grace with awe and with confidence, to receive from the God who is a consuming fire both mercy and grace to help in time of need. Amen.

Theme: Transformation

'Deserts into pools of water' (Psalm 107:35)

He turns a desert into pools of water,
  a parched land into springs of water.
And there he lets the hungry dwell,
  and they establish a city to dwell in;
  they sow fields and plant vineyards,
  and get a fruitful yield...
Whoever is wise, let him give heed
  to these things;
  let men consider the steadfast
  love of the Lord.

Psalm 107: 35-37 and 43, RSV

WEEK

44

Ah! Wilderness!

The Spirit immediately drove him into the wilderness. And he was in the wilderness forty days, tempted by Satan; and he was with the wild beasts; and the angels ministered to him.

The tempter came to him and said to him, 'If you are the Son of God, command these stones to become loaves of bread.'

I will allure her and bring her into the wilderness, and speak tenderly to her. And there I will give her vineyards and make the valley of Achor a door of hope.

As the Holy Spirit says,'Today, when you hear his voice, do not harden your hearts as in the rebellion, on the day of testing in the wilderness.'

Great multitudes gathered to hear and to be healed of their infirmities. But he [Jesus] withdrew to the wilderness and prayed.

I will make the wilderness a pool of water, and the dry land springs of water.

Blessed are those who hunger and thirst for righteousness, for they shall be satisfied.

(Mark 1:12-13; Matthew 4:3; Hosea 2:14-15; Hebrews 3:7-8; Luke 5:15-16; Isaiah 41:18; Matthew 5:6 — all RSV)

The wilderness is an ambiguous place. The prophets speak of it as the setting of God's and Israel's shared intimacy of love and duty. But it was also the occasion of God's fierce disappointment: 'for forty years I loathed that generation.' It is a place of ambiguity for us also. It is the time in our lives when we are separated from our working, where disappointment and failure get to us and yet from which we return clearer in mind for having heard the unwelcome truth, refreshed in spirit in having been alone with God. We perceive the truth also that you cannot lead people out of the wilderness unless you have been there yourself (Henri Nouwen). It is the time of trial, of temptation, and so important to God is it that Jesus was led there, or was 'driven' there. He sees to it that we have times there also.

In the wilderness illusions are tested and destroyed, true motives, real weaknesses made plain; when our busyness, for which people praise us and in which we may feel secure, is revealed as flight. We fly from suspected fractures of integrity, the declaiming of large, round home truths and the suspicion that we are more hollow than we appear. When we are by ourselves, left to ourselves, do we experience ourselves as dry, restless, impatient? Do we fear the risk of shame before God? This is the wilderness. What can we learn from it?

Jesus had prophetic hope for his ministry, so movingly declared at Nazareth (and so thoroughly rejected by the congregation there). The adversary tested these hopes, sounded the disappointment. He probed for the falsities of illusion. Was there in Jesus desire, ambition, self-confidence enough, to draw him away from his centre in the Father? Did he really live in God? Did he really love the Father more than the mission? Might he be led to consider that the end might baptise the means? Could he be persuaded to by-pass disappointment and loss? Would he always wait for God? We hear echoes of these questions in our wildernesses.

Physical hunger is not an illusion, but the belief that it is the chief of our hungering is. Risk is not an illusion, but the belief that we can create risks for which God will then deliver us is. It is possible to gain the whole world and lose our soul. Yet God means that our desert experiences shall give us opportunities of looking for him beyond our darkness, feeding upon him in our hunger, resting on him from our labours, looking at the bones he shows us to be broken, that they may rejoice (Psalm 51:8).

The Father said, This is a stone. The Son would not say, That is a loaf.

George MacDonald, *Unspoken Sermons*

I have discovered that all the unhappiness of men arises from one single fact, that they cannot stay quietly in their own chamber... We do not content ourselves with the life we have in ourselves and in our own being; we desire to live an imaginary life in the mind of others, and for this purpose we endeavour to shine. We labour unceasingly to adorn and preserve this imaginary existence, and neglect the real. And if we possess calmness, or generosity, or truthfulness, we are eager to make it known, and so attach these virtues to that imaginary existence... We are so presumptuous that we wish to be known by all the world, even by people who shall come after, when we shall be no more...

Blaise Pascal, *Pensees*

The reward of the good man is to be allowed to worship in truth.

Soren Kierkegaard, *Purity of Heart*

Stanley Spencer has painted his 'Christ in the wilderness' in such a way as to bring out, in an unexpected key, the tone of Mark's 'and the wild beasts were with him'. Jesus sits on his heels in a desert empty of all life except a scorpion, which he holds in his hands and looks upon, meditatively. Isn't it a marvellous way of bringing to us both the value of solitude, of reflection, and the need for companionship in pilgrimage?

Yes, there is a sense of shame that is favourable to the Good, woe to the man who casts it off. This sense of shame is a saving companion through life. Woe to the man who breaks with it. It is in the service of sanctification and true freedom... Each one who is not more ashamed before himself than all others, if he is placed in difficulty and much tried in life, will in one way or another end by becoming the slave of men. For to be more ashamed in the presence of others than when alone, what else is this than to be more ashamed of seeming than being?

Soren Kierkegaard, *Purity of Heart*

A man does not live by his feelings any more than by bread.

George MacDonald, *Unspoken Sermons*

A most imposing gate led out on the north side, and beyond this, as far as the eye could reach, was an undulating desert over which the wintry wind was blowing... The scene was desolate beyond all words, and if ever human sorrow has left an impress on the atmosphere of a place it is surely at Kiayukwan, through whose portals for centuries past a never-ending stream of despairing humanity has filed. Disgraced officials, condemned criminals, homeless prodigals, terrified outlaws, the steps of all these have converged to that one sombre portal and through it have forever left the land of their birth. The arched walls are covered with poems wrung from broken hearts, nor can anyone leave China by this road without peculiar pain, and even tears... Among all those tragic inscriptions, from the day of our visit, one message of hope now hangs, printed in crimson letters so large and clear, that every tear-filled eye can see it:

'Christ Jesus came into the world to save sinners'.

Mildred Cable and Francesca French
Through Jade Gate and Central Asia

Father, in my imagination I sit with Jesus in his wilderness experience. I allow the silence and the solitude to come to me, become part of me. I let go all distractions, yesterday's profits and loss, tomorrow's plans and expectations. What I spend minutes in doing, my Lord spent days. Such a long time, Father, to pray and meditate, such a long time being tried, discovering your will freshly and making it his own with joy. Let me wait before you Father, surrendering my gifts and strengths and experience so as to find your strength perfect in my weakness. I should be afraid, Father, of learning of my hidden weaknesses, my flights into busyness, my sometimes testy virtue, if I did not realise that you know me through and through, and love me dearly. Teach me, Father, and let me always be learning about the way you see me — your desire to reach the real me, hidden from myself but coming to be, becoming more and more a blessing to those you give me to care about.

A Benediction

Christ be with me, Christ within me,
Christ behind me, Christ before me,
Christ beside me, Christ to win me,

Christ to comfort and restore me,
Christ beneath me, Christ above me,
Christ in quiet, Christ in danger,
Christ in hearts of all that love me,
Christ in mouth of friend and stranger.

St Patrick, tr. by C.F. Alexander

WEEK

45

Like the corners of my mind

(Alan and Marilyn Bergman)

This day shall be for you a memorial day, and you shall keep it as a feast [Passover] to the Lord: throughout your generations you shall observe it as an ordinance for ever.

You shall remember that you were a servant in the land of Egypt, and the Lord your God brought you out thence with a mighty hand and an outstretched arm.

By the waters of Babylon, there we sat down and wept, when we remembered Zion . . . How shall we sing the Lord's song in a foreign land? If I forget you, O Jerusalem, let my right hand wither! Let my tongue cleave to the roof of my mouth, if I do not remember you.

And when he had given thanks, he broke it and said: 'This is my body which is for you. Do this in remembrance of me.'

'Why do you seek the living among the dead? Remember how he told you, while he was still in Galilee, that the Son of man must be delivered into the hands of sinful men, and be crucified, and on the third day rise.' And they remembered his words.

As I remember your tears, I long night and day to see you, that I may be filled with joy.

(Exodus 12:14; Deuteronomy 5:15; Psalm 137:1,4-6; 1 Corinthians 11:24; Luke 24:5-8; 2 Timothy 1:4 — all RSV)

The totality of our experience is stored in our memories, but, paradoxically, most of us spend an inordinate amount of energy trying to forget some of our past. We're prepared to linger over 'happy memories' but many of our memories appear to be too painful to recall. They remind us of past grief or loss; they evoke feelings of guilt or failure — so we repress them.

To a certain extent, this way of dealing with painful memories is probably necessary. Without the use of defence mechanisms such as repression, the burdens of the past may become too difficult to bear. But indiscriminate repression is unhealthy. If we never come to grips with our hurtful memories, we fail to learn from the experiences which caused us pain, stunting our growth and development as persons. We become enslaved by the tyranny of our past and don't really live in the present. Feelings of anxiety and pain lie embedded in our subconscious and because we have suppressed the memories associated with them, we have forgotten the cause of those feelings. Unidentifiable painful feelings are more crippling than their original cause. They can even cause us to become afraid of the future, in case the future brings us further pain.

Henri Nouwen (*The Living Reminder*) points out that whilst good memories are visible in outer signs such as trophies, decorations, diplomas, gifts and portraits, painful memories tend to remain hidden, even from ourselves, in the corners of forgetfulness. It is only as we're prepared to make a conscious effort to remember them, as part of our life-story, that they again become available to us. Only as they are available to us can they be confronted and healed.

The Jewish concept of remembrance stressed that creative memory is able 'to make present' the past so that it could become contemporaneous. Normally, the closest we Christians come to acknowledging the validity of this concept is in our celebration of the Lord's Supper. Perhaps it's time to apply it to other aspects of our Christian lives. Perhaps it's time to use our God-given talent for creative memory, recalling our hurtful memories so that God can heal them.

When I use my memory, I ask it to produce whatever it is that I wish to remember. Some things it produces immediately; some are forthcoming only after a delay, as though they were being brought out from some inner hiding place; others come spilling from the memory thrusting themselves upon us when what we want is something quite different, as much as to say 'Perhaps we are what you want to remember?' . . . All this goes on inside me, in the vast cloisters of my memory. In it are the sky, the earth, and the sea, ready at my summons, together with everything that I have ever perceived in them by my senses... In it I meet myself as well. I remember myself and what I have done, when and where I did it, and the state of my mind at the time... The power of the memory is prodigious, my God. It is a vast immeasurable sanctuary. Who can plumb its depths? And yet it is a faculty of my soul.

Augustine, *Confessions*

Most of our human emotions are closely related to our memory. Remorse is a biting memory, guilt is an accusing memory, gratitude is a joyful memory, and all such emotions are deeply influenced by the way we have integrated past events into our way of being in the world. In fact, we perceive our world with our memories.

Henri Nouwen, *The Living Reminder*

Enter into yourself, then, and see that your soul loves itself most fervently; that it could not love itself unless it knew itself, nor know itself unless it remembered itself, because our intellect grasps only what is present to our memory.

Bonaventure, *The Soul's Journey into God*

The personal unconscious contains lost memories, painful ideas that are repressed (i.e. forgotton on purpose).

Carl Jung, *'On the Psychology of the Unconscious'*

Remembering is the beginning of freedom from the covert power of the remembered thing or occurrence.

Max Scheler, *On the Eternal Man*

Now there are some men who resemble the animal known as the lynx: according to Saint Jerome, they remember only what is before them, and once they turn their backs, they forget everything they cannot see. Then there are some we call idiots and fools because they wander about unaware with their mouths open wide to catch flies. Seneca says of them that they waste their lives because they do not think of the past... Memory is the place wherein is stored the treasure of the wise; it is the ark of truth, the living book of man, the womb where the soul cherishes her sons so that they are not killed by forgetfulness... Do not be a sickly stomach unable to digest what it has eaten, for if you are you will not retain the food of good teaching in the stomach of your memory and spiritually your life will be depleted.

Francisco de Osuna, *'The Third Spiritual Alphabet'*

For the past which we remember through Jesus Christ is not the serial but the enduring past. When we speak of the past in internal history we do not refer to events which no longer have reality in the world... Our past is what we are... Our past is our present in our conscious and unconscious memory. To understand such a present past is to understand one's self and, through understanding, to reconstruct.

H. Richard Neibuhr, *The Meaning of Revelation*

What is the ground for such faith in God's sovereignty and deliverance? As throughout the biblical record, it is *memory*. Remembrance of what God has done in the past gives rise to hopes for what he yet shall do to deliver his people. Just as Old Testament experience and faith grew out of reflection on memories of the exodus and covenant when God's mighty arm delivered his people from bondage to Egypt, so here God's great gift of himself and his forgiveness in Christ is the sufficient ground for confidence about what is really happening in present and future... Faith is grounded in memory but lives in hope.

Gordon D. Kaufman, commenting on Romans 8 in *Systematic Theology: A Historicist Perspective*

Memory came to my aid and made me feel God's presence; my heart, taking comfort, sought to embrace the cross.

Jacopone da Todi, *The Lauds*

Almighty God, right now I'm allowing my memory to wander haphazardly through the past events of my life. It's like retracing my footsteps through a long corridor, occasionally stopping outside a closed door, having forgotten what was in that particular room.

Somewhat timidly I'm opening the first door, Lord... I'm looking upon the experiences of my childhood... The next door is slightly ajar and as I peek in memories of my adolescence and young adulthood come flooding back... I had forgotten that those people ever existed. They were so much a part of my life then... How could I have forgotten?

I'm savouring the happy moments, Lord — but one or two memories are a little painful. I'm not sure if I want to open any more doors, especially not the one in that dark part of the corridor. I have the feeling that it leads to a room with very hurtful memories. See, there's a big padlock with chains on that door!

Lord, give me the courage to open that door after all. I want you to help me to deal with whatever I have to confront... Where forgiveness is called for, may I have the assurance of your forgiveness. Where reconciliation needs to be effected, grant me your strength to approach the person whom I have allowed to become estranged. Where the loneliness of grief is re-awakened, may I be comforted by the knowledge that you share my grief.

A Benediction

Seek the Lord and his strength, seek his presence continually! Remember the wonderful works he has done, his miracles and the judgments he uttered. Have no anxiety about anything, but in everything by prayer and supplication with thanksgiving let your requests be known to God.

(Psalm 105:5; RSV; Philippians 4:6, RSV)

Talk is cheap

Suppose a brother or a sister is in rags with not enough food for the day, and one of you says, 'Good luck to you, keep yourselves warm, and have plenty to eat', but does nothing to supply their bodily needs, what is the good of that? So with faith; if it does not lead to action, it is in itself a lifeless thing.

Religion that is pure and genuine in the sight of God the Father will show itself by such things as visiting orphans and widows in their distress, and keeping oneself uncontaminated by the world.

At the beginning God expressed himself. That personal expression... was God. So the word of God became a human being and lived among us.

Let what you say be simply 'yes' or 'no'; anything more than this comes from evil.

How beautiful on the mountains are the feet of one who brings good news, who heralds peace, brings happiness, proclaims salvation, and tells Zion 'your God is King'.

(James 2:15-17, NEB; James 1:27, Phillips; John 1:1,14, Phillips; Matthew 5:37, RSV; Isaiah 52:7, JB)

Communication is the first essential ingredient in any relationship: between marriage partners, parents and children, labour and management or in international affairs. Failure to communicate lies at the root of all tension, friction and fear. Mankind's objects — to achieve peace and reconciliation — are possible only through real human communication. Communication is a bridge fashioned out of words, feelings, gestures, 'body language' and attitudes. Words are the most common vehicles of communication.

Words are amazingly powerful. They can sway crowds for

good or ill. They can bring relief, hope, encouragement. The gospel is couched in words — the greatest words in the world: love, forgiveness, grace, reconciliation, faith. It is the good news about Jesus which has the power to save and dignify human life.

But words, rather than being a *vehicle* of deep communication, can be a barrier to effective communication. Words are too often substituted for action. They can be offered instead of sacrificial and loving involvement in another's needs. Words can be the world's most devalued currency.

The most powerful temptation to beset the preacher — or any Christian who wants to communicate the gospel — is to offer words (however true and orthodox those words may be) instead of offering him/her self. Great Christian words of faith all too easily become mechanical formulas.

Words are a cop-out whenever they are cheapened.

God's means of person-to-person communication extended beyond the words of the law and the prophets, to incarnation — the Word becoming flesh!

Christians dare not forget that incarnation lies at the heart of the gospel and its communication. There is no escape for the Christian who takes Christ's commission and method seriously.

The whole anguish of religious broadcasting is that we are transmitting a message of love and it is costing us nothing. It costs us nothing to say 'I love you' or 'God loves you' except the breath it takes to speak into a microphone. There is a powerful missionary movement being built up around the use of private satellites and cable television, based mainly in the United States. From these sources, electronic missionaries placed 23,000 miles in the air will preach the gospel to the people of Africa, Asia, and South America. But you see, it costs nothing. In terms of personal cost — of the real giving of self — it doesn't cost a thing. Therefore it is a ghost, a distortion of what Christianity is about. Unless I actually stand alongside you — not as an electronic ghost, but as someone who shares your life, who sweats, fears and hungers, and who risks the same diseases, it is not what Christianity is all about.

Colin Morris, Head of Religious Broadcasting, BBC

The most immutable barrier in the world is between one person's thoughts, and another.

William James

That blackguard who uses the science of speech more to blackmail and swindle than to teach.

Henry Higgins, in Lerner and Lowe's *My Fair Lady*

Words are, of course, the most powerful drug in the world.

Rudyard Kipling

The finest possible communication... (brings another) into a relationship instead of isolating him.

Berthold Brecht, *Radio as an apparatus for Communication*

In the beginning was the Word. The Word was made Flesh. His word was his bond. He was true to his word... And it is startling to discover that 'the word', whose possession marks man off from the rest of creation, whose employment is the key to his self-knowledge, his relationship with others, and his intellectual, spiritual and material evolution, leads his understanding as far as it can go into the inmost nature of the Trinity. The word plies between heaven and earth, has application to both God and man, and is the sign through which each, in that many-layered expression, gives himself away...

The Word which is Christ is the most translucent window opening onto the inner nature of God. And the words we use in everyday life are in similar fashion windows through which we know each other. The word is not our only means of communication. But since the dawn of language — and how awesome and mysterious must that dawn have been — words have been the most universal, most serviceable and most flexible vehicle of human communication.

Words are hard to pin down. Far worse is the damage we human beings inflict upon words by negligence or malice. Words are the coin of mutual trust. When we use them carelessly, twist them out of shape, force them into the service of falsehood and half-truths, we debase that coinage and undermine the trust that keeps society functioning. Christ tells us that he is Truth. It is the Devil who is the father of lies. To be a follower of Christ entails being a servant of the truth; and that service requires that we keep the vehicle of truth, our language, our words, in good repair.

John Harriott, 'Words and the Word', *The Tablet*

Words and magic were in the beginning one and the same thing, and even today words retain much of their magical power. By words one of us can give to another the greatest happiness or bring about utter despair... Words call forth emotions and are universally the means by which we influence our fellow creatures. Therefore *let us not despise the use of words.*

Sigmund Freud

In Hebrew the term *dabar* means both 'word' and 'deed'. Thus to say something is to do something. 'I love you.' 'I hate you.' 'I forgive you.' 'I am afraid.' Who knows what such words do, but whatever it is, it can never be undone. Something that lay hidden in the heart is irrevocably released through speech into time, is given substance and tossed like a stone into the pool of history, where the concentric rings lap out endlessly.

Words are power, essentially the power of creation. By my words I both discover and create who I am. By my words I elicit a word from you. Through our conversation we create one another...

God never seems to weary of trying to get himself across. Word after word he tries in search of the right word. When the Creation itself doesn't seem to say it right — sun, moon, stars, all of it — he tries flesh and blood... Jesus as the *mot juste* of God.

Frederick Buechner, *Wishful Thinking*

Lord, give us grace, and give us the spirit of adventure and sacrifice that will transform each of us from being a mere vehicle of words, to becoming living words of life and hope, a word of God to others.

O Lord, I know that men and women in past ages have heard your word, for it is so true today; it changed their lives and made them feel part of a great purpose. Grant that I may relate the truth of your word in the past, to life today. I pray also to speak to me anew, new things under new conditions, for the sake of him who was the word made flesh and is the eternal word, revealing meaning and truth, even Jesus Christ, my teacher and my Lord.

George Appleton, *Journey for a Soul*

Lord, never once did you substitute words for actions. You achieved the perfect balance between what you said and what you did. Of all people who ever lived, you are the only one whose actions were the personification of his words. And whose words were the commentary on his actions. You did not shrink from total involvement with individuals in their need, nor even humanity in its suffering and lostness. And the word you brought was yourself. Offering words, even good words, is so often for us a way to avoid offering ourselves. Help us to follow your paths of costly caring and true communication, because it is in the same way as the Father sent you — the way of incarnation — that you send us. It frightens us, but we know it is the only way to touch, heal and save others. Lord give us this grace. Amen.

A Benediction

Go forth into the world in peace; be of good courage; hold fast that which is good; render to no one evil for evil; strengthen the faint-hearted; support the weak; help the afflicted; honour everyone; love and serve the Lord, rejoicing in the power of the Holy Spirit. Amen.

WEEK

The Sunday menu

(Paul Scherer)

The language of the cross may be illogical to those who are not on the way to salvation, but those of us who are on the way see it as God's power to save. As scripture says: I shall destroy the wisdom of the wise and bring to nothing all the learning of the learned. Where are the philosophers now? Where are the scribes? Where are any of our thinkers today? Do you see now how God has shown up the foolishness of human wisdom? If it was God's wisdom that human wisdom should not know God, it was because God wanted to save those who have faith through the foolishness of the message that we preach.

Herald and preach the Word! Keep your sense of urgency (stand by, be at hand and ready, whether the opportunity seems to be favourable or unfavourable, whether it is convenient or inconvenient, whether it be welcome or unwelcome, you as preacher of the Word are to show people in what way their lives are wrong) and convince them, rebuking and correcting, warning and urging and encouraging them, being unflagging and inexhaustible in patience and teaching. For the time is coming when [people] will not tolerate (endure) sound and wholesome instruction, but having ears itching [for something pleasing and gratifying], they will gather to themselves one teacher after another to a considerable number, chosen to satisfy their own liking and to foster the errors they hold, and will turn aside from hearing the truth and wander off into myths and man-made fictions.

In my vision I saw another angel, flying in mid-heaven, with an eternal gospel to proclaim to the inhabitants of the earth, to every nation and tribe and language and people.

'Reverence God,' he shouted for all to hear, 'and give him the glory, for the hour of his judgment has come! Worship him who made heaven and earth, the sea and the springs of water!'

(1 Corinthians 1:18-23, JB; 2 Timothy 4:2-4, AMP; Revelation 14:6-7, Barclay)

Rudolf Bultmann was one who took preaching most seriously, so seriously in fact that he believed the salvation occurrence was in the very act of preaching and only there. Bultmann held that Christ meets us in the preaching of the cross and resurrection. He believed that 'the sermon is the proclamation of the word of God as attested in the Bible, that it must be understood as an address which strikes the heart, and in that address Jesus Christ speaks to us.' For Bultmann, the 'risen Christ is present in the proclaiming word'.

The pulpit is not simply a talkplace, but rather a powerhouse. Unfortunately, we've become like Humpty Dumpty in Lewis Carroll's *Through the Looking Glass*. Humpty said, 'When I use a word it means just what I choose it to mean — neither more nor less.' Yet the preacher is commissioned to declare God's word as being full of power. After all, when God spoke, the word came into being. Hebrews 4:12 reminds us, 'For the word of God is living and active.' Preaching must forever hover between the cross and the empty tomb and the preacher must declare the redemptive power of Christ to an audience who have ears to hear what the Spirit is saying to the churches.

For those who listen

Preachers are under almost irresistible pressure from their congregations to become counsellors, managers of an important community enterprise, administrators of a highly organised and going concern dedicated to the spiritual, social, and cultural improvement and welfare of mankind, both locally and nationally; while the magnitude of the demands made on them is matched only by the ludicrous inadequacy of what is provided by way of resource in finance and personnel; so that the Sunday menu is likely to consist largely of half-hour homilies on handicaps and happiness. There is no time for anything else; and often enough to constitute a frightening conspiracy against the pulpit, there is comparatively little desire for anything else.

If there are not many great preachers today, neither are there great listeners. If criticism can be levelled at the pulpit, it must be also at the pew. D.L. Moody is reputed to have said on one occasion, 'If you freeze me in the vestry, how do you expect me to burn in the pulpit?' And, we may add, the refrigeration can be in the pew too. We have lack of prayer and preparation before the service, a lack of expectancy — as though God were not present, or at least not interested in manifesting himself. This can all be inferred by the rush to church on the part of some — strangely, the same minority being late each time, or the chatter, noise and movement beforehand of those who are in time. In some churches the worshippers give the impression that they expect nothing to happen *before* the sermon, and in others that they expect nothing to happen *during* it! The truth is that if we have no Spurgeon, Maclaren or Alexander Whyte, we also have few who would tolerate the weight and length of their sermons. The demand for shorter sermons, while well-directed in some cases, may well be symptomatic of the decline in the ability to listen fruitfully.

Source unknown

A divine means of communication is the teaching and preaching of the Word of God. It is God who has taught us to communicate. His method has become our method. Verbal symbols express the thought of God which we are to hear and heed. We are to communicate one with another in every good thing. The art of Christian communication is the supreme means of transmitting divine truth into mortal and unilluminated human minds.

'There is a law of propagation of divine life analogous to the propagation of vegetable and animal life. The various productions of the vegetable kingdom are not new and independent products. The life of the parent plant is in the seed which it produces. The life of the parent animal passes over to its offspring. So in the church it is the general law that the spiritual life is communicated through and by living members of the church. This is not always the case with communication of spiritual life. We might as well ask why the Spirit does not operate without the written word, as why he so seldom operates without the living preacher. In both cases, we can only say: "Even so, Father, for so it seemed good in thy sight" ' (B.P. Warfield).

The objective of hearing is salvation, spiritual edification, emerging in obedience to God's holy will. 'Take heed *how* ye hear.' Each mind must be prepared for the reception of the truth.

Article from the *Watchman Examiner*

Preaching is about *his* story... the story of the creative Logos, the story of the people of God of the Old Testament, but supremely, preaching is about his story, the Christ story. Preaching is about the once-for-all there-and-then saving acts of God in Christ. If it is not about *that* then, however interesting or edifying, it is not Christian preaching. At the heart of all Christian preaching (implicitly or explicitly) lies Christian dogma. Does that sound dull? Dorothy Sayers was right when she said: 'The dogma is the drama.'

But preaching is also about *our* stories... the story of our world, our societies, our churches, our individual lives in all the infinite complexity of the strange amalgam of glory and shame that *they* present. God did not close up shop on the day of the Ascension or the day of Pentecost. Christ is not sitting at the right hand of God slumped half asleep waiting for someone to nudge him awake when he is due back on the stage of human history for his second coming. Christ is awake and alive, our great high priest and advocate, active and potent in our world here-and-now.

Ian Pitt-Watson, *Theology, Notes and News*

For those who preach

We will make our greatest impact in preaching when we dare to make available to the woundedness of others what we have learned through an honest grappling with our own woundedness. Instead of trying to dazzle people with the breadth of our learning or to pass on lists of secondhand information that may or may not be existentially relevant to their situations, I can help most when I am honest enough to lay bare my own wounds and acknowledge what is saving and helping me. Truth that I have found, or better still, truth that has found me — this is the sort of material that rightly belongs in the preaching event. Lloyd Ogilvie once observed that only the things that have happened to us can happen through us. I believe this is correct. One of the qualities that gives authenticity and urgency to our preaching is our own involvement in the very realities we proclaim.

John R. Claypool, *The Preaching Event*

The methods of the nineteenth-century preachers were largely effective for their age, but they have become increasingly less so as culture has shifted its interest. This is the reason many preachers sound sadly Victorian, or like chaplains to a literary society. What has happened to the sermon is what McLuhan also describes — the lively communication medium for one generation has become the art form for the next generation.

Clyde E. Fant, *Preaching for Today*

Do not regard preparations for the pulpit as a trifling thing; and do not rush upon your holy duties without devout preparation for the hallowed service... Get your message fresh from God.

Charles Haddon Spurgeon

Great God of the spoken word, help me to hear your message to me through preaching. Help me prepare myself whether I deliver your word or hear your word. Make me tune myself to the wind of the Spirit, listening carefully to what the Spirit is saying.

Father in heaven, help me not to cast the matter of preaching aside lightly but to take the whole matter of preaching seriously and to understand that through the mystery of preaching you present your divine message to your creation.

Loving Lord, help me prepare well as I get ready to send out an interpretation of your word to those who listen. Give me a perceptive mind as I search the scriptures, a ready tongue as I deliver your word and an understanding heart so that my hearers may see Christ in me as their hope of glory.

Gracious Lord, may the vehicle of preaching be the means of many coming to understand your ways with your people.

May we all — preachers and listeners — place prime importance on the place of your word in our worship, when we gather, and when we are scattered in the world.

A Benediction

May your word, O Lord, which brought creation into being, which brought redemption to the human race in the life and death and resurrection of Jesus, empower us who preach, or who listen, to be your 'lived word' in our world. Through Jesus Christ our Lord. Amen.

WEEK

Birds never sing in caves

(Henry David Thoreau)

Then the Lord said to Moses, 'Go in to Pharoah and say to him, "Thus says the Lord, Let my people go, that they may serve me..." ' And he gave to Moses, when he had made an end of speaking with him upon Mount Sinai, the two tables of the testimony, tables of stone, written with the finger of God.

You shall hallow the fiftieth year and proclaim liberation in the land for all its inhabitants. You shall make this your year of jubilee... You must not victimise one another, but you shall fear your God, because I am the Lord your God. Observe my statutes, keep my judgments and carry them out; and you shall live in the land in security.

I was a stranger and you received me... in prison and you visited me.

The Spirit of the Lord is upon me... to proclaim liberty to the captives... to set free the oppressed.

If the Son sets you free, then you will be really free.

Freedom is what we have — Christ has set us free! But do not let this freedom become an excuse for letting your physical desires control you.

Paul, a slave of Christ.

(Exodus 8:1 and 31:18, RSV; Leviticus 25:10 and 17-18, NEB; Matthew 25:35-36, GNB; Luke 4:18, GNB; John 8:36, GNB; Galatians 5:1 and 13, GNB; Romans 1:1, RSV footnote)

Only one in five individuals in our world's 200 nations enjoys full political and civil freedoms. That is, only twenty per cent can participate in bringing about changes in their government, may assemble, speak or worship freely, or may sue the authorities and have a chance of winning the case in court.

In the biblical world, notions of 'freedom' existed in the context of widespread slavery. Slaves were totally owned by their masters. They could be set free only if the appropriate price was paid. So the Bible constantly refers to God as Redeemer of his people, the One who pays the price to ransom us.

There are, of course, many kinds of captivities. Every human being is a slave to something. Those two influential nineteenth-century determinists, Marx and Freud, claimed we are all unfree. Marx saw us controlled by the dialectic of history. Freud saw unconscious forces as being omnipotent.

But think about it for a moment. If there is no human freedom, then ideas like 'true' and 'false', 'good' and 'bad' have no significance. Albert Schweitzer was free to minister to sick Africans at Lambarene; Adolph Hitler was free to slaughter Jews in Europe.

Into this world of 'slaves whose wills are free' comes the Son of God promising deliverance from all the sinful, selfish entanglements of our lives. Jesus calls us and liberates us to become his servants and co-redeemers. Service for him is 'perfect freedom', the ultimate liberation.

Stone walls do not a prison make
Nor iron bars a cage;
Minds innocent and quiet take
That for a hermitage.

If I have freedom in my love
And in my soul am free,
Angels alone, that soar above
Enjoy such liberty.

Richard Lovelace, *To Althea, From Prison*

Some people think they can imagine a creature which was free but had no possibility of going wrong; I cannot. If a thing is free to be good it is also free to be bad... Free will, though it makes evil possible, is also the only thing that makes possible any love or goodness or joy worth having... Nothing that you have not given away will ever be really yours.

Nothing in you that has not died will ever be raised from the dead. Look for Christ and you will find him, and with him everything else thrown in.

C.S. Lewis, *Mere Christianity*

'Give us more freedom!' is the constant cry today. This is valid when directed against tyranny or oppression or exploitation, but many have pushed the concept far beyond that. The freedom they now claim has come to mean freedom from all unpleasantness; from hardship, from discipline, from the pain of self-sacrifice.

Arthur Gordon, 'Freedom is a Two-edged Sword'

We were never more free than during the German occupation. We had lost all our rights, beginning with the right to talk. Every day we were insulted to our faces and had to take it. Because the Nazi venom seeped into our thoughts, every accurate thought was a conquest. Because an all-powerful police tried to force us to hold our tongues, every word took on the value of a solemn declaration of principles. Because we were hunted down, every gesture had the weight of a solemn commitment.

Jean Paul Sartre, describing life in the French Resistance in *The Republic of Silence*

It is a rare peasant who, once promoted to overseer, does not become more of a tyrant towards his former comrades than the owner himself.

Paulo Freire, *Pedagogy of the Oppressed*

Sooner or later, money covers the eyes with dangerous scales and freezes the lips, the hands, and the heart . . .

Dom Helder Camara, *The Church and Colonialism*

The New Testament describes three major tyrants from which Christ can set us free. They concern our past (freedom from guilt), the present (freedom from self) and the future (freedom from fear). One of the most thrilling notes of the gospel is the freedom from guilt, self and fear which Christ offers us today. By his death our guilt can be expunged. By the power of his resurrection we can be turned inside out, from self to unself.

And his exaltation to God's right hand assures us that all the ogres of which we are afraid are under his feet. Once freed from these tyrants we are free for God and for others.

John Stott, 'Authority and Freedom'

In Jesus' famous parable of the prodigal son, the young man comes running home shattered by the world as it really is, and says: 'Father, make me a hired servant. Take over my life. Now I don't want any freedom at all.' This young man was fortunate in the kind of father he had. All of us are tempted to do what the prodigal did — to be so beaten by failure or complexity that we run from freedom into some form of cosy bondage. This is why people drink too much or conform or lamely acquiesce to some authoritarian structure. It is easier to be an object than a subject.

John Claypool, from an unpublished sermon

Licence they mean when they cry liberty.

John Milton, *Sonnets*, 12

Make me a captive, Lord,
And then I shall be free;
Force me to render up my sword
And I shall conqueror be.

I sink in life's alarms
When by myself I stand;
Imprison me within thine arms,
And strong shall be my hand.

George Matheson

Long my imprisoned spirit lay
Fast bound in sin and nature's night.
Thine eye diffused a quickening ray —
I woke, the dungeon flamed with light.
My chains fell off, my heart was free,
I rose, went forth, and followed thee.

Charles Wesley

You said there is perfect freedom in your service, Lord. Well, I don't feel perfectly free. I'm a captive to myself. I do what I want. I have it all my own way. There is no freedom at all for me in this, Jesus. Today I feel like a slave bound in chains and branded by a hot iron because I'm a captive to my own will and don't give an honest damn about you or your will. You're over there where I'm keeping you, outside my real life. How can I go on being such a lousy hypocrite? Come over here, where I don't want you to come. Jesus, help me to let you be yourself in my life — so that I can be myself.

Malcolm Boyd, *Are You Running with Me, Jesus?*

Lord, I'm thinking about my own captivities. I name the areas of my bondage in your presence... Lord, help me to be free. Sometimes I'm 'driven' by the very things that are meant to be fulfilling. There's both a death-wish and a life-wish within me, striving for mastery. Free me from any slavery to my passions and desires, and help me to be disciplined, self-controlled.

Lord, free me from such common tyrannies as:

* *others' opinions, so that I'm too concerned with their adulation.*
* *my own self-despisings, of being 'allergic to myself'.*
* *the insecurity of believing I'm always right.*
* *legalisms of many kinds, so that I'm more known for what I don't believe than for what I do believe.*
* *easy formulas, which save me from the hard work of thinking too much.*

Father, help me to be the kind of 'freedom fighter' Jesus was. First help me to serve God — above any of this world's pharoahs. Then enable me to hear the cries of the wretched of the earth and do what I can to alleviate their sufferings. God of the Exodus-event, of the Easter-event, deliver us from our sins and our selfishness. You, Lord, have been in the business of liberating slaves for a long time. You lead the march to freedom. Deliver me out of my bondage, sorrow and night. And, perhaps through me, be present with those who today do not experience freedom from want, freedom from fear, or freedom of belief and worship.

A Benediction

Depart now in the fellowship of God the Father and, as you go, remember: in the goodness of God you were born into this world; by the grace of God you have been kept all the day long, even to this hour; and by the love of God, fully revealed in the life of Jesus, you are being redeemed. Amen.

WEEK

49

The power of powerlessness

The Lord said, '. . .my power is made perfect in weakness.'

The weakness of God is stronger than men.

God chose what is weak in the world to shame the strong.

When I am weak, then I am strong.

If anyone strikes you on the right cheek, turn to him the other also.

And I was with you in weakness and in much fear and trembling; and my speech and my message were not in plausible words of wisdom, but in demonstration of the Spirit and of power.

My God, my God why have you forsaken me?

. . .sown in weakness, . . .raised in power.

(2 Corinthians 12:9; 1 Corinthians 1:25; 1 Corinthians 1:27; 2 Corinthians 12:10; Matthew 5:39; 1 Corinthians 2:3-4; Psalm 22:1; 1 Corinthians 15:43 — all RSV)

Popular religion sometimes has trouble with the helplessness of the cross. Something within us seems to resist identifying powerlessness with God. How can such a God help with all the problems of the world? How can such a God help me with the issues that drag my life down? The classic image of God as the *deus ex machina* makes a lot more sense to many people. Pray hard enough and he swoops down and patches things up, the all-powerful deity at our 'beck and call' if we have faith enough. But God as helpless — never.

Well, I have a tale of discovery to tell. I have at times felt overwhelmed with life. It was just such a time, a very specific time, when I sat down at my desk wanting to give up. Nothing was working out. I felt tension over just about everything in my life — my work, my relationships, God, you name it. I felt bereft, without direction.

I picked up a hymn book, and flipping through I came eventually to the hymn printed out below, *Men go to God when they are sorely placed,* the extraordinary testimony of Dietrich Bonhoeffer. But it was not the message about going to God for help that touched me. It was rather the message of God's helplessness, powerlessness, and *our* going to his support in his hour of need. It was this that touched me and broke open my soul. I wept deeply, hungrily, as something within my helplessness touched the helplessness of God in Christ on the cross. God himself identified with me, and I with him in a moment of loneliness and helplessness. Nothing is in vain after such a moment of recognition. This most terrible helplessness is the ultimate power that will draw all things to itself, resisting nothing and in time carrying all before it.

It's not easy to be the same after such a moment. Recognition of God's helplessness is transforming, opening the soul to new energies and peace as life is accepted deeply in all its countless confusions.

In a generation when the most active Christianity seems to be strongly influenced by the charismatic movement and spiritual enthusiasm generally, the helplessness of God can be an unwelcome message. But it is really the very counterbalance St Paul offered the Corinthian church, under stress from spiritual enthusiasm. Without the cross, with God helpless and dead, the Spirit in Christian consciousness remains something external, something coming to us from without. And it often doesn't take much for the ego to start to try and manipulate the Spirit conceived in such a way. But with recognition of God's powerlessness in Christ's death, the message of the cross, the Spirit becomes for us an indwelling, transforming energy from within, changing us personally. It is this second conception that is the Christian conception of Spirit, I believe.

So the message of God's powerlessness, of his helplessness is crucial. Without it there is no basis for the identification of God with us, no lever for the mystery of Christ in us to go to work in our consciousness, humbling us by helpless love and raising us in eternal Spirit.

Men go to God when they are sorely placed,
pray him for succour, for his peace, for bread,

for mercy, for them sinning, sick or dead
All men do so in faith or unbelief.

Men go to God when he is sorely placed,
find him poor, scorned, unsheltered, without bread,
whelmed under weight of evil, weak or dead
Christians stand by God in his hour of grief.

God goes to man when he is sorely placed
body and spirit feeds he with his bread
For every man, he as a man hangs dead:
forgiven life he gives me through his death.

Dietrich Bonhoeffer, versified by W.H. Farquharson

. . . theology has succeeded for centuries in keeping at arm's length the full conceptual implications of discovering God among the dispossessed and disfigured and dead. We have lacked the daring to allow the presence of God in the cross, and his affirming of those represented by its suffering and incapacity, seriously to reform our static, painless and authoritarian categories of divine being and doing. Only recently, when the external circumstances of our history and culture have finally compelled us to come to terms with the weakness of the Reign of God have we begun to rethink such notions as power, agency, causality, perfection: basic building blocks of theological ontology.

Alan E. Lewis, 'God as Cripple: Disability, Personhood and the Reign of God'

He saved others . . . and yet he cannot, or will not save himself from the hostile powers that close in upon him as his ministry proceeds . . . Finally he is bound, nailed helpless to a cross and left to die. The Saviour cannot save himself . . . The saving power of God is to be carried and communicated by those who have no power to save themselves . . . The strange truth about the Church is that when it can claim to be strong it is weak, and when it shares in the weakness of Christ it is truly the bearer of the power of God for the salvation of men and women everywhere.

Leslie Newbigin, 'Not whole without the handicapped'

The SS hung two Jewish men and a boy before the assembled inhabitants of the camp. The men died quickly but the death struggle of the boy lasted half-an-hour. 'Where is God? Where is he?' a man behind me asked. As the boy, after a long time, was still in agony on the rope, I heard the man cry again, 'Where is God now?' And I heard a voice within me answer, 'Here he is — he is hanging here on this gallows. . .'

Elie Wiesel Night, tr. by Stella Rodway, quoted by John Shea, *Stories of God*

A life of true sacrifice
we here proclaim
be lifted up O sweet Jesus
in suffering and shame.
Your life is broken open now
you hang upon your cross
the pain and agony of life
are summed up in your lot.

Your mouth from which sweet poetry flowed
your hands that healed the lame
your eyes that shone with righteous love
all sunk in sin and shame
O shattered spirit, crushed and dead
O broken, naked frame
in this dreadful hour of agony
your glory lays its claim.

Gather people, gather round
come from far and wide
life's meaning lies within that breast
so bruised and lifted high.

David Oliphant

In the deep places of my being
where light trickles
In the caverns of my soul
where time has no meaning
In the alley ways inflicted with the stench
of broken promises
Clinging to the rhythms of my mind
It's here I weep and wonder.

Was it like this for you, Lord?

It's here a faint hope dawns
and creeps round jagged edges,
It is here inmost laughter
breaks in hollow rings,
Life's daring, reckoning, cries,
in great and clanging cymbals
and the fear of being lost
crushes every hopeful stirring.

Was it like this for you, Lord?

And it's here the lingering moment
and the invitation to embrace
sifts the marrow of my being
and stirs the blackness sleeping.
It's here faint light gathers itself
into blazing day,
revealing not an empty dream
but a truth that passes reason,
a life unquenchable, with nail prints in his hands,
coming walking on the water of my mind.

Thank you, Jesus, thank you, thank you.

Father, help us to surrender to your powerlessness in Christ, so that our souls may be imbued with the power and mystery of 'Christ in us, the hope of glory'. Grant, Lord, a true knowledge of the cross and what this means for our daily lives, the lives of our families, our nation, the world. Keep us from wanting only a God who intervenes and fixes things up, and grant us rather deep hunger for the God eternally present in the powerlessness of life, manifesting transformation from within. This God is you, Father, the God of Jesus Christ. Amen.

A Benediction
Let the powerlessness of God on the cross embrace you in every aspect of your life. No longer strive to emulate someone

who acts out of desire and power, but rest in that terrible grace that emerges out of nothingness. Go now, in this grace, this life. It is eternal. It is God. It is you, *in so far as you dare to live in it.* Amen.

WEEK

Time is my inheritance

(Goethe)

I trust in you, O Lord; I say, 'You are my God.' My times are in your hands... Let your face shine on your servant; save me in your unfailing love.

How many are your works, O Lord! In wisdom you made them all; the earth is full of your creatures... These all look to you to give them their food at the proper time. When you give it to them, they gather it up; when you open your hand, they are satisfied with good things.

There is a time for everything, and a season for every activity under heaven... He has made everything beautiful in its time.

When the time had fully come, God sent his Son.

'The time has come,' [Jesus] said. 'The kingdom of God is near. Repent and believe the good news!'

'My time has not yet come...' 'The right time for me has not yet come...' They tried to seize him, but no-one laid a hand on him, because his time had not yet come.

'The hour has come for the Son of Man to be glorified...' 'Now my heart is troubled, and what shall I say? "Father, save me from this hour"? No, it was for this very reason I came to this hour...' Jesus knew that the time had come for him to leave this world and go to the Father... 'Father, the time has come. Glorify your Son, that your Son may glorify you.'

Let us not become weary in doing good, for at the proper time we will reap a harvest if we do not give up. Therefore, as we have opportunity, let us do good to all people, especially to those who belong to the family of believers.

Teach us to number our days aright, that we may gain a heart of wisdom.

(Psalm 31:14-16; 104:24, 27-28; Ecclesiastes 3:1,11; Galatians 4:4; Mark 1:15; John 2:4; 7:6,30; 12:23,27; 13:1; 17:1; Galatians 6:9-10; Psalm 90:12 — all NIV)

Observation of the world around us might tempt us to deny one of the most crucial tenets of our faith — the providence of God. The regular succession of 'natural disasters', the proliferation of wars, the seemingly undeserved suffering or untimely death of unknown millions (or perhaps of known individuals) may prompt us to ask whether the God we believe to have been in control of the events of biblical days is still 'alive and well' in these last decades of the twentieth century.

Can God still deliver those who trust in him from their enemies — the contemporary enemies of injustice, oppression, persecution, secularism, nuclear threat? Does God still undertake to satisfy the basic needs of the creatures he has created, even in an era when the gulf between rich and poor grows constantly wider? Has the coming of Christ and the establishment of the kingdom of God really brought good news to the poor, freedom for the prisoners, sight to the blind and release for the oppressed? Has the expectation of the church that a lifestyle faithful to the gospel will eventually result in the reaping of a harvest been vindicated by results? Is our belief in the providence of God just a figment of our imagination, or a reality that has practical, observable implications in our lives?

While it would be naive to imagine that we can rightly discern all the detailed purposes of God in our times, and while it might seem glib to say to the oppressed, the hurting, the bewildered, that God is still in control, we must constantly hold onto the biblical notion of *kairos* time — the right time, the proper time, the time of opportunity and decision. God never promised us that all the facets of human life would fall into place according to *our* timetable and wisdom. But he does encourage us to see him at work in *his* time, both in the affairs of humanity and in our personal lives. Jesus' ministry, characterised as it was by a strong awareness of *kairos* time, is a perfect model for us, as we seek to discern the ways of God in the world.

All of life can be transformed as we come to realise, not just in theory, but in the everyday dilemmas and decisions of life, that 'time is our inheritance'. The perfect timing of God in the events of our individual and corporate lives can be trusted, and will enrich us beyond any earthly treasure. And God's purpose for us is that we should be so alert to the wisdom that he promises to provide, that we respond to his prompting to act on his behalf, in his time, in a world that so desperately needs to experience that God has made everything 'beautiful in its time'.

Time is not an enemy to be killed. It is a gift to be used. It has to be used right now, because time is not a circle, it is a line. The face of a clock is round, seducing some people into believing that time is unlimited because it keeps going round and round. If time is a circle, they think they will always have another chance. The calendar is round, and some people think they will always have a chance to do next year what they failed to do this year. Time is not round. Time is a line! Every second that passes flies off into space and is gone.

Oswald C.J. Hoffman, a sermon entitled 'The Gift of Time'

The Word Incarnate
brings eternal things
to time from
Nazareth to Calvary.

'My hour' He says
'is come,' ending
a beginning for a
beginning without end.

Day after day
He nurtures faith and friendship
and drinks a Father's will
at each new dawn.

Susan McGowan, 'The Hour is at Hand'

There is a difference between acceptance and resignation. One is positive; the other negative. Acceptance is creative, resignation sterile.

Resignation is barren of faith in the love of God. I say, 'Grievous circumstances have come to me. There is no escaping them. I am only one creature, an alien in a vast unknowable creation. I have no heart left even to rebel. So I'll try to make a virtue out of patient submission.' So resignation lies down quietly in the dust of a universe from which God seems to have fled, and the door of Hope swings shut.

But turn the coin over. Acceptance says, 'I trust the good-will, the love of my God. I'll open my arms and my understanding to what He has allowed to come to me. Since I know that He means to make all things work together for good, I consent to this present situation with hope for what the future will bring.' Thus acceptance leaves the door of hope wide open to God's creative plan.

Catherine Marshall, *Beyond Our Selves*

The Christian response to God's providence... ought not to express itself in a quietist withdrawal from human responsibilities or from involvement in the problems facing our world and our immediate society. Rather the Christian who accepts these responsibilities has the immense reassurance that the just, pure and godly values which he pursues in the everyday world are reflections of the essence of the Lord who rules and orders all things; and further, in spite of the vastness of many of the problems which confront us, these values are destined to endure in the new age of God's rule which is to appear.

Bruce Milne, *Know the Truth*

'Wait on the Lord' is a constant refrain in the Psalms, and it is a necessary word, for God often keeps us waiting. He is not in such a hurry as we are, and it is not his way to give more light on the future than we need for action in the present, or to guide us more than one step at a time. When in doubt, do nothing, but continue to wait on God. When action is needed, light will come.

J.I. Packer, *Knowing God*

The time factor in Galatians 6:9 is important — 'When the time comes.' There is always an interval between sowing and reaping. The process of germination and maturation takes time and is largely invisible. But 'when the time comes,' the proper time, harvest is certain.

J. Oswald Sanders, *Enjoying Intimacy with God*

Something was wrong somewhere. What? Suddenly it came over me. It was only that I had had my day all planned out and did not want my plans interfered with. Because they had been interfered with, I had done nothing but sulk. All the things I might have enjoyed I had not enjoyed at all. I had made myself miserable for a whole day, just because my time had been disposed of by someone else, and not by me.

'Lord,' I said, 'I'm not going to go through this again! I know it was really You who disposed of my day when I wanted to do something else with it! Give me an open mind, Lord, so that whenever I start a new day, I'll be able to accept whatever comes, and rejoice in it!'

Mabel Williamson, *Have We No Right?*

If we decide ahead of time what has to happen and then demand this of reality, we are almost sure to be disappointed. But if we can remember that God has different gifts for different moments in life and that he can be trusted to give us what we need when we need it, then help will become available. A trust in his adequacy and a humility of spirit that is willing to accept what is offered are the keys to receiving what he gives.

John R. Claypool, *The Light Within You*

It is far from easy to decide how to balance all the various demands upon our limited time, so that it becomes a harmonious whole, a living, dramatised psalm of praise to the glory of our God. It is so easy to use time disproportionately... We need to pray for ourselves and for each other, as Paul did, that we may 'discern what is important.'

Michael Griffiths, *Take My Life*

In his time, in his time,
He makes all things beautiful in his time.
Lord, please show me every day,
as you're teaching me your way,
that you do just what you say
in your time.

In your time, in your time,
You make all things beautiful in your time;
Lord, my life to you I bring,
may each song I have to sing
be to you a lovely thing,
in your time.

Dianne Ball, 'In His Time'

You who are beyond time, Lord, you smile to see us fighting it.
And you know what you are doing.
You make no mistakes in your distribution of time to me.
You give each one time to do what you want him to do.

But we must not lose time,
waste time,
kill time,
For time is a gift that you give us,
But a perishable gift,
A gift that does not keep.

Lord, I have time,
I have plenty of time,
All the time that you give me,
The years of my life,
The days of my years,
The hours of my days,
They are all mine.
Mine to fill, quietly, calmly,
But to fill completely, up to the brim,
To offer them to you, that of their insipid water
You may make a rich wine such as you made once in Cana of Galilee.

I am not asking you tonight, Lord, for time to do this and then that,
But your grace to do conscientiously, in the time that you give me, what you want me to do.

Michel Quoist, 'Lord I have time'

A Benediction

May God our Father, through whose providence we have been given the gift of time, and his Son, Jesus Christ, whose earthly life demonstrated the supreme importance of timeliness, and the Holy Spirit, through whom alone we are empowered to fulfil the purposes for which we have been given time as our inheritance, so teach us to number our days aright, that we may gain a heart of wisdom.

WEEK

51

To do as little as a Christian can

(F.H.C. Doyle)

So Jesus answered them, 'I am not trying to do what I want, but only what he who sent me wants.'

Come to me, all of you who are tired from carrying heavy loads, and I will give you rest . . . For the yoke I will give you is easy, and the load I will put on you is light.

For God is at work within you, helping you want to obey him, and then helping you do what he wants.

'Whenever you did this for one of the least important of these brothers of mine, you did it for me!'

Do not love the world or anything that belongs to the world. If you love the world, you do not love the Father. Everything that belongs to the world — what the sinful self desires, what people see and want, and everything in this world that people are so proud of — none of this comes from the Father; it all comes from the world. The world and everything in it that people desire is passing away; but he who does the will of God lives forever.

'Much is required from the person to whom much is given.'

'This is my body, which is given for you.'

'You received without cost: give without charge.'

First they gave themselves to the Lord; and then, by God's will they gave themselves to us as well.

(John 5:19,30, GNB; Matthew 11:28-29, GNB; Philippians 2:13, LB; Matthew 25:40, GNB; 1 John 2:15-17, GNB; Luke 12:48, GNB; Luke 22:19, GNB; Matthew 10:8, NEB; 2 Corinthians 8:5, GNB)

'Merry Christmas!' is the greetin',
'Hope you are happy,' they say.
But that's more easy said than done,

when it's less than a week away!
Takes at least a month to prepare
to have fun for just one day.

The tree is the first thing I've got to decide on,
the fake one no longer stands up on its own.
A real one moults needles all over the carpet
but if we don't have one, the kids will all moan.
'Why does one bother?' Because it's tradition!
Wouldn't be Christmas without the addition.
Don't ask me why, I haven't time to reply.

Christmas tucker, nothing like it,
but it takes a deal to make.
Stuff the turkey, boil the pudding,
stir the sauce while you ice the cake.
'Remember the *hungry*?' You've got to be joking!
I'm flat out recalling what I've got to bake!

Now the presents, where was I?
Must remember all the band.
Something solid in bright paper,
that I can put into their hand.
My list is full, of time I've nil,
no time to lend a hand.
'Someone's birthday?' at Christmas?
What a nuisance! How ill-planned!

Sending cards to the rest of the cobbers,
must send a card to keep in touch.
'Why not ring, it's a whole lot cheaper?'
Haven't the time and don't like the mush.
No time to *care*, just sign my name there.
'Forgotten Someone? In all the rush?'
'Whose birthday *is* it?' Well I dunno,
I've sent a card to all those I know.

Got the grog? That's the main thing.
The windows need washing for the party tonight.
Shampoo the carpet, get down the spiders,

mow the lawns and hang up the lights.
'Stop and listen? Reflect and wonder?'
Maybe tomorrow, if the kids don't fight.

Good old Santa, life without him
for the children would be dull.
Greedy eyes sparkle for the presents
they hope to get to fill the lull.
Can't disappoint 'em, get the biggest;
the Jones's is bigger than you can believe.
'Feed a mother?' 'Help a poor kid?'
Ask another. Can't afford it.

Clean the boat out, fill the van up,
hope to start out at first light.
Check the car, call the milkman,
cancel papers, snatch a bite.
To get away will be a pleasure,
we deserve a break.
'Someone we're indebted to?'
Well that takes the cake!
I'm a self-made man, a real good bloke.
Why, of all the nerve!
I've fought my way to where I am,
what I've got is what I deserve.

'Stop the rushin'?' That's a laugh.
I'll do that on Boxing Day.
Me taken in? *Me* taken for a ride?
Not me. I take all I can score.
'Missed something?' Never. I've been through my list;
cards, tree, food, presents.
How *can* there be something more?

Bronwyn Pryor, 'A Blank Christmas'

Advent in Australia could well be the busiest in the world, combining as it does the end of the school year with all its farewells and celebrations, and the beginning of the long summer vacation. Christmas is sandwiched in the middle.

Added to that, the competition put up by Santa and the commercial interests — and where does God find a place? 'No room!' is often the result, unless we make a definite commitment to put him at the head of our list of priorities.

In all the busy-ness that is our Advent, is it possible to be still enough and empty enough to contemplate the meaning of it all? Very often, we know what God wants us to do, but we try to do both his will and our own. So life becomes overburdened and strained and the peace that God wants for us at Christmas is just not there.

We need at this time more than ever to surrender our decision-making to the will of God. 'Lord, what do you want me to do next. . . and next. . . and next?' is the key question in finding a victoriously efficient way through the maze of our Advent. 'To do as little as a Christian can' under one's *own* strength and direction would leave room for *God* to move and have his way within us and through us.

Let not our hearts be busy inns
That have no room for Thee,
But cradles of the living Christ
And His nativity.

An old Welsh grace

As I went into [their] kitchen for more coffee, I heard one of the women say, 'Where can they stay tonight?' . . . they expected no help from me. Hadn't I shut out even my closest friends for months? No room, I thought. Then, in that moment God spoke to me, and I knew, for the first time since my loss, that I had made contact with him again. Here was a night such as might have been ages ago — a young man, and an expectant mother in deep distress. . . When we finally got home, I threw open the door to the [closed and dark] guest room and flooded it with light. . . But the real blessing was mine, for I had opened another door at the same time, my heart's door. . . for the spirit of Christmas to enter and heal my grief.

Betty Banner, 'The empty room'

My father stopped short, 'You shouldn't treat a man like that — Christmas Eve or any other time.' 'But Dad,' I said, 'he's a bum.' 'There's no such thing as a bum, Norman,' my father said. 'There may be some people who haven't made the most of their lives, but all of us are still children of God.' *'Love one another,'* Jesus said. No ifs, ands or buts. No reservations. And that's how Jesus loved. He loved the poor, the diseased, the prostitutes, the criminals, the 'bums'. He loved those who ridiculed, hated and abused him. To me, Christmas is about that way of loving.

Norman Vincent Peale, 'Words to grow on'

We must understand that faith is rest... when faith in its struggling gets to the end of itself, and just throws itself upon God and rests on him, then comes joy and victory... It is a great thing when a man comes to rest on God's almighty power for every moment of his life, in prospect of temptations to temper and haste and anger and unlovingness and pride and sin... You say: 'Won't that make me slothful?' I tell you it will not. No one who learns to rest upon the living Christ can become slothful, for the closer your contact with Christ the more of the Spirit of his zeal and love will be borne in upon you... The cause of the weakness of your Christian life is that you want to work it out partly, and to let God help you. And that cannot be. You must come to be utterly helpless, to let God work, and God will work gloriously... God does not ask you to give the perfect surrender in your strength, or by the power of your will; God is willing to work it in you.

Andrew Murray, *Absolute Surrender*

Children, take every moment as of my planning and ordering. Remember your Master is the Lord of the day's little happenings. In all the small things yield to my gentle pressure on your arm. Stay or go, as that pressure, Love's pressure, indicates... And when things do not fall out according to your plan, then smile at me indulgently, a smile of Love, and say, as you would to a human loved one, 'Have your way then' — knowing that my loving response will be to make that way as easy for your feet as it can be.

'The Two Listeners' in *God Calling*

At the height of holiday shopping, in the middle of a bustling mall store, my children began to squabble. All day we'd been impatient with each other. 'You two are fighting like cats and dogs,' I said to Bob and Ann, trying not to remember that I was feeling as angry and sullen as they were. . . *Go to the pet store!* said the voice in my thoughts. So we walked back. There in the window. . . were a puppy and a kitten. They were asleep, curled around each other like two spoons in a drawer. A cat and a dog! 'They get along good,' said Ann. . . the Christmas puppy and kitten became a quiet small symbol of reconciliation and peace. . . 'I'm sorry about all the fighting,' I said. 'Me, too,' each replied. I wrapped my arms around them, and felt their embrace in return. And there was peace. . . good will among us all.

Sue Monk Kidd, 'Sincerely'

Go placidly amid the noise and haste, and remember what peace there may be in silence.

Max Ehrmann, 'Desiderata'

May my great aim, Lord, this Advent be to bring happiness to you, through the giving of myself — my time, my plans — for you to use as you see fit. My gift to you must take precedence over my gifts to my family and friends. For it is your birthday, Lord — not mine, not the children's, not friends', but yours. Part of my gift to you must include my response to those lonely souls whom the world passes by; those whose need is so great that they cannot repay me; those whom I know, but have never felt attracted to, and criticised. Forgive me, Lord.

So the spring-cleaning of my spiritual house will take precedence over our physical one; the nourishment of our souls comes before the Christmas dinner; the beauty of loving hearts in harmony be more important to me than an array of tinsel and coloured lights. And good, in-filling times alone with you, must happen alongside good, outpouring times with friends and family. Help me, Lord, to get my priorities right, so that the busy burden of this time may be turned into blessing.

May an awareness of your presence fill my every waking hour, so that far from being squeezed out, you may come with me into my days, as my guide. For you are the only one who can help me find those surprising, secret springs of Christmas joy that you planted for us amongst the responsibilities, temptations and heartaches of our world.

A Benediction

The Lord fill you with his peace and trustfulness as you go into the busy day ahead, relaxing about the things you want to see accomplished before the twenty-fifth and being totally responsive to the promptings of the Master.

Give up your own desires, surrendering the rudder of your will in the small decisions as well as the big, knowing that you will be infinitely more pleased with his dreams for you, than you would be with your own. You are in God's keeping. He is working out your life for you. Thus may your Christmas be wonderfully blessed. Amen.

WEEK

He hides in the bushes

For you shall go out in joy, and be led forth in peace; the mountains and the hills before you shall break forth into singing, and all the trees of the field shall clap their hands.

Now Moses was tending the flock of Jethro his father-in-law, the priest of Midian, and he led the flock to the far side of the desert and came to Horeb, the mountain of God. There the angel of the Lord appeared to him in flames of fire from within a bush.

There were some shepherds in that part of the country who were spending the night in the fields, taking care of their flocks. An angel of the Lord appeared to them, and the glory of the Lord shone over them. They were terribly afraid.

Then he climbed into the boat with them, and the wind died down. They were completely amazed.

As he sat at table with them, he took the loaf, and said the blessing, and broke it in pieces, and gave it to them. Suddenly they saw! And they recognised him.

For in him we live and move and have our being.

But just as dawn began to break, Jesus stood there on the beach, although the disciples had no idea that it was Jesus. 'Have you caught anything, lads?' Jesus called out to them.

(Isaiah 55:12, RSV; Exodus 3:1-2, NIV; Luke 2:8-9, GNB; Mark 6:51, NIV; Luke 24:30-31, Barclay; Acts 17:28, NIV; John 21:4-5, Phillips)

I discovered it while washing nappies. There I was at the laundry sink, muttering over what is surely one of the most unenviable tasks allotted our race, when it struck me: this is human. This dismal, mucky business is irredeemably part of being human.

And then, by an intuitive leap that caught me completely off-guard, I saw, as if for the first time, the Incarnation. The Word become flesh: the ultimate affirmation of humanness.

The ultimate affirmation of the goodness of washing dismal, mucky diapers.

If human life was good enough for Jesus, it had to be good enough for me. *All* of it . . .

So many of our encounters with God are like that. We meet him in the mundane. The scrap of desert scrub bursts into flames before Moses' eyes. On the shepherds' night shift, angels suddenly fill the sky. Jesus walks beside the lake and asks, 'How's the fishing?'

We don't need to be mystics to meet God in the things he's made, or in ourselves. The filigree of frost, the peeling of vegetables, the struggle with inner doubts and contradictions — at times his Spirit makes things like these throb with him.

Everywhere we go we find God waving flags, God semaphoring, God jumping up and down and waving his arms to attract our attention like a man on a desert island. Only it is we who are on the island, and God is on the rescue ship, waving to let us know that help is near, even though we are too obtuse or blind or accustomed to island life to see it.

To see it. That is what we need. To allow the Spirit-Surgeon to remove our cataracts, correct our astigmatisms, restore our sight. He will; it is our choice.

All the world is one great sacramental loaf. We are not — nor will we ever be, God save us — solitary intelligences spinning in the void of space. He crowds upon us from Sheol to the sea; he jostles our thoughts along the pathways in our brains. He hides in the bushes, jumping out in flames to startle us into seeing. He sequesters himself in stables and swaddling so as to take us unawares. He veils himself in flesh, the same flesh that drips into fingers at the end of my arms and sprouts into hair on my head.

Virginia Stem Owens, *And the Trees Clap Their Hands*

There is nothing so secular that it cannot be sacred, and that is one of the deepest messages of the Incarnation.

Madeleine L'Engle, *Walking on Water*

We are all of us more mystics than we believe or choose to believe — life is complicated enough as it is, after all. We have seen more than we let on, even to ourselves. Through some moment of beauty or pain, some sudden turning of our lives, we catch glimmers at least of what the saints are blinded by; only then, unlike the saints, we tend to go on as though nothing has happened. To go on as though something has happened, even though we are not sure what it was or just where we are supposed to go with it, is to enter the dimension of life that religion is a word for.

Frederick Buechner, 'Summons to Pilgrimage'

God passes through the thicket of the world, and wherever his glance falls he turns all things to beauty.

St John of the Cross, 'The Spiritual Canticle'

The world is charged with the grandeur of God.
It will flame out, like shining from shook foil;
It gathers to a greatness, like the ooze of oil
Crushed. Why do men then now not reck his rod?

Gerard Manley Hopkins, 'God's Grandeur'

To some, God is discoverable everywhere... send a saint up in a space ship and he'll find God in space as he found God on earth. Much depends on the seeing eye.

C.S. Lewis, 'The Seeing Eye'

Ezekiel excoriates false prophets as those who have 'not gone up into the gaps.' The gaps are the thing... The gaps are the clefts in the rock where you cower to see the back parts of God; they are the fissures between mountains and cells the wind lances through, the icy narrowing fiords splitting the cliffs in mystery. Go up into the gaps. If you can find them; they shift and vanish too. Stalk the gaps.

Annie Dillard, *Pilgrim at Tinker Creek*

I have become convinced that the very contradictions in my life are in some ways signs of God's mercy to me; if only because someone so complicated and so prone to confusion and self-defeat could hardly survive for long without special mercy.

Thomas Merton

These shepherds are the first practitioners of what Dietrich Bonhoeffer called *religionless Christianity*. They encounter the angels in their work place and they worship the divine presence in a human baby. They do not meet God in the temple in the liturgy or in any pious pursuit. They worship the 'beyond in their midst.' In their present joy they have a down-payment of their future liberation.

Trevor Jordan, 'Joy to the World'

For some of us the contrast between God and world is so great that we abandon the spiritual quest. We turn away from God's brilliance and walk in shadows because we do not wish to see ourselves in an unbecoming light.

Parker J. Palmer, *The Promise of Paradox*

When I am made aware of the sinfulness of my heart, the manger of Bethlehem becomes a source of comfort. Jesus did not abhor a dirty place. Therefore, I praise him. It is his greatness that he chooses a lowly place, even my heart, as his dwelling place.

Vishal Mangalwadi

The essence of prayer is to hear the voice of another, of Christ, but likewise to hear the voice of each person I meet in whom Christ addresses me. His voice comes to me in every human voice, and his face is infinitely varied... God became incarnate so that man might contemplate his face in every face. Perfect prayer seeks this presence of Christ and recognises it in every human face.

Catherine de Hueck Doherty, *Poustinia*

I praise you, Lord: with the psalmists, with the saints, with the angels, with all creation, I praise you!

I roar like the sea and its creatures! I sing like the earth! I clap hands like the rivers and shout for joy like the trees of the wood! For the king of the universe has come to rule the earth, and everywhere the marks of his coming can be seen.

Yet my sight is weak, Lord; and when you are in the distance I search at my feet, and when you are nearby, I scan the horizon. Nonetheless, you have opened my eyes! I am like the man you healed who saw people like walking trees; at least I see them, and I trust you to complete my healing.

I ask your forgiveness:

* *for the times I've failed to recognise you,*

* *for the times I've refused to acknowledge what I've seen,*
* *for the times I've allowed myself to be dazzled by the world's neon brightness,*
* *for the times I've permitted myself to be deceived by the prince of darkness masquerading as an angel of light.*

Teach me to recognise the many signs of your coming, both in the world around me and the world within. And when your presence burns with its brilliance, searing my eyes with its dazzling demands, give me strength not to turn my head away.

There are many I know and love who are still blind to you, Lord. You know them... In the name of the One who came to give sight to the blind, rescue them for your kingdom; and help me to see in their faces the sweet, whole, human face of Christ.

I stand in awe at the mystery of how the infinite Creator became part of his creation in order that his creation could be redeemed. I praise you, Lord: for you are the Father of Lights, and everywhere — like a million million fireflies — you and your people defy, drive back, transform the darkness.

A Benediction

The ridiculously rich, fabulously free grace of God surrounds you like the air. Move through it like a weatherman, always alert for the unexpected, unpredictable rush of the wind. Tornado or breeze, it always blows love.

Postlude

Uttered through a reed

OUTSIDE THE CITY IN A MARSH near the river grew a reed. She had lived in the green and yellow marsh all of her life, and she was happy.

When it rained, the young reed thanked God; she felt clean on the outside and on the inside. Within her, life surged and she grew strong. When the red sun beat on the marsh, she thanked God too (but not so loudly as before). She knew that although it scorched her outside and hurt her inside, her roots were digging into rich black soil, but most of her days were like yours and mine — sunny, overcast, windy, or drizzly.

One day (I'm not sure of the date), the Son of God walked through the marsh. He liked it out there at times, away from the whirlpool city. He saw the speckled reed and stopped to look at her.

It wasn't that she was particularly beautiful, but the Son of God needed a reed to pipe on and, with a little fixing up, she would do. He studied the reed and finally said: 'Little reed, I need a pipe to play a melody. Would you let me pluck you by the roots? I can fix you for my purpose and that may hurt, but I wish to sing a song of love through you.'

The little reed could hardly believe her ears; she could hardly believe what was happening to her or what the Son of God was saying to her.

Finally, she strangely enough said, with no hesitation:

'Yes, yes, let it be done.'

And as the Son of God pulled up the reed by the roots (and it did hurt), she lay in his hand and didn't mind. Even when he took his knife and cut away her throbbing roots, she just cried:

'Yes, yes, let it be done.'

The Son of God whittled her to fit his palm and emptied the clutter in her heart. And when she was hollow, virgin, empty, the Son of God kissed her with his lips and uttered through her a beautiful song of love.

A Sister of Carmel

Abbreviations

Abbreviations of versions of the Bible used in this book

Amp.:	*The Amplified New Testament*, The Lockman Foundation, Zondervan, Grand Rapids, 1958
GNB:	*Good News Bible*, The Bible in Today's English Version, The American Bible Society, New York, 1976
JB:	*Jerusalem Bible*, Darton, Longman and Todd Ltd, 1968
KJV:	*The Holy Bible, King James Version*, 1611
LB:	*The Living Bible*, Tyndale House Publishers, Wheaton, 1971
Moffat:	*The Moffat translation of the Bible*, Hodder and Stoughton, London, 1982
NASB:	*New American Standard Bible*, The Lockman Foundation, 1963
NEB:	*The New English Bible*, OUP and CUP, 1970
NIV:	*Holy Bible, New International Version*, New York International Bible Society, New York, 1973
Phillips:	J.B. Phillips, *The New Testament in Modern English*, The Macmillan Company, New York, 1958
RSV:	*Revised Standard Version*, Thomas Nelson and Sons, London, 1952
Weymouth:	R.F. Weymouth *New Testament in Modern Speech*, James Clarke, London, 1929

Bibliography

Other sources used in the weekly readings

Week 1

Augustine, *Confessions*, I, 15 and 24, Albert C. Outler (tr.), (Vol.VII in *The Library of Christian Classics*), SCM Press, 1955, pp.31-45

An Australian Prayer Book, Anglican Information Office, 1978, pp.41-42

Catherine of Siena, *The Dialogue of the Seraphic Virgin*, Algar Thorold (tr.), Burns and Oates, 1925, pp.342-345

Dietrich Bonhoeffer, *Life Together*, Harper and Row, 1954, pp.79 and 84

Catherine de Hueck Doherty, *Poustinia*, Ave Maria Press, 1979, p.92

Thomas à Kempis, *The Imitation of Christ*, Ronald Knox and Michael Oakley (trs.), Sheed and Ward, Bk II, p.60

Henri Nouwen, *With Open Hands*, Ave Maria Press, 1978, p.48

Edwin McNeill Poteat, Exposition, Psalm 46:10, *The Interpreter's Bible*, Abingdon, 1955, Vol. 4, p.244

Brother Roger of Taizé, *The Wonder of a Love*, Mowbray, 1981, p.34

W.E. Sangster, *The Pure in Heart: A Study in Christian Sanctity*, Epworth, 1955, pp.197-209

Clifton Wolters (tr.), *The Cloud of Unknowing*, Penguin, 1980, p.145

Week 2

Carlo Carretto, *The Desert in the City*, Collins/Fount, 1981, p.19

Catherine de Hueck Doherty, *Poustinia*, Collins/Fount, 1975, p.30

Richard Foster, *Freedom of Simplicity*, SPCK, 1981, p.14

Frank Laubach, *Open Windows Swinging Doors*, G/L Regal Publications, 1955, p.54

Brother Lawrence, *The Practice of the Presence of God*, Spire Books, 1958, p.29

Thomas Merton, *No Man is an Island*, Image Books, 1967, p.65

Henri Nouwen, *Out of Solitude*, Ave Maria Press, 1974, p.26

Gerhard Tersteegen, 'God Himself is Present' from *Australian Hymn Book*, No.47, v.1 and 2, Collins, 1977

Week 3

W. Cowper, in *The Preacher's Dictionary*, E.F. Cavalier (ed.), Hodder and Stoughton, 1904, p.605

Matthew Henry, in J. Blanchard, *Gathered Gold*, Evangelical Press, 1984, p.11

E. Stanley Jones, in J. Blanchard, op. cit., p.78

J.H. Jowett, *Thirsting for the Springs*, Allenson, 1907, p.59

Rollo May, in *A Sense of Wonder*, S. Moskawitz (ed.), New English Library, p.7

H.H. Munro (Saki), in *Quotations for Speakers and Writers*, Allen Andrews (ed.), Sun, 1981.

Isaac Newton, in Allen Andrews, op. cit., p.502

John Owen, in J. Blanchard, op. cit., p.16

J.I. Packer, *Knowing God*, Hodder and Stoughton, 1973, p.18

Francis de Sales, in H.E. Kirk, *The Vision of God* (Bampton Lectures), Longmans, Green, 1941, p.406

W. Secker, in J. Blanchard (ed.), op. cit., p.180
R. Sockman, in Allen Andrews, op. cit., p.502
C.H. Spurgeon, *Behold the Throne of Grace*, Marshall, Morgan and Scott, p.106
A.W. Tozer, *The Pursuit of God*, Oliphants, 1969, pp.36-39 and 67
J.G. Whittier, *The Poetical Works of John Greenleaf Whittier*, Ward, Lock & Co., 1911, p.311

Week 4
Richard Foster, *Celebration of Discipline*, Hodder and Stoughton, 1981, pp.77 and 168
Tim Hansel, *When I Relax I Feel Guilty*, David C. Cook Publishing Co., 1981, introduction, pp.44 and 113

Week 5
S. Kierkegaard, *Gospel of Sufferings*, James Clarke & Co., 1955, p.13
George MacDonald, in *An Anthology*, C.S. Lewis (ed.), Macmillan, 1978, p.47
Thomas Merton, *Spiritual Direction and Meditation*, Anthony Clarke, 1975, p.59
Jurgen Moltmann, *Experiences of God*, Fortress, 1981, p.33
Fritz Rosenweig, in Jurgen Moltmann, *Experiences of God*, Fortress, 1981, p.17
W.H. Vanstone, *The Stature of Waiting*, Darton, Longman and Todd, 1983, pp.50, 70 and 96

Week 6
Horatius Bonar, in M. Stacey, *The Divine Love*, Currawong, 1982, p.42
John Byrom, in *The Lion Book of Christian Poetry*, Lion, 1981, p.41
Arch Hart in *Grid* Magazine, 1984
A.J. Heschel, *The Sabbath, its Meaning for Modern Man*, 1951-52, p.73f
Toki Miyashina, in *The Lion Book of Famous Prayers*, Lion, 1983, pp.114-115
Henri Nouwen, in *The Lion Book of Famous Prayers*, Lion, 1983, p.106
Bruce Prewer, *Australian Prayers*, Lutheran Publishing House, 1983, p.146
G. von Rad, *Moses*, Lutterworth, 1961, pp.52-53
Claus Westermann, *Creation*, Fortress, 1974, p.65
John Greenleaf Whittier, *Australian Hymn Book*, Collins, 1977, p.519
H.W. Wolff, *Anthropology of the Old Testament*, SCM, 1974, p.137ff

Week 7
Carlo Carretto, *Letters from the Desert*, Darton, Longman & Todd, 1980
C.S. Lewis, *Prayer: Letters to Malcolm*, Collins, Fontana Books, 1974
Henri Nouwen, *Out of Solitude*, Ave Maria Press, 1974
Henri Nouwen, *With Open Hands*, Ave Maria Press, 1979
Karl Rahner, *Encounters with Silence*, Burns & Oates, 1978
St Teresa of Avila, *The Collected Works of St Teresa of Avila*, Kieran Kavanaugh and Otilio Rodriguez (trs.), ICS Publications, 1976 and 1980 (two volumes)

Week 8
T.S. Eliot, *Four Quartets*, Faber and Faber, 1959, pp.19 and 28
Richard Foster, *Celebration of Discipline*, Hodder and Stoughton, 1978, p.84
Gerard Manley Hopkins, *A Selection of Poems and Prose*, Penguin, 1953
Morton T. Kelsey, *The Other Side of Silence: A Guide to Christian Meditation*, SPCK, 1976, p.98
Thomas à Kempis, *The Imitation of Christ*, Penguin, 1953, p.49
Anthony de Mello, *Sadhana: A Way to God*, Gujarat Sahitya Prakash Anand, 1978, p.108ff
Henri Nouwen, *With Open Hands*, Ave Maria Press, 1972, pp.44 and 154

Henri Nouwen, *The Way of the Heart: Desert Spirituality and Contemporary Ministry*, Darton, Longman and Todd, 1981, pp.81-82
Bruce Prewer, *Australian Prayers*, Lutheran Publishing House, 1983, p.21
St Teresa of Avila, *The Collected Works of St Teresa of Avila*, Kieran Kavanaugh and Otilio Rodriguez (trs.), ICS Publications, 1976 and 1980 (two volumes)
J.G. Whittier, *The Australian Hymn Book*, No.519, Collins, 1977

Week 9

W.E. Andersen, *The Christian Concept of Maturity*, a study booklet, based on lectures to the Australian Teachers' Christian Fellowship, 1960, pp.11 and 15
John Claypool, 'Absurdity, Causality and Mystery', a sermon preached on May 6, 1979
John Claypool, 'Slow Learners and Hope', a sermon preached on September 7, 1980
Richard Foster, *Celebration of Discipline*, Hodder and Stoughton, 1980, pp.1 and 9
Michael Griffiths, *Give Up Your Small Ambitions*, IVP, 1970, p.147
I. Howard Marshall, 'Towards Maturity', editorial of TSF Bulletin, No.52, Autumn, 1968
Ken Medema, 'Tree Song', Word Music, 1976
Bob Mumford, *The Purpose of Temptation*, Fleming H. Revell Company, 1973, p.13
Henri Nouwen, *Reaching Out: The Three Movements of the Spiritual Life*, Collins, 1976, pp. 133-134
Orville S. Walters, 'Maturity: When?' an article in *Christianity Today*, January 8, 1969

Week 10

Professor E.M. Blaiklock, 'Our Lord's Teaching on Prayer', in Francis Foulkes' paper 'In Touch with God'
Lewis Carroll, *Alice in Wonderland*, The Children's Press, 1976, pp.140-141
John Donne, *The Metaphysical Poets*, Helen Gardner (ed.), Penguin Books, 1961, p.83
Ralph Waldo Emerson, *Penguin Dictionary of Quotations*, J.M. and M.J. Cohen (eds.), Penguin Books, 1964, p.154
Rev. Francis Foulkes, paper given at Evangelical Conference in MBI, Melbourne
Dr Os Guinness, from a clergy's and pastors' conference in Melbourne
Gary Inrig, *Life in His Body*, Harold Shaw Publishers, 1975, p.76
Dr J.I. Packer, *Knowing God*, Hodder and Stoughton, 1975, p.277
Dr Paul Rees, Pastors' Conference, Melbourne
A.W. Tozer, in Warren Wiersbe, *The Best of Tozer*, Christian Publications Inc.

Week 11

William Barclay, *The Letters to the Corinthians*, Daily Study Bible, The St Andrews Press, 1954, p.85
Dietrich Bonhoeffer, 'Outline for a Book', in *Letters and Papers from Prison*, Collins/Fontana, 1959, p.166
Richard Foster, *Celebration of Discipline*, Hodder & Stoughton, 1980, p.115
Thomas à Kempis, *The Imitation of Christ*, Ronald Knox and Michael Oakley, (trs.), Burns and Oates, 1959, pp.138-139
Andrew Lansdown, *Counterpoise*, Angus and Robertson, 1982, p.28
William Law, *A Serious Call to a Devout and Holy Life*, Dent, in Foster, op.cit., p.114
Madeleine L'Engle, *Walking on Water*, Harold Shaw Publishers, 1980, p.60
C.S. Lewis, 'Christianity and Literature', *Christian Reflections*, Eerdmans, 1967, p.7
Ranald Macaulay and Jerram Barrs, *Being Human*, IVP, 1978, pp.134-135

Leon Morris, *1 and 2 Thessalonians*, Tyndale New Testament
Andrew Murray, *Humility*, Oliphants, 1961, p.58
Commentaries, IVP, 1958, p.71
Helen Roseveare, *Living Sacrifice*, Hodder and Stoughton, 1979, p.119
Mother Teresa, in Kathryn Spink, *A Chain of Love*, SPCK, 1984, p.103

Week 12

R. Girard, *My Weakness: His Strength*, Zondervan, 1981, p.148
John Helm, *Weak But Strong*, Anzea, 1985, p.87
Calvin Miller, *The Philippian Fragment*, IVP, 1982, p.80
Henri Nouwen, *Creative Ministry*, Doubleday, 1971, p.110
Henri Nouwen, *The Living Reminder*, Gill and Macmillan, 1977, p.68
J.B. Phillips, *Young Church in Action*, Bles, 1975
Charles Povey, *The Paradox of Weakness*, (unpublished poem)
J.O. Sanders, *Your Best Years*, Moody, 1982, p.14
J.S. Stewart, *Thine is the Kingdom*, St Andrews, 1956, p.34
P. Tournier, *Learning to Grow Old*, SCM, 1972, p.222

Week 13

Sherwood Eddy, in *Everyday Encyclopaedia of Religious Quotations*, Peter Davies, 1965, p.151
Frederick W. Faber, in *The Baptist Hymnbook*, Psalms and Hymns Trust, 1962, No.419
M. Green, *Choose Freedom*, IVP, 1965, p.68
C.F. Horne, 'Liberation', in *Pulpit Digest*, March/April 1984, p.41
F.C. Laubach, *Christ Liveth in Me*, Fleming H. Revell, 1951, p.13
W. McWilliams, *Free in Christ*, Broadman Press, 1984, p.126
F. Pollard, *Keeping Free*, Broadman Press, 1983, p.18

Week 14

Richard Rothe, in John Baillie, *A Diary of Readings*, OUP, 1957, Day 28
Augustine, *Confessions*, Penguin, 1961
Walter Raleigh, in Derek Kidner, *Proverbs*, IVP, 1964
William Barclay, *Colossians*, St Andrews Press, 1959, p.130
Robert Browning, in Oswald Chambers' *Baffled to Fight Better*, Simpkins Marshall, 1947, p.105
William Cowper, in *Australian Hymn Book*, No.54, Collins, 1977
John Goodwin, USCL *World Christian Books*, No.47, 1963, p.29
Derek Kidner, *Proverbs*, IVP, 1964, pp.31-32
George MacDonald in C.S. Lewis, *George MacDonald: An Anthology*, Geoffrey Bles/The Century Press, 1946, p.95
J.I. Packer, *Knowing God*, Hodder and Stoughton, 1973, p.116
John Paterson, *The Wisdom of Israel*, Lutterworth, 1961, p.54
A.W. Tozer, in Warren Wiersbe, *The Best of Tozer*, Christian Publications Inc., 1978, pp.22-23

Week 15

Bernard of Clairvaux in J. Claypool, *The Light Within You*, Word, 1983, p.214
J.S. Bonnell, in W. Scott McPheat, *Coping with Life — But not alone*, Hodder, 1979, p,15
J. Claypool, *The Light within You*, Word, 1983, p.214
Romano Guardini in W. Trobisch, *Love Yourself*, Evangelical Tracts, 1976, p.15
Hermann Hesse in W. Trobisch, *Love Yourself*, Evangelical Tracts, 1976, p.11
W. Scott McPheat, op.cit.
John V. Taylor, *The Go-Between God*, SCM, 1972, p.172
P. Tillich, *The Courage to Be*, Fontana, 1952, p.160
P. Tillich, *The Shaking of the*

Foundations, Penguin, 1962, p.163
W. Trobisch, *Love Yourself*, Evangelical Tracts, 1976, p.26
J.S. Whale, *Christian Doctrine*, CUP, 1956, p.78f

Week 16
D.H. Lawrence, *Selected Poems*, Penguin, 1950, p.119
C.S. Lewis, *The Last Battle*, Puffin, 1964, pp.154-155
Song of Solomon, 8:6-13 (RSV)
John V. Taylor, *The Go-Between God*, SCM, 1972, p.243

Week 17
L. Christenson, *The Christian Family*, Bethany Fellowship, 1974, p.204
A. Grams, *Changes in Family Life*, Concordia, 1968, p.112
T.C. Myers, *Happiness is Still Home Made*, Word, 1969, p.49
C.M. Sell, *Family Ministry*, Zondervan, 1981, p.9
H.N. Wright, *Premarital Counseling*, Moody Press, 1982, p.9

Week 18
Dom Helder Camara, *A Thousand Reasons for Living*, Darton, Longman and Todd, 1981, pp.75 and 92
John Claypool, adapted from a sermon, 'Absurdity, Causality and Mystery', May 6, 1979
John Claypool, *The Light Within You*, Word, 1983, p.119
Ruysbroeck, in David Walker, *God is a Sea*, Alba House, 1977, p.13
A.C. Swinburne, *A Midsummer Vacation*, in William James, *The Varieties of Religious Experience*, Collins/Fount, 1977, p.406
David Walker, *God is a Sea*, Alba House, 1977, p.13

Week 19
Leslie Brandt, *Psalms Now*, Concordia, 1973, p.56
George Herbert, in *The Metaphysical Poets*, W.H. Gardner (ed.), Penguin, 1957, p.126
Gerard Manley Hopkins, in *Poems and Prose of Gerard Manley Hopkins*, W.H. Gardner (ed.), Penguin, 1953, p.62
Herman Kohlbrugge, in *The Minister's Prayer Book*, John W. Doberstein (ed.), Collins, 1959, p.241
Austin Pardue, 'Why Learn to Pray' in *Partners in Prayer*, Charlotte M. Clough (ed.), Doubleday, 1953, p.13f

Week 20
Jamie Buckingham, in Anne S. White, *Healing Adventure*, Logos International, 1972
Jim Glennon, *Your Healing is Within You*, Hodder and Stoughton, 1982, pp.70 and 72
C.S. Lewis, *Mere Christianity*, Collins/Fount, 1978, pp.143-144
Dennis Linn and Matthew Linn, *Healing of Memories*, Paulist Press, 1974, p.8
S.I. McMillan, *None of These Diseases*, Marshall, Morgan and Scott, 1966, p.7
Francis MacNutt, *Healing*, Ave Maria Press, 1978, pp.178 and 181
Francis MacNutt, *The Prayer that Heals*, Ave Maria Press, 1981, pp.101 and 107
John and Paula Sandford, *The Transformation of the Inner Man*, Bridge Publishing Inc., 1982, p.170
William Shakespeare, *Macbeth* Act 5, scene 3, line 40, in McMillan, op.cit., p.68
Barbara Leahy Shlemon, *Healing Prayer*, Ave Maria Press, 1976, p.79
Ruth Carter Stapleton, *The Gift of Inner Healing*, Hodder and Stoughton, 1979, p.77
Betty Tapscott, *Inner Healing through Healing of Memories*, Marshall, Morgan and Scott, 1984, p.20

Week 21
John Calvin, in Jurgen Moltmann, *Theology of Hope*, SCM, 1975, p.189
T.O. Chisolm, *Hymns for Today's Church*, M. Baughan (ed.), No.260, Hodder and Stoughton, 1982
T. Falla, *Be Our Freedom Lord*, Lutheran Publishing House, 1983, pp.27 and 149
David Hubbard, 'Hope in the New Testament', in *Tyndale Bulletin 34*, 1983, p.58
Martin Luther King, in *Lion Book of Famous Prayers*, 1983, p.122
Henry Miller, in S. Travis, *I Believe in the Second Coming of Jesus*, Eerdmans, 1982, p.227
Jurgen Moltmann, *The Experiment Hope*, SCM, 1975, p.189
Jurgen Moltmann, in S. Travis, *I Believe in the Second Coming of Jesus*, Eerdmans, 1982, p.223
Edward Mote, in *Daily Readings from the Works of Martyn Lloyd-Jones*, Hodder and Stoughton, 1973, p.103
Lesslie Newbigin, 'The Other Side of 1984', WCC, in *Eremos Newsletter*, August 1984, p.26
Pericles, in D.W.B. Robinson, *Hope for Christ's Coming*, Evangelical Tracts and Publications, 1963, p.7
Alexander Pope in A. Farrer, *A Celebration of Faith*, Hodder and Stoughton, 1970, p.119
Jean-Paul Sartre in S. Travis, *I Believe in the Second Coming of Jesus*, Eerdmans, 1982, p.227
E. Schillebeeckx, *God the Future of Man*, Sheed and Ward, 1969, p.183
H.W. Wolff, *Anthropology of the Old Testament*, SCM, 1974, p.155

Week 22
Francis Bacon, 'Essay on Death' in *Oxford Book of English Prose*, OUP, 1952
John Donne, 'Death the Leveller', Sermon XV, in *Oxford Book of English Prose*, OUP, 1952
John Dryden, 'Aureng-Zebe iv-i', in *Oxford Book of Quotations*, OUP, 1950
The Office of Compline, *The Priest's Book of Private Devotions*, A.R. Mowbray and Co., 1978, p.72
Robert Scott, 'Death of Captain Oates', retold by Charles Tinley, 'Scott's Last Expedition', in *Oxford Book of English Prose*, OUP, 1952
William Shakespeare, *Antony and Cleopatra*
Alfred, Lord Tennyson, 'The Two Voices', No.cxxxii, in *Oxford Book of Quotations*, OUP, 1950
Paul Tournier, *The Person Reborn*, SCM/Heinemann, 1967, p 232
Charles Wesley, 'O Thou who camest from above' *Hymns Ancient and Modern*, No. 329, William Clowes and Sons Ltd

Week 23
Aime Ceasaire in W.H. Vanstone, *The Stature of Waiting*, Darton, Longman and Todd, 1982, p.114
Carmen Bernos de Gasztold, *Prayers of the Ark*, The Viking Press, 1965, p.21
Mahatma Gandhi in Ernest J. Campbell, *Locked in a Room with Open Doors*, Word Books, p.67
John Hazelwood, in *Anglican Spirituality*, John Bayton (ed.), Anglican Media Publication, 1982, p.55
Harry Kemp, 'Blind' in *Great Poems of the English Language*, Wallace Briggs (comp.), Tudor Publishing Co., 1936, p.1294
Martin Luther King, *Strength to Love*, Fontana, 1974, pp.65-66
C.S. Lewis, *The Great Divorce*, Bles, 1945, p.29
W.H. Vanstone, *The Stature of Waiting*, Darton, Longman and Todd, 1982, p.114

Week 24
Leslie F. Brandt, *A Book of Christian Prayer*, Kingsway, 1978, p.78
Frederick Buechner, *Wishful Thinking*, Collins, 1973, p.47
John Donne, *Sermons*, No.28
Richard Foster, *Freedom of Simplicity*, SPCK, 1981, p.102
John N. Gladstone, 'Weeping and Whistling', sermon preached at Yorkminster Park Baptist Church, Toronto
Vernon C. Grounds, 'Soar with the Eagles, Sing with the Angels', Christianity Today, August 27, 1976
Oswald C. J. Hoffman, 'In the Reality of Joy', a Lutheran House Address, No. 996, Adelaide, January 3, 1965
Helen Howarth Lemmuel, *Scripture Union Chorus Book*, No.278, Scripture Union, 1921
George Matheson, *Christian Praise*, No.147, Tyndale, 1957
J.I. Packer, 'Joy', sermon preached at Peninsular Bible Church, Palo Alto, Discovery Papers No.3269, Discovery Publishing, February 20, 1977

Week 25
F.F. Bruce, *This is That*, Paternoster Press, 1976, p.40
John Dryden, An Epistle to John Dryden 1/164, *Oxford Dictionary of Quotations*, OUP, 1941
Herman Hesse, *Siddhartha*, Picador, 1973, pp.78-79
Frank Houghton, *Amy Carmichael of Dohnavur*, SPCK, 1954, p.36
Hannah Hurnard, *Hind's Feet on High Places*, The Olive Press, 1977, pp.76-77
Samuel Johnson, *The History of Rasselas, Prince of Abbisinia*, Penguin, 1982, p.97
Brother Lawrence, *The Practice of the Presence of God*, E.M. Blaiklock (tr.), Hodder and Stoughton, 1981, p.67
C.S. Lewis, *The Great Divorce*, Fontana, 1942, p.52
Alexander Pope, 'Essay on Man' ('The Lansdowne Poets'), *The Poetical Works of Alexander Pope*, Frederick Warne and Co., p.222
Pyrrhus, after defeating the Romans at Asculum in 279 BC, in Plutarch, *Makers of Rome*
Schopenhauer, 'On the Suffering of the World', in *Essays and Aphorisms*, R.J. Hollingdale (tr.), Penguin, 1981, p.41
Robert Southey, 'Battle of Blenheim', in *The Poetical Works of Robert Southey*, Green and Longmans, 1850, pp.449-450
William Shakespeare, *Much Ado About Nothing*, Act 1, Scene 1
John Stott, *God's New Society*, IVP, 1979, p.266
Paul Tillich, *The Boundaries of Our Being*, Fontana, 1973, p.191
John White, *The Fight*, IVP, 1979, p.216

Week 26
E.L. Allen, *Thou Must Venture*, Nisbett & Co., 1942, p.146
Metropolitan Anthony, *God and Man*, Hodder and Stoughton, 1974, p.47
F.R. Barry, *Asking the Right Questions*, Hodder and Stoughton, 1960, p.166
R.E.C. Browne, *The Ministry of the Word*, SCM, 1958, p.51
Herbert Butterfield, *Christianity and History*, G. Bell & Sons, 1950, p.146
Baron von Hugel, *Letters from Baron Friedrich von Hugel to a Niece*, J.M. Dent, 1928, xvi
John Macquarrie, *God and Secularity*, Westminster, 1967, pp.108-109
W.B.J. Martin, *Five Minutes to Twelve*, Collins, 1957, p.42
Christopher Morley, *No Coaching, from Steamlines*, J.B. Lippincott, 1933

John V. Taylor, *The Go-Between God*, SCM, 1975, p.146
A.E. Whitham, *The Pastures of His Presence*, Hodder and Stoughton, 1939, p.94

Week 27
Jerome B. Berryman (ed.), *Life maps: Conversations on the Journey of Faith*, Word Books, 1978, p.10
Horatius Bonar in Lord David Cecil, *The Oxford Book of Christian Verse*, OUP, 1940, p.394
John Bunyan, *Pilgrim's Progress*, The Pocket Library, 1957, pp.51 and 291
Lewis Carroll, *Alice's Adventures in Wonderland*, International Pocket Library
Rex Chapman, *A Kind of Praying*, SCM, 1970, p.13
Wallace B. Clift, *Jung and Christianity: the Challenge of Reconciliation*, Dove Communications, 1983, p.28
St Cyril of Jerusalem in Gerald O'Collins, *The Second Journey: Spiritual awareness and the mid-life Crisis*, Dove Communications, 1978, p.64
T.S. Eliot, *Four Quartets*, Faber and Faber, 1959, p.59
Robert Frost, *The Poetry of Robert Frost*, E.C. Latham (ed.), Holt, Rinehart and Winston, 1969
Lolande Jacobi and R.F.C. Hull (eds.), *Psychological Reflections*, Princeton University Press, Princeton, 1970
J.H. Newman in *The Australian Hymn Book*, No.493, Collins, 1977
Frances J. Roberts, *Come Away My Beloved*, King's Farspan, 1973, p.16
C.G. Rosetti, in *Major British Poets*, Oscar Williams (ed.), Mentor, 1963, p.319
Alfred, Lord Tennyson, 'Ulysses', in *The Concise Oxford Dictionary of Quotations*, OUP, 1964, pp.177 and 230

Week 28
H. Drummond, *The Will of God*, Hodder and Stoughton, 1906, p.43
W.E. Sangster, *God Does Guide Us*, Hodder and Stoughton, 1950, p.23
R.L. Stevenson, in *Living Quotations for Christians*, Sherwood Eliot Wirt and Kirsten Beckstrom (eds.), Harper and Row, 1974, p.101
C.R. Swindoll, *God's Will*, Multnomah Press, 1982, pp.9 and 13
L. Weatherhead, *The Will of God*, Epworth Press, 1944, p.25

Week 29
William Blake, 'The Little Black Boy', in *The Concise Oxford Dictionary of Quotations*, OUP, 1964, p.39
Merlin Carothers, *Power in Praise*, Kingsway, 1972, pp.145f, 153
Catherine Marshall, *Something More*, Hodder and Stoughton, 1974, pp.163-166
Raymond A. Moody, *Life after Life*, Bantam, 1975, pp.58-59
Agnes Sanford, *The Healing Light*, Arthur James, 1949, pp.28, 32, 39f, 52
William Wordsworth, in *The Concise Oxford Dictionary*, OUP, 1964, p.246

Week 30
Dietrich Bonhoeffer, *The Cost of Discipleship*, SCM, 1959, p.49
F.F. Bruce, *The Hard Sayings of Jesus*, Hodder and Stoughton, 1983, p.165
Frederich Buechner, *Wishful Thinking*, Harper and Row, 1973, p.82
John Bunyan, *To Be a Pilgrim*, OUP
William Sloane Coffin, *The Courage to Love*, Harper and Row, 1982
Emily Henrietta Hickey,

'Beloved, it is Morn', in *Oxford Book of Quotations*, 1953, p.248
John Laird, *No Mere Chance*, Hodder/SU, 1981, p.72
Andrew Murray, in *The Topical Encyclopedia of Living Quotations*, Bethany House, p.60
C.S. Lewis, *The Last Battle*, Penguin, 1964, p.88
J.I. Packer, *Freedom, Authority and Scripture*, IVP, 1981, p.31
J.I. Packer, *I Want to be a Christian*, Tyndale, 1983, p.33
Polycarp, in *Documents of the Christian Church*, Henry Bettenson (ed.), OUP, 1954, p.14
Ronald Wallace, *The Lord is King*, IVP, 1979, p.107

Week 31
Soren Kierkegaard, *Purity of Heart*, Fontana, 1961, p.158
Brother Lawrence, *The Practice of the Presence of God*, Epworth Press, p.46
B. Pascal, *The Pensees*, Penguin, 1961, p.287
J.B. Phillips, *Your God is Too Small*, Wyvern Books, 1957, p.61
F.M. Segler, *Christian Worship*, Broadman Press, 1961, p.58
R. Webber, *Worship Old and New*, Zondervan, 1982, p.97

Week 32
Sheila Cassidy, *Prayers for Pilgrims*, Collins/Fount, 1980, pp.39 and 40
Howard Clinebell, *Growth Counseling for Mid-Years Couples*, Fortress, 1977, p.33
Richard Foster, *Freedom of Simplicity*, SPCK, 1981, pp.78-80
Michael Green, in *The Work of an Evangelist*, World Wide Publications, 1984, p.49
Howard Hendricks, in *The Work of an Evangelist*, World Wide Publications, 1984, p.62
George Matheson, *The Australian Hymn Book*, No.525, Collins, 1976
Henri Nouwen, *Reaching Out*, Collins/Fount, 1976, pp.63, 65, 68-73

Week 33
Thomas Aquinas, *Summa Theologica*, Great Books of the Western World, Vol. 20, R.M. Hutchins (ed.), Encyclopaedia Britannica, 1952, p.520
Augustine, *The City of God*, Great Books of the Western World, Vol.18, op.cit., p.617
Augustine, *Confessions*, op.cit., Vol.18, p.93
John Bunyan, *The Pilgrim's Progress*, Books Inc., 1945, p.151
Dante, *The Divine Comedy*, Great Books of the Western World, Vol.21, R.M. Hutchins (ed.), Encyclopaedia Britannica, 1952, p.152
G.M. Hopkins, 'That Nature is a Heraclitean Fire', in *Poems and Prose of Gerard Manley Hopkins*, Penguin Books, 1953, p.66
C.S. Lewis, *The Last Battle*, Penguin Books, 1964, p.165
D. Winter, *Hereafter*, Hodder and Stoughton, 1972, pp.77 and 79

Week 34
Steven L. Fry, *Scripture in Song*, Vol.2, No.13, Scripture in Song, 1974
C.S. Lewis, *Mere Christianity*, Collins, pp.62-63
Bruce Milne, *The End of the World*, Kingsway, p.23
C.M. Noel, 'At the Name of Jesus', *Baptist Hymn Book*, Psalms and Hymns Trust, 1962, p.361
Ruth Paxson, in J. Oswald Sanders, *Certainties of Christ's Second Coming*, Kingsway, p.118
J. Oswald Sanders, *The Incomparable Christ*, Moody Press, pp.254-255
Ray Stedman, a sermon, 'Are These the Last Days?', June 8, 1980

Helmut Thielecke, *The Waiting Father*, James Clarke, 1966
Television commercial, 'The Age', Melbourne, April 13, 1981, p.2
A.W. Tozer, *The Knowledge of the Holy*, STL Productions, p.118
Charles Wesley, in *Christian Hymns*, No.605, Evangelical Movement of Wales, 1977
Avery Willis Jr, *Biblical Basis of Missions*, Convention Press, p.145

Week 35

W.H. Auden, *New Year Letter*, Faber and Faber, 1941, p.27
D.M. Baillie, *God was in Christ*, Faber and Faber, 1948, p.121, footnote
Rupert Brooke, *Collected Poems*
F.A. Cockin, in *The Christian Faith*, W.A. Matthews (ed.), Eyre and Spottiswood, 1944, p.184
Peter de Rosa, *Not I, not I, but the wind that blows through me*, Argus Communications, 1975, p.12
Andrew M. Greeley, *The Friendship Game*, Doubleday, 1971, frontispiece
John Macquarrie, *Paths in Spirituality*, SCM, 1973, p.45
John Oman, *Grace and Personality*, Cambridge, 1942, p.30
Paul Ramsay, *Basic Christian Ethics*, SCM, 1950, p.103
John V. Taylor, *The Go-Between God*, 1975, pp.18 and 33
Evelyn Underhill, *The School of Charity*, Longmans, Green, 1934, p.84

Week 36

John Donne, 'Holy Sonnet 14', *Poems*, J.M. Dent, 1947, p.254
Angus I. Kinnear, *Against the Tide*, Victory Press, 1976, pp.229-230
Soren Kierkegaard, *The Gospel of Sufferings*, James Clarke, 1955, pp.70, 72 and 85
Sebastian Moore, *The Crucified is No Stranger*, Darton, Longman and Todd Ltd, 1978, p.71
Watchman Nee, in Angus I. Kinnear, *Against the Tide*, Victory Press, 1976, p.230
Shaw Neilson, 'The Poor can feed the Birds', *Selected Poems*, Angus and Robertson, 1980, p.264
John A. Sanford, *The Man who wrestled with God*, Paulist Press, 1981, p.41
Paul Tournier, *Creative Suffering*, SCM, 1982, p.58

Week 37

Augustine, *Confessions*, Pocket Books Inc., 1957, p.196
Veronica Brady, *A Crucible of Prophets*, Theological Explanations, 1981, p.14
Monica Furlong, *Cousins*, Weidenfeld and Nicholson, 1983, p.130
Ernst Kasemann, *Jesus Means Freedom*, Fortress , 1977, p.54
Jurgen Moltmann, *The Church in the Power of the Spirit*, SCM, 1977, p.293
Elizabeth O'Connor, *Eighth Day of Creation*, Word Books, 1977, p.22
Noel Paul Stookey, *On Being*, February 1985, p.24
Paul Tillich, *The New Being*, Charles Scribner and Sons, 1955, pp.6-7
Paul Tillich, *The Shaking of the Foundations*, Charles Scribner and Sons, 1976, pp.93 and 161
Patrick White, *Flaws in the Glass*, Penguin, 1981, p.145

Week 38

Gene Beerens, in *Sojourners* Magazine
Dietrich Bonhoeffer, *The Cost of Discipleship*, SCM, 1959
Michael Crosby, *The Spirituality of the Beatitudes*, Orbist Books, 1981
Clarence Jordan, *The Sermon on the Mount*, Judson Press, 1970
Johannes Baptist Metz, *Poverty of*

Spirit, Newman Press, 1968
Jurgen Moltmann, *The Power of the Powerless*, SCM, 1983

Week 39
Augustine, *Soliloquies*
E.M. Bounds, *Power through Prayer*, Marshall, Morgan and Scott, p.96
John Bunyan, in *Spiritual Riches of John Bunyan*, World Publishing Company, 1952, pp.304-305
P.T. Forsyth, *The Work of Christ*, Independent Press, 1958, p.62
A.J. Gossip, preface to *The Making of a Preacher*, W. M. McGregor, SCM, 1945, p.10
D.M. Lloyd-Jones, *Preaching and Preachers*, Hodder and Stoughton, 1971, p.97
H.E. Luccock, 'Reality in Preaching', in *Effective Preaching*, C.B. Oxnam (ed.), Abingdon, 1929, p.25
T.H.L. Parker, *The Oracles of God*, Lutterworth, 1947, p.140
C.H. Spurgeon, *Lectures to My Students*, Marshall, Morgan and Scott, 1964, p.310

Week 40
George Appleton, *Journey for a Soul*, Fontana, 1974, p.189
William Sloane Coffin, *The Courage to Love*, Harper and Row, 1982, pp.85-86
Mohandas Gandhi, in *Hodder Book of Christian Quotations*, Hodder and Stoughton, 1982, p.72
E. Stanley Jones, *The Christ of the Mount*, Hodder and Stoughton, 1931, p.57
Martin Luther King, *Strength to Love*, Fontana, 1969, p.48

Week 41
Benediction, *An Australian Prayer Book*, Anglican Information Office, 1978, p.28
Changing Australia, Dove Communications, 1983, p.12
David Hollenbach, in *The Faith that does Justice*, J.C. Haughey (ed.), Paulist Press, 1977, p.100
David Sheppard, *Bias to the Poor*, Hodder and Stoughton, 1983, p.191
Brian Wren, *Education for Justice*, SCM, 1977, p.52

Week 42
Mary Butler, *Baptist Hymn Book*, London, 1963, p.557
Edward Fitzgerald, 'Omar Khayyam', *Oxford Book of Quotations*

Week 43
T.S. Eliot, *Murder in the Cathedral*, Faber and Faber, 1965, p.77f
P.T. Forsyth, *The Work of Christ*, Collins, 1965, p.178
Michael Green, *The Empty Cross of Jesus*, Hodder and Stoughton, 1984, p.76
C.S. Lewis, *The Great Divorce*, Geoffrey Bles, 1946, p.66f
C.S. Lewis, *Screwtape Proposes a Toast and other pieces*, Fontana, 1965, p.109
Hugh Silvester, *Arguing with God: A Christian examination of the problem of evil*, IVP, 1971, p.90
J.W. Wenham, *The Goodness of God*, IVP, 1974, p.68f

Week 44
Mildred Cable and Francesca French, *Through Jade Gate and Central Asia*, Hodder and Stoughton, 1943, p.107
Soren Kierkegaard, *Purity of Heart*, Collins/Fontana, 1961, pp.59 and 78
George MacDonald, *An Anthology*, C.S. Lewis (ed.), Macmillan, 1978, pp.12 and 13
Blaise Pascal, *Pensees*, J.M. Dent, 1947, pp. 39 and 45

Week 45
Augustine, *Confessions*, R.S. Pine-Coffin (tr.), Penguin, 1961, pp.214-216

Bonaventure, 'The Soul's Journey into God, the Tree of Life, the Life of St Francis', in *The Classics of Western Spirituality*, E. Cousins (tr.), SPCK, 1978, pp.79-80
Jacophone da Todi, 'The Lauds', S. and E. Hughes (trs.), in *The Classics of Western Spirituality*, SPCK, 1982, p.212
Francisco de Osuna, 'The Third Spiritual Alphabet', M.E. Giles (tr.), in *The Classics of Western Spirituality*, SPCK, 1981, pp.294-295
C.C. Jung, 'On the Psychology of the Unconscious', in *Two Essays on Analytical Psychology*, Princeton University Press, 1972, p.66
G.D. Kaufmann, *Systematic Theology: a Historicist Perspective*, Charles Scribner and Sons, 1968, p.400
H. Richard Niebuhr, *The Meaning of Revelation*, Macmillan, 1941, pp.85-86
Henri Nouwen, *The Living Reminder*, Seabury, 1977, p.19
M. Scheler, *On the Eternal in Man*, Harper and Brothers, 1960, p.41

Week 46
George Appleton, *Journey for a Soul*, Fontana, 1974, pp.200-201
Berthold Brecht, *Radio as an Apparatus for Communication*, 1932
Frederick Buechner, *Wishful Thinking*, Collins, 1973, p.96f
John Harriott, 'Words and the Word', in *The Tablet*, December 24/31, 1983, p.1256f
William James, *Hodder Book of Christian Quotations*, Hodder and Stoughton, 1982, p.39
Rudyard Kipling, in *Hodder Book of Christian Quotations*, Hodder and Stoughton, 1982, p.259
Lerner and Lowe, *My Fair Lady*
Colin Morris, *Love and the Electronic Ghost*, Mediacom Associates, Editors' Clip Sheets, Vol.5, No.10, October 1984

Week 47
J.R. Claypool, *The Preaching Event*, Word, 1980, p.87
C.E. Fant, *Preaching for Today*, Harper and Row, 1975, p.113

Week 48
Malcolm Boyd, *Are you running with me, Jesus?*, Heinemann, 1967, p.13
Dom Helder Camara, *The Church and Colonialism*, Sheed and Ward, 1969, p.34
C.S. Lewis, *Mere Christianity*, Macmillan, 1960, p.52
George Matheson, 'Make me a captive, Lord,' *Baptist Hymn Book*, Psalms and Hymns Trust, No. 478
John Milton, *Sonnets*, 12, Dent and Sons, 1962, p.80
Charles Wesley, 'And can it be?', *Baptist Hymn Book*, op. cit., No. 426

Week 49
Dietrich Bonhoeffer, in *The Australian Hymn Book*, No.182, Collins, 1977
Alan Lewis, 'God as Cripple', in *Pacific Theological Review*, San Francisco Theological Seminary, Fall 1982, p.17
Lesslie Newbigin, 'Not whole without the handicapped', in *Partners in Life*, Gecks Muller-Fahrenholz, Faith and Order Paper No.89, World Council of Churches, p.17
Elie Wiesel Night, in John Shea, *Stories of God*, Thomas More Press, 1978

Week 50
John R. Claypool, *The Light Within You*, Word, 1983, p.140
Michael Griffiths, *Take My Life*, IVP, 1967, p.64
Oswald C.J. Hoffman, 'The Gift of Time', A Lutheran Hour Address,

No.914, June 23, 1963
Susan McGowan, 'The Hour is at Hand', in *An Anthology of Christian Verse*, Rigby, 1985, p.83
Catherine Marshall, *Beyond Ourselves*, Hodder and Stoughton, 1969, p.102
Bruce Milne, *Know the Truth*, IVP, 1982, p.89
J.I. Packer, *Knowing God*, Hodder and Stoughton, 1975, p.268
Michel Quoist, 'Lord, I have time,' in *Prayers of Life*, Gill and Son, 1963, pp.76-78
J. Oswald Sanders, *Enjoying Intimacy with God*, Moody, 1980, pp.149-150
Mabel Williamson, *Have We No Right?*, OMF, 1958

Week 51
Betty Banner, 'The empty room', *Guideposts*, Guideposts Associates Inc., December 1977, p.17
Max Ehrmann, 'Desiderata', *Guideposts*, Guideposts Associates Inc., December 1982, p.6
Sue Monk Kidd, 'Sincerely', *Guideposts*, Guideposts Associates Inc., December 1984, p.45
Andrew Murray, *Absolute Surrender*, Whitaker House, 1981, pp.8, 64, 106, 107 and 116
Norman Vincent Peale, 'Words to grow on', *Guideposts*, December 1984, pp.32-33
'The Two Listeners', in *God Calling*, A.J. Russell (ed.), Fleming H. Revell Co., 1977, p.277
An old Wesh grace, *Guideposts*, Guideposts Associates Inc., December 1977, p.9

Week 52
Frederick Buechner, 'Summons to Pilgrimage', in *A Room Called Remember*, Harper and Row, 1984, p.152
Annie Dillard, *Pilgrim at Tinker Creek*, Picador/Pan, 1976, p.235
Catherine de Hueck Doherty, *Poustinia*, Collins/Fount, 1975
Madeleine l'Engle, *Walking on Water*, Harold Shaw Publishers, 1980, p.50
Gerard Manley Hopkins, 'God's Grandeur', in *Poems and Prose of Gerard Manley Hopkins*, W.H. Gardner (ed.), Penguin, 1953, p.27
St John of the Cross, 'The Spiritual Canticle', Stanza 5, in Evelyn Underhill, *Worship*, Fontana, 1962, p.16
Trevor Jordan, 'Joy to the World', in *Dayspring*, Dayspring, December 1984, p.7
C.S. Lewis, 'The Seeing Eye', in *Christian Reflections*, Eerdmans, 1967, p. 171
Vishal Mangalwadi, Personal Newsletters, December 3, 1984
Thomas Merton, in Parker Palmer, *The Promise of Paradise*, Ave Maria Press, 1980, p.16
Virginia Stem Owens, *And the Trees Clap Their Hands*, Eerdmans, 1983, pp.141-142
Parker J. Palmer, *The Promise of Paradox*, Ave Maria Press, 1980, pp.18-19

Contributors

Personal profiles of contributors

The following profiles describe our contributors as at the time of original publication. Since then, their life situation may have changed.

Neil Adcock has recently retired as pastor of the Canberra Baptist Church, before which he ministered in Adelaide, Sydney, Melbourne and Perth. He has been involved for many years in all sections of the media, especially radio. He and his wife, Joan, have three married children.

Colin Alcock was a founding director of Eremos Institute in Sydney, a ministry committed to developing Christian spirituality in the Australian context.

Vaughan Bowie is senior lecturer in Youth Work at the Macarthur Institute School of Community and Welfare Studies and is involved in support areas for Christian workers, especially stress management. He is a deacon in a Church of Christ.

John Campbell is senior pastor of Albany Baptist Church in Western Australia. His church is developing a 'triune' project of aged units, school and a worship centre. He lectures across Australia and overseas at theological conferences and Christian schooling conventions. John and Rosemary have two sons.

Allan Chapple, a Uniting Church minister in Western Australia, is currently staffworker for the Perth area of the Australian Fellowship of Evangelical Students. Married with three children, he has completed doctoral studies in New Testament and has taught in a seminary in Malaysia.

Marlene Cohen, a trained school teacher, has a Masters Degree in Theology and has been Sydney Convenor of the Movement for the Ordination of Women.

Rowland Croucher has pastored churches in New South Wales, Victoria and British Columbia. For the past twelve years, he has ministered to clergy, church leaders and their spouses — first with World Vision, now with John Mark Ministries. He and Jan have two married children and two daughters in secondary school.

Arthur Cundall was the principal of the Bible College of Victoria and before that a lecturer at the London Bible College. He has had considerable pastoral and lecturing experience in Australia, England and other places. He is also known as a convention speaker and the author of many books and articles. He is married to Janet and has three adult children in England.

Rod Denton is now senior pastor of Clovercrest Baptist Church. He is married to Sue and has two daughters.

Majorie Donellan, a mother and grandmother, is a member of Gymea Baptist Church in New South Wales, where she is involved with young people and adults and works part-time in the pre-school kindergarten. She is a trained midwife. Her hobbies are bush-walking, photography and reading.

Greg Elsdon is principal of the Churches of Christ College, Victoria. He has recently undertaken post-graduate studies in New Testament at Ruschlikon Theological Seminary in Switzerland. He is married to Elaine and they have two young daughters.

Ron Ham was formerly pastor at Collins Street Baptist Church, Melbourne. He has had previous pastorates in Victoria and New South Wales, completing a Master of Divinity, and been a lecturer in theology. Janice and he have two teenage chldren.

John Helm is pastor of the Knightsbridge Baptist Church in Adelaide. He has spent most of his twenty-six years of ordained ministry in pastoral situations in New South Wales. He is married to Betty.

David Hewetson has ministered for over thirty years in a number of capacities — parish minister, teaching missioner, missionary administrator, principal of a theological college in Tanzania, writer. He and his wife Ann have three adult children. In recent years, e has served as international chairman of Africa Enterprise.

Jenkins, born and educated in New Zealand, is a pastor's wife ree children. She lectures in Christian Education and con- peaking and writing ministry. She and her husband have ndertaken post-graduate studies in the USA.

John Key was field director of World Vision in Bangladesh and worked in the international office of World Vision in California, USA. As an Anglican priest, he spent fifteen years in parish ministry in England and four years in Papua New Guinea. He and his wife Loveday have two sons and a daughter. Since then, he has become national director of the Good News Broadcasting Association, based in West Ryde, Sydney.

Tom Keyte was ordained in 1934. He served Baptist churches in Victoria until 1972, interrupted by AIF chaplaincy from 1941 to 1945 and six years as general superintendent of the Baptist Union of Victoria. Thence until 1984 he served part-time in team ministries, majoring in pastoral counselling.

John Lane is a member of the national staff of Scripture Union in Australia, serving as Literature and Media Director. He lives in Melbourne with his wife, Wendy, and three children, and is an elder and lay preacher of the Uniting Church.

John Mallison, a Uniting Church leader and educationalist in New South Wales, Australia and overseas, is a lecturer, consultant and trainer in many fields of church renewal. A prolific writer, especially on the role of small groups, he is married with five children.

Ken Manley was the pastor of Epping Baptist Church in Sydney until he became the principal of Whitley College — the Baptist College of Victoria — in 1987. He has lectured at Baptist colleges in Adelaide and Sydney. He is author of books and articles on church history. He is married to Margaret and they have two teenage daughters.

Peter Newall is a Uniting Church minister and a member of the South Australian Synod's Spiritual Development Taskforce. He has pictures in his study of Martin Luther, Peter Taylor Forsyth and George MacDonald and has a special interest in mystical theology. He is married with two children.

David Nicholas was senior minister at the Menai Baptist Church, New South Wales, is a graduate of the NSW Baptist Theological College and has completed Masters studies in journalism and radio television overseas. He has written many articles in both the religious and secular press, and is married with three children.

Alan Nichols worked with World Vision Australia. Prior to that, he was executive director of the Mission of St James and St John,

Melbourne, until his appointment as archdeacon of Melbourne in 1986. Alan has served with several organisations concerned with social justice, including work with refugees in Thailand. He is currently the rector of St Mark's Anglican Church, Camberwell. He and his wife Denise have five children.

David Oliphant, formerly an architect, is vice-principal of the Anglican College of Ministry in Canberra. His main interests are in theological reflection and the philosophy of religion. He is married to Alison and they have three children.

Gordon Preece, previously a youth worker, was an Anglican minister at Malabar in Sydney's eastern suburbs. Before joining the staff of Ridley Theological College, Melbourne, he lectured part-time at the Baptist Theological College of NSW in Ethics, a subject on which he has written a book, and is working on a Master of Science and Society degree. He and Susan have three children.

Bronwyn Pryor, a trained infants teacher prior to marriage, with subsequent studies in Arts and Theology, enjoys working as a team with her husband Robin. They have three teenage children. Bronwyn concentrates on children's ministry (puppets, musicals and religious education) and women's ministry (women in prayer, work with mothers coping on their own).

Robin Pryor is a Uniting Church presbytery minister with a special concern to link issues of spirituality and social justice, and to develop approaches to stress management (especially in ministry) via prayer, meditation and spiritual direction. He was previously a demographer in various Australian universities and with the UN.

Eric Reid came to Australia from Dublin in 1951 with his wife and two children. He is a pastor of a Christian Brethren Assembly in Melbourne. He has spoken at Keswick Conventions in Australia and has had long association with a number of Christian organisations.

Owen Salter was editor of the monthly Australian Christian magazine, *On Being*. He is part of an inner-city Baptist community in Melbourne, where he serves as an elder. He and his wife Jane have one son.

rnard Shah, a Carmelite monk, made his vows in 1960 and was ained priest in 1966. He has worked in parishes, been an editor, written articles in Catholic papers and magazines. His present is retreats and spiritual direction. He is a member of the community in Port Melbourne.

Ann Siddall is a journalist with *New Times*, the monthly publication of the Uniting Church in South Australia. She is also involved in a spiritual development task group within that Synod, and is a lay preacher and a church elder at Maughan Church, Adelaide.

Jim Stebbins lives with his wife and family in Melbourne. He has worked as a pastor in churches in Melbourne, Canberra and Los Angeles, and as a public servant in Canberra and Melbourne. He has a BA Hons and MDiv, and has written papers for the Zadok Centre and elsewhere.

Bill Tabbernee was principal of the College of the Bible, the theological hall for the Churches of Christ, based in Glen Iris, Victoria. He is editor of two recent books published by the Victorian Council of Churches' Faith and Order Commission. He and Sandra have three children.

Grace Thomlinson currently divides her time three ways: looking after husband, Geoffrey; teaching Christian Ethics at the Bible College of Victoria; and contributing to the musical ministry at Blackburn Baptist Church.

Peter Walker was pastor of the Ashburton Baptist Church in Victoria. From 1978–1984, he was senior staffworker with the Australian Fellowship of Evangelical Students in Melbourne. He is married to Anne and has four school-age children. He is particularly interested in the area of spiritual formation.